The Vegetarian Traveller
A guide to Europe and the Mediterranean for
vegetarians abroad

The
Vegetarian Traveller

by

Andrew Sanger

THORSONS PUBLISHING GROUP
Wellingborough, Northamptonshire
——————— ● ———————
Rochester, Vermont

First published 1987

©ANDREW SANGER 1987

British Library Cataloguing in Publication Data

Sanger, Andrew
The Vegetarian Traveller.
1. Vegetarians – Europe – Handbooks,
manuals, etc. 2. Europe – Handbooks,
manuals, etc.
I. Title
641.3'0094   D923

ISBN 0-7225-1196-5

Printed and bound in Great Britain

Contents

For Gerry

Thank You

First, to the many friends who helped with ideas, information and advice, especially Hilary Munt, Rachel Magowan and her sister Caroline, Leon and Ulrike, Els Dykstra, Marlie, Jane Mendelssohn, my parents Joe and Hilda Sanger and, above all, to my friend and travelling companion of many years, Gerry Dunham.

And for their freely offered time and knowledge, thanks to Claire Milne, Barry Gray, Tim Salmon, Florica Kyriacopoulos, Enza Ferreri, Violeta Zaječaranović and Beba Radulović.

And to all the people who so kindly contacted me with useful information or suggestions, in particular Margaret Barr, Cynthia Boskett, Joy Charnley, Edith Kilner, Leah Leneman, Maria Mann and Rosemary Stevens; as well as Edwin Heller and Ruth de Roche (of *Regeneration* magazine, Switzerland), Philip Brown (of the Vegan Society, Oxford), Jacqueline André (of Infor-Végétarisme, Belgium), Godfrey Fischer (of Better Life Holidays), Ianthe Hoskins, Martyn Lowe, Maurizio Lipparaini and Miriam Mayver.

And for the future — if you wish to see anything added to a future edition, or if you think there's something inaccurate in the book, please do write to me, c/o the publishers.

Starters

Foreign food is one of the great delights of travelling. Vegetarians should not willingly forgo this pleasure. Uncertainty about what is available, and timidity about asking, have been an obstacle to the full enjoyment of many a holiday. This book sets out to solve the problem and give all the information needed to find a meal without meat or fish wherever you are in Europe or the Mediterranean area.

In any case no traveller can reasonably expect to find everywhere the familiar food of home. Vegetarians who complain — and there are many — that they cannot find brown rice in Greece or wholewheat pasta in Italy, or that too much dairy produce is eaten in Switzerland or Israel, are missing the point of being abroad, and have much in common with those meat-eating tourists who always insist on having steak and chips. The markets and menus of almost every country can offer something tasty and meatless. Perhaps it is not quite as 'balanced' or wholesome as your usual everyday dinner; but now each mouthful contains something of another land, another history, another climate: eat and enjoy. Bon courage!

Cheese

I have written with the conventional European-style lacto-vegetarian in mind, that is, a diet of plants, eggs and milk products. Where we each draw the line on what to eat is entirely a personal decision, but it must be said that the blind spot of most vegetarians is cheese. The rennet used in traditional cheese-making (to coagulate and 'set' the milk) normally comes from the stomachs of young animals slaughtered for their meat. With knowing indifference, many vegetarians continue to make great use of cheese, and indeed it is an invaluable resource when travelling. While neither condoning nor condemning this, I too have assumed throughout that cheeses will be eaten, regardless of how they were made, although where I know of local cheeses in which animal rennet is not used, these have been especially pointed out.

Vegans
People who avoid all animal products — vegans — clearly encounter more difficulties finding something suitable to eat. Certain countries can be recommended though. Those with a selection of traditional dishes with neither meat (or fish) nor milk are Italy, Israel, Turkey and Greece. Those with a good number of vegetarian restaurants where vegan meals can be found are Holland, Germany, Britain and Sweden.

What to take
Anyone heading east towards Russia and Eastern Europe, north into Scandinavia, or south as far as North Africa, certainly ought to consider packing a few dietary supplements or ready-to-eat snacks. Self-caterers holidaying in any country - except Holland, Belgium, Germany, Switzerland, Israel and Britain, where health foods can be found easily — might be wise, if they are anxious about having enough to eat, to pack a little emergency supply of muesli and instant vegetarian foods. Real Eat's *Vege-Burger* and other mixes have been praised by mountain climbers and explorers on major expeditions, their advantage over other prepared foods being that nothing needs to be added except water. Personally I regard a small bag of porridge oats mixed with dried fruit and nuts and plenty of milk powder as an excellent standy-by on walking expeditions lasting several days, or long journeys of uncertain destination or in areas with few facilities, because again, if only water is available that will be enough to make a digestible and nourishing light meal.

Babies

It is not as hard to travel with babies as some people think. Airlines are far more ready to make arrangements for babies than for vegetarians! Channel ferries (though not ships in the Mediterranean) have baby-care rooms on board. Trains are less convenient, although French Railways have introduced 'family trains' on a number of routes, having playrooms and child-care facilities on board. If you require processed or prepared baby foods which are wholesome and free of meat products, it would be wise to take plenty of packets (for example, Robinsons) with you. Conventional baby foods generally have some meat and/or sugar added. Countries where vegetarian baby foods should be easier to find are Britain, Holland and Switzerland

Vegetarian restaurants and information

Countries fall into three groups: those where the normal cuisine offers little to vegetarians but where there are many vegetarian restaurants (Britain, Holland, Denmark, Belgium, Sweden, Germany, Switzerland); those where the normal cuisine is to varying degrees adaptable to vegetarian needs, and where there may be in some cases quite a number of suitable restaurants as well (Italy, France, Greece, Israel and the Middle East); and those where the normal cuisine is fairly difficult for vegetarians and there are few alternative facilities (Portugal and Spain, Ireland, most of Scandinavia, North Africa, Eastern Europe).

At the end of the section on each country details have been given of how to find out about hotels and restaurants catering specifically for vegetarians, as well as any other useful information. Names and addresses of individual establishments have not been given here, except in rare instances of a place which has been in business for many decades. Such enterprises normally come and go so fast that almost any list would be out of date before it reached the printer. This is precisely the problem which besets *The International Vegetarian Handbook* (published by The Vegetarian Society). This is extremely useful as a list of places which *did* exist; it is important that no holiday plans should be made on the basis of addresses in the Handbook without checking that they *still* exist. Within days of receiving a review copy of the Handbook, I did a spot check in a number of foreign cities: in every case many of the restaurants listed had already closed down, while new ones had opened too late to be included in the book. Where it excels is in information on the UK.

British vegetarian/health-food magazines carry advertisements for UK and foreign vegetarian restaurants. Best of these by far is *The Vegetarian* (Parkdale, Dunham Road, Altrincham, Cheshire [phone: (061) 928 0793],. For more literature, by the way, visit The Vegetarian Centre and Bookshop, 53 Marloes Road, London W8 (open Mon.–Fri. 9.30–5.30). Other possible sources of information might include the Esperanto clubs and societies in various countries, because Esperantists encourage vegetarianism; the world-wide Theosophical Society (in UK at 50 Gloucester Place, London W1), most of whose members are vegetarian; and the Hare Krishna Organization (9 Soho Street, London W1), which runs excellent little vegetarian restaurants in a number of European cities. And it is always worth asking the National Tourist Offices of the different countries for information of use to vegetarians — they may not have any but it helps to make them aware of the need.

—Trains, Boats & Planes—
. . .and Package Holidays

PACKAGE HOLIDAYS

A vegetarian cannot simply leaf through the brochures and book a fortnight by the Mediterranean. Whether it's full board, half board, or just bed and breakfast, he (or rather she, since most vegetarians are women) is likely to feel very short-changed at hotel mealtimes. True, at many hotels breakfast is nothing more than the miserable roll and coffee which the travel industry calls a 'continental breakfast', while lunch can sometimes be presented in buffet style with a good range of salads, so that meat can easily be avoided. Only dinner then poses a few problems if it follows the usual 'international' format (typical example: soup; chicken and chips or sole meunière with buttered boiled potatoes; chocolate mousse). Certainly one option is to take holidays like these, but having checked with travel agent, tour operator and, if possible, with the hotel itself that vegetarian meals can be supplied. (If you can extract some sort of written agreement to this effect it will be easy to sue should the type of food requested not be available after all). It would be wise to specify precisely what can or can't be eaten. Do not expect hotels to buy health foods especially for you: the most they can normally manage is meatless meals prepared from their usual grocery order. In many cases this consists only of a plate of boiled vegetables.

There's no reason why you should not book a hotel package — very often the cheapest way of getting to a foreign country — and have all your meals at local restaurants or in the form of picnics. Another option, the obvious one for anyone with an unconventional diet, is self-catering. This ranges from camping or caravanning right up to luxuriously comfortable detached houses (or 'villas' in brochure-language) with a rental car included in the price. Some countries offer far more self-catering facilities than others. France leads the way in both variety and availability. Before booking-up, satisfy yourself, perhaps by using this book, that a sufficient range of the sort of food you want can be found in the area. Visitors staying in purpose-built holiday apartment complexes frequently depend upon overpriced shops built into the complex itself, where a predictable and, for a vegetarian, inadequate selection of foods is offered. Shops on campsites too suffer from this problem. Far better would be to rent a real house, be it humble cottage or splendid villa, and do all shopping in the market and shops of the local town or village. Making your own meals is not everyone's idea of a holiday, so when looking at self-catering possibilities, remember to choose a destination where you can do some eating out as well.

For a third option, perhaps the most enticing, book an entirely vegetarian holiday. To make the arrangements yourself, simply find the names and addresses of suitable hotels and guesthouses either from the sources of information mentioned after each country in this book or by studying the advertisements and recommendations in *The Vegetarian* and the health-food magazines (especially in the January/February and Spring issues), and write or phone directly with your booking requirements. To have the arrangements made for you, in the form of an inclusive package, there are a number to choose from. Ideas include, for example, vegetarian cycling or canal cruising holidays (both advertised in *The Vegetarian*); or ocean cruising on a luxury liner: the QE2, and indeed most cruise liners, will provide whatever kind of food passengers require provided advance notice is given. Several travel firms have from time to time tried to put together vegetarian package holidays but have been unable to make them viable. Correspondence in the trade publication *Travel Trade Gazette* reveals that Regent Travel (of Shanklin, Isle of Wight), who arrange occasional group visits to European hotels which offer vegetarian meals, receive many enquiries but few bookings. Another firm, Mohandas Travel (Ashton-under-Lyne, Lancs.), say they have been trying for years to organize tours for vegetarians, but have met with little response. The one company which has been able to make a success in this field, perhaps because they deal *only* with vegetarian holidays, is The House of Fischer Better Life Holidays (of Chapel Place, Ramsgate [phone: (0843) 583164],. Their brochure details hotel, farmhouse and guest-house packages for vegetarians and vegans in eight countries ranging from Finland to Israel, and adds that mixed vegetarian and non-vegetarian families can be catered for.

AIRLINES

What could be more irritating, when you have made a point of notifying the travel agent, the tour operator and even the airline itself that vegetarian meals will be required in flight, than being asked with insincere and disbelieving politeness by a stewardess (who happens to have no food on board for you) whether you are quite sure you have requested a vegetarian meal? It has happened to me on scores of flights, more than I could possibly remember, and must be regarded as one of the hazards of air travel.

Nearly all airlines cheerfully claim to cater for vegetarians. The reality is rather different. Most, it would seem, regard dietary peculiarities as a confounded nuisance, and by a careful process of accidentally overlooking special meal requests actually make little or no provision for them at all. Least interested in special requests are the charter airlines flying fully loaded with package holiday-makers. It would be unusual to have the opportunity to choose which charter airline to fly as part of an all-in package deal, but for the record the worst charter I have flown, from the vegetarian point of view, was Monarch; and the best, Air Europe (although they too have managed to forget my meal on occasion).

When it comes to scheduled flights though, the choice is all yours. Few airlines do their own catering: they employ specialist contractors located at the major airports. Trusthouse Forte, International Catering and Dobbs are three situated at or near Heathrow. Fleet Vegetable Company, close by, provides much of the produce, including exotic fruits. Some airlines, notably

British Airways, El Al, Air Canada and SAS, do their own catering — supplying other airlines too — and have their own kitchen complexes at the airports. Cost dictates how good or bad a tray meal can be assembled for each airline. On the whole, trans-continental passengers get better food than those on short trips. Certain of the airlines operating within the area covered by this book deserve to be singled out for particular praise and recommendation. They are El Al, Swissair and now at last British Airways, all of which recognize different types of vegetarianism and have shown themselves willing and capable in supplying meatless meals as good as one can hope to find in an aeroplane.

The main problem faced even by these airlines is that while food loaded in Britain may be exactly as requested, tray meals picked up at stopovers or loaded at a foreign airport from which you are returning home may not be so acceptable. Indeed on returning flights the likelihood is high that your vegetarian meal will have been overlooked or, if not, that it will not be properly vegetarian. Always make an official complaint — ask the steward or stewardess for a Complaint Form — if your requested meal has not been provided (this helps to make airlines aware of the problem). Often sympathetic flight staff will make up a suitable impromptu meal from spare trays or from their own rations. It would still be sensible to make the complaint, duly mentioning what you were eventually given to eat.

The procedure I recommend to maximize the chances of getting a vegetarian meal on board is:

1. **When booking** the holiday or flight state that vegetarian food will be required, and whether it should be lacto-vegetarian, vegan or oriental.

2. **Shortly after,** phone the airline itself if possible to confirm that your request has gone on to the computer.

3. **When checking in** at the airport, ask the check-in clerk to confirm that your meal has been ordered. If it has not, ask him or her to order one, and if necessary that a call be made to the airline's reservations department to confirm that you had already made the request.

4. **When on the plane**, as meals are about to be served, notify a steward or stewardess that they should have a vegetarian meal tray on board booked in your name.

5. **If they do not have it**: ask for the Chief Steward, explain that the meal was pre-booked and confirmed, and ask if he or she can put something together for you. **Later**, whether or not something was made for you, ask for a Complaint Form (but be polite and friendly to the flight staff — you may need their help in case of emergencies).

6. **At any stopover or change of planes**: it's important to reconfirm the request for vegetarian food.

7. **A couple of days before returning home**: contact the airline to confirm your flight. This is advisable for all passengers, to avoid problems in the event of overbooking. Take the opportunity to remind them of your special meal request, and ask them to check that a record has been made of it.

Two more tips: first, take some fruit or bread or other pocket-sized snack on to the plane, and secondly, avoid travelling again on an airline which fails to provide reasonable vegetarian food.

TRAINS

Although meals are provided on many trains throughout Europe, vegetarians rarely find much beyond salad and chips, an omelette if extremely lucky, or a horrible moist plastic-wrapped cheese and tomato roll. Take your own already-cut bread, cheese, fruit and nuts — and for a long journey, a bottle of water.

FERRIES

The food on ferries from Britain to Ireland and to the Continent ranges from quite dreadful to more-or-less acceptable depending on the ferry company. And in most cases the choice, for vegetarians, ranges from practically nothing to hardly anything.

```
              ✓ PURE VEGETARIAN DIET

  NO ANIMAL PRODUCTS - POLYUNSATURATED
  MARGARINE ONLY
```

<u>0720566</u>	2ND M/M PURE VEGETARIAN 'Y'
0720548	VEGETARIAN SPECIAL 2ND MEAL 'Y'
0720533	ONIONS ESCOFFIER HORS D'OEUVRE 'Y'
0720539	FRUIT SALAD 120 GM & STRAWBERRY 'Y'
	BREAD ROLL RYE ROUND 1 NO
	MARGARINE DIET 1 NO
	MACADAMIA NUTS IND.

<u>0720621</u>	HOT B/FAST PURE VEGETARIAN 'Y'
0720599	BREAKFAST VEGETARIAN 'Y'
0720603	FRUIT COMPOTE 'Y'
	BREAD ROLL SOFT ROUND 2 NO
	MARGARINE DIET 2 NO
	MARMALADE IND.
	HONEY IND.
	MACADAMIA NUTS IND.

<u>0720624</u>	CONT. B/FAST PURE VEGETARIAN 'Y'
0720603	FRUIT COMPOTE 'Y'
	BREAD ROLL SOFT ROUND 2 NO
	MARGARINE DIET 2 NO
	MARMALADE IND.
	HONEY IND.
	MACADAMIA NUTS IND.

72ØØØ4I

```
PAX: _____

FLT. NO.: _____   DATE: _____

SECTOR: _____
```

Behind-the-scenes instructions for British Airways catering staff preparing the airline's imaginative in-flight vegetarian meal trays.

LACTO OVO VEGETARIAN DIET

NO MEAT PRODUCTS TO BE USED

0720571 | 1ST M/M LACTO OVO VEGETARIAN 'Y'

0720547 | VEGETARIAN SPECIAL 1ST MEAL 'Y'
0720531 | PINEAPPLE CHAT HDO 'Y'
0720536 | KIWI & STRAWBERRIES 120GM 'Y'
BREAD ROLL RYE ROUND 1 NO.
BUTTER PAT INDIVIDUAL
VINTAGE CHEESE
SAO PLAIN INDIVIDUAL
MACADAMIA NUTS INDIV.

0720627 | REF. COOKIES ONLY LACTO OVO VEG 'Y'

COOKIE POLYUNSATURATED 1 PKT

0720630 | REF SANDW & COOKIES LACTO OVO VEG 'Y'

0720593 | REFRESHMENT VEG 'Y' WHOLEMEAL
COOKIE POLYUNSATURATED 1 PKT.

0720633 | COLD MEAL REF LACTO OVO VEG 'Y'

0720590 | COLD MEAL PREPLATE 'Y'
0720606 | MELON DICED FRESH 120GM 'Y'
BREAD ROLL RYE ROUND 1 NO.
BUTTER PAT INDIVIDUAL
VINTAGE CHEESE
SAO PLAIN INDIVIDUAL
MACADAMIA NUTS INDIV.

2312

7200002

PAX: SANGER

FLT. NO.: BA12   DATE: 13 3 .

SECTOR: BNE SYD

The rare exceptions deserve special mention: while not catering specifically for vegetarians, Sally Line (Ramsgate-Dunkirk) has an excellent *smörgåsbord* on every crossing — a Scandinavian-style buffet of salads, open sandwiches and hot and cold cooked vegetables. A number of the items have no meat or fish in them. DFDS (to Scandinavia) put on a similar first-rate *smörgåsbord*, and will additionally provide vegetarians who give advance notice with some sort of hot meal, while their cheaper restaurant has egg and chips.

On the shortest Channel crossings, Townsend Thoresen ships to Calais have three eating places on board: the least interesting is the self-service cafeteria, perhaps with bowls of cereal, rolls, or egg and chips; however, there is a pleasant small restaurant with waiter service, having omelettes and salads on the menu and, until about 11 a.m., breakfasts of cereal and toast; and the Salad Bar, basically a rather superior self-service cafeteria with a small but edible selection of salads. Townsend's Boulogne crossing does not compare, having only a poor self-service cafeteria.

Sealink (Calais and Boulogne) vessels vary considerably. One has a pleasant wine bar with a couple of meatless dishes (for example quiche and salad) while others have just a ghastly cafeteria in which the only possibility is a portion of chips. It is hard to predict which ship you will be using: as a general rule though, the car ferries have more and better facilities than the foot-passenger ships which connect with rail services. Dieppe Ferries (Newhaven-Dieppe), a member of the Sealink family, closely resembles a poor-quality Sealink crossing with basic cafeteria and a mediocre waiter service restaurant.

On longer crossings, food choice and quality improves over all. In order of preference at this end of the Channel, Brittany Ferries (Portsmouth/Plymouth–Caen, St Malo, Roscoff, Santander) leads the way with a good buffet restaurant, an acceptable cafeteria with egg and chips, bread, cheese, cereals, etc. . . . and fresh croissants, baked on board, for breakfast. Brittany's 'Les Routiers' service (Poole–Cherbourg) offers only a French-style set meal. Sealink's expensive Portsmouth–Cherbourg crossing, as long as it stays in business, also has an eat-all-you-want buffet restaurant with good wines. Townsend Thoresen (Portsmouth--Cherbourg/Le Havre) have a reasonable waiter-service restaurant with imaginative food on an à la carte menu, including two specifically vegetarian main dishes; and their self-service cafeteria, though grubby and unappetizing by comparison, has a couple of Indian vegetarian hot snacks. Lagging behind comes Sealink's Weymouth–Cherbourg crossing, with uninteresting waiter and self-service restaurants plus limited and unappealing 'bar snacks'. Equally bad are ships on the rough crossing to Ireland.

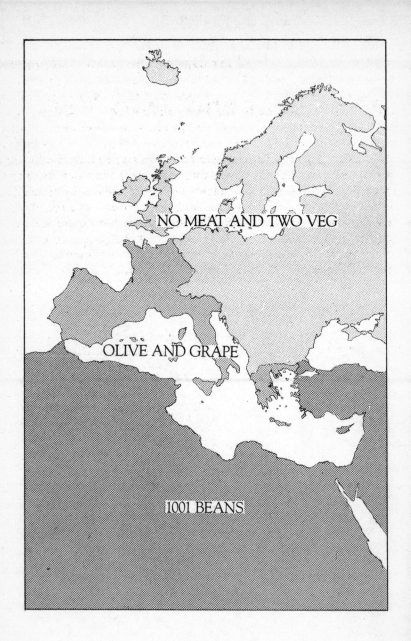

NO MEAT AND TWO VEG

OLIVE AND GRAPE

1001 BEANS

Part One

No Meat and Two Veg

Extending in a broad sweep over northern and eastern Europe are those countries in which the basic meal (unless it be a Scandinavian *smörgåsbord* or a Hungarian goulash) is a plate with a piece of meat or fish accompanied by two or three plainly cooked vegetables. Sometimes the meat can be substituted with an omelette, sometimes it cannot. Most of the countries with really big and well-established vegetarian movements are in this part of the world: Britain, Holland, Denmark, Sweden, Germany, and Switzerland.

Belgium and Luxembourg

BELGIUM

Belgium is perhaps Europe's most unloved country, seat of the pernicious rule-makers of the Common Market and butt of a thousand French cruel jokes. Largely flat and industrial, this tiny nation is further riven into two by the factionalism of its rival cultures — Flemish and French. Everywhere north of Brussels (even right on the French border) is entirely Flemish-speaking; south of Brussels the people speak only French and are also more French in their character and lifestyle. Yet Belgium's cities and towns have a good deal of charm and history. The North in particular has some superb examples — Brugge, Ypres, magnificently rebuilt after war damage, and many others. The South too has some attractive old towns, as well as pretty countryside — the Ardennes — which has not been much developed for tourism. Brussels, the capital, has a splendid old centre, with elaborate and gilded mansions reflecting the immense power and wealth that Flanders once possessed.

Another point in Belgium's favour is the food. There's some good eating to be done here. Gastronomically, as in language (and, of course, in geography), Belgium falls between France and Holland, but unlike the language rivalry, in food the mixture has been entirely harmonious and successful. Hearty, substantial dishes, enriched with plenty of cream or butter, are typical. Most Belgians eat vast amounts of sausage and other meats, but cheese and milk products are very important too. Baking plays a major role in the diet, not just in the form of delicious pastries, cakes and waffles, but in the variety of wholesome breads on offer. Brown bread is the norm both at home and in restaurants. Ordinary

Belgian restaurants and cafés have long menus with lots of choice, and it is usually possible to find something meatless to eat.

Breakfast and snacks

For the simplest and best breakfast, buy a fresh roll, croissant, *pain au chocolat* or other pastry from a bakery and take it to a bar (they serve all sorts of beverages, not just alcoholic drinks). This is normal practice. Failing this, a café (rather than a bar) may be able to provide breakfasty things of its own. The coffee itself will be served with a little bite of something – a biscuit or a nibble of chocolate. Hotels generally serve up a pot of coffee or tea, with rolls, butter, jam and thin slices of cheese.

Cafés and cheap ordinary restaurants have great varieties of hot and cold food available all day, and you can order a meal, a snack or quick bite at any time. In bigger or busier places, menus are likely to be in both French and Flemish, and sometimes English as well. You can ask for practically anything in these places, from a coffee or a glass of wine to a complete meal, a light lunch, afternoon tea, just a plate of bread and cheese, or some ice cream. They have marvellous cakes, crisp light waffles with a tremendous choice of toppings, and the sandwiches are something of an artform. Omelettes also appear on most menus. Vast amounts of coffee are drunk: it's made strong, from freshly ground beans, and comes with either milk or cream; a cappuccino, Belgian-style, is a large, strong coffee covered with a thick layer of whipped cream decorated with real grated chocolate. *Lait Russe* means a cup of hot milk with instant coffee. Tea, though not popular, can be ordered almost everywhere, as can decaffeinated coffee and herb teas

Standards tend to be high, ingredients good, and there is a reasonable choice of meatless dishes. And just about every eating place has its *potage du jour* — soup of the day, usually (though do always ask to be sure) mixed vegetable or tomato, served with brown bread. In Brussels, several fast-food, pizza and hamburger places have sprung up, and quite a few of these, including hamburger restaurants, have an excellent salad bar.

An informal eating place called a *Friture*, or *Frituur*, specializes in fried snacks, especially chips *(frites)*. Chips are served with 'sauce', usually mayonnaise, but alternatives — on request — include sauce tartare or ketchup (never vinegar!). Fritures by the roadside may have nothing but chips, while indoor fritures also make fried eggs and omelettes: more of a meal than a snack.

And all day long, you can sit down in a pastry shop, which may be called a tea room, conditorei, patisserie, etc., to a choice of pastries and cakes. *Mattetaarte*, in the Flemish area, for example, are little pies containing sweetened white cheese. *Gaufres de Bruxelles* are sweet waffles covered with cream and fruit. *Pralines* — filled chocolates — are another sweet-toothed national speciality.

Lunch and dinner

A light lunch and a filling dinner is the Belgian pattern. The midday meal is hardly more than a snack, for vegetarians best found in an ordinary cheap café or friture. The same type of place could also provide the evening meal. More 'proper' restaurants are less likely to have anything suitable, though announce that you are a vegetarian and they will probably indulge you with an order of boiled vegetables, salad, potatoes or macaroni, sometimes rice. Red cabbage, asparagus, chicory, and of course brussel sprouts, are among the commonest vegetables. You probably won't go hungry, though you may at times have to pluck up the courage to *ask* for something with no meat or fish. When the going get tough, luckily Belgium has large numbers of foreign restaurants, especially in the centre of Brussels. Italian, Chinese and Indian come in particularly useful. Vegetarian/health food restaurants are not uncommon either: many towns have at least one. For their names and addresses, municipal tourist offices are the best source of up-to-the-minute local information.

Self-catering and picnics

Belgian food shops reflect the cultural diversity and the national love of eating. Most larger supermarkets throughout the country stock brown rice, cous-cous, polenta and wholemeal flour, as well as '5-cereal flour' made from wheat, rye, oats, rice and barley. Not only honey and peanut butter, but hazelnut butter and other nut butters, and curiosities like pear syrup, number among the array of spreads. Canned foods, which might contain 'animal fat' in the UK, in Belgium specify 'butter' and no other animal fat. But beware of *bouillon* as an ingredient: it could be meat stock. There's a good selection of oils for cooking, masses of fresh or frozen vegetables and fruit, huge jars of the ever-popular mayonnaise and a big coffee section with dozens of varieties of beans and ground coffee, many of them decaffeinated. A lot of shops have a self-service machine where customers can grind the coffee beans for themselves. Look for organic rice, brown sugar or molasses, muesli, wheat germ and meatless baby foods in the health food section. Real soya sauce may be stocked with Chinese foods, and the pasta shelf almost invariably has wholemeal pasta.

In the fridge is a wide choice of yogurts (whole-milk and low-fat), butter, creams, buttermilk, quark, French, Dutch and Belgian cheeses, and many processed cheeses, but although Belgians like dairy foods they are not keen on fresh milk (they prefer UHT) — though it is available. At the bread section, brown varieties outnumber white, including not only wholemeal, with or without currants, but 7-grain, soya bread, and other flours.

Better still, leave the supermarket and buy bread from a bakery, where you'll find substantial circular loaves of brown bread, together with rolls, scones, heavy cakes either plain or with fruit, and some French-style patisserie. In French areas, they have French bread as well, and a wider choice of patisserie, though everything is more sturdy than in France. Among other interesting food shops, particularly in the Flemish area, are the cheese specialists. Belgium produces an enormous amount of cheese. It is confusing to discover that many foreign varieties are manufactured here, including English Cheddar. Native Belgian cheeses worth trying include the many soft, moulded types — Boulette, Brusselsekaas, Herve and Remoudou. All have a strong taste . . . and a strong smell! Cheese shops are useful too for their prepared take-away dishes like cheese pastry roll (*kaasrollen*), pancakes (*pannekoekjes*) and slices of pizza. The big and colourful local street markets, if you happen to be in the right place at the right time, are yet another source of fresh fruit, salad vegetables and dairy produce.

LUXEMBOURG

The Grand Duché de Luxembourg, poised at the meeting point of France, Germany and Belgium, has curiously more in common with Belgium than either of its larger neighbours. All the countryside of this small state falls within the Ardennes, handsome wooded hills that extend across south-east Belgium and into northern France. Apart from an obscure local *patois*, the people of Luxembourg speak French, and for money they use the Belgian franc.

There are no vegetarian establishments, but Luxembourg would be easy to manage. The local food, like Belgium's, has a strong bias towards bakery and dairy produce as well as meat. The main difference is a stronger 'international', touristy influence. Luxembourg city, the only town of any note in the Duchy, is attractive, supremely prosperous, and packed with grand, elaborate buildings — many of them are banks. There's a pleasant cosmopolitan atmosphere, and large numbers of foreigners living or working there, or just passing through. The city has dozens of Italian, Chinese and fast-food eating places. Italian restaurants in particular have meatless choices on the menu: and in any ordinary snackbar, salads, omelettes, chips, good bread and nice pastry are easy to get.

Worth a special mention — though you may find others just like it — is Taverne Diekirch, at 25 rue Philippe II (next to a splendid bakery). This well-established, inexpensive restaurant calls itself a 'gratinerie, omeletterie & creperie', and while also doing meat meals, its speciality is cheese and egg dishes.

Information

Infor-Végétarisme, 80 av.de Versailles, 1120 Bruxelles (phone: 02/268.22.76), or 34 rue des Bollandistes (1st floor), 1040 Bruxelles (phone: 02/736.92.72) — this is an information service about vegetarianism, for both vegetarians and meat-eaters. Belgian National Tourist Offices abroad do not have much useful information, but local offices within the country have good up-to-date information on vegetarian restaurants. The Brussels tourist office is in the Grasmarkt, 61 rue du Marché aux Herbes, 1000 Bruxelles (phone: 02/512.30.30).

For French vocabulary — see 'France' (page 141). For Flemish vocabulary — see 'Holland' (page 60).

Britain

(a quick guide for vegetarian visitors)

A great, civilized and humanitarian people, yet when it comes to food the British have a quite uncanny instinct for getting everything wrong. Production of traditional cheeses has been encouraged to go into decline by policies of the Milk Marketing Board (buyers and redistributors of all the nation's milk) which at the same time is busily inventing new, tasteless factory-made varieties. Chemical food additives outlawed in the rest of Europe continue to be used by British manufacturers. Nowhere else is instant coffee preferred to the real thing. Vegetables are driven to London's New Covent Garden market from all over the country — and driven back to the provinces to be consumed. And in a score of other ways the national indifference to food makes itself felt. It's not true, though, that the British have no cuisine of their own, although it has so declined in the last fifty years as to become almost clandestine, but it is extraordinarily heavy and meaty. The modern replacement takes the form of an endless succession of boiled, fried or grilled meats accompanied by vegetables reduced to a flavourless disintegration by a long period in boiling water. Salads are not popular at all. A cup of strong tea with milk (the national drink) is often drunk with meals, especially by clients of cafés and cheap restaurants. Wine, though lately becoming more accepted, remains the preserve of the relatively well off and sophisticated. For social class permeates all things in Britain: people of different classes — which, incidentally, is not the same thing as money — eat different food, in different places, at different times of day, and call meals by different names. Most pubs, for example, have two bars — one, called the Saloon, is carpeted, comfortable and supposedly for a 'better class' of customer, while the other, called the Public Bar, is plainer and simpler and intended for common folk!

The middle class drink a lot of coffee, eat 'lunch' at midday and 'dinner' in the evening ('supper' if it's late), and eat out in restaurants; they have something called 'teatime' in mid- or late-afternoon which consists of tea or coffee, a sandwich or two, and a biscuit or cake. The working class drink a lot of tea, eat 'dinner' at midday and 'tea' in the evening, and eat out in pubs, cafés and fast-food chains; by 'breakfast' a working man may mean a traditional British fry-up of eggs, bacon, etc. eaten about 10 a.m. as a *second* breakfast (the first was a cup of tea and buttered toast). Disraeli's description of Britain as 'two nations' remains apt today. And the country is sharply divided in yet another way — North and South. The North possesses both the best of the wild country and the worst of industrial conurbation. The South is more densely populated, more prosperous, and relatively middle class.

For well over a century there has been a sizeable vegetarian minority in Britain. Today they number in the millions. An annual opinion poll (Gallup Poll, commissioned by Real Eat) clearly shows that most are women, young, middle class, and live in the South. Their motivation traditionally has been concern for animals rather than with health, although nowadays all sorts of other reasons are cited. The arrival in Britain of Hindu immigrants has given a great boost to the national vegetarian tradition. In the southern half of the country, almost every town has its health food shop and perhaps a vegetarian restaurant (or two) as well. In London there are dozens, and many other restaurants which feature a vegetarian main dish on the menu. But all over Britain, though the choice may not be extensive, any café, sandwich bar, snackbar, pub or cheap restaurant probably has something without meat. There's no clear dividing line between snacks and meals — most of these places serve both — and aside from 'proper' restaurants which open only at lunch and dinner times, and pubs which are bound by the limited licensing hours, nearly all eating establishments can provide a hot meal at any time ('Breakfast served all day' is a sign you'll see in the steamed-up windows of popular cafés).

A FEW EATING PLACES

Cafés	Basic, unpretentious 'working man's restaurant', colloquially known as a 'caff'. Either counter or table service. Choice of (white bread) sandwiches and filled rolls, hot snacks and meals, tea, coffee and soft drinks. Some vegetarian options: cheese, egg, or salad sandwich; hot snacks on toast; egg, chips and beans.
Chip Shops	The 'chippy', the original take-away of oily french fries generously sprinkled with salt and vinegar. Used to be accompanied by fried fish, now it's as often fried chicken.
Fast Food Restaurants	Either take-away or eat on the premises; not all concentrate on hamburgers — one chain, Spud-U-Like, specializes in baked potatoes with a variety of toppings.
Foreign Restaurants	Extremely numerous all over the country, especially: Indian — very important to vegetarians since most have a selection of non-meat dishes and a few are entirely vegetarian; Chinese — often with a limited selection of meatless meals; Italian — should always be able to manage a reasonable three-course meal without meat; French — often not run by French people, but this is where the British

go for 'good food' . . . and it may be possible to put together a satisfactory meal by having a second hors d'oeuvres in place of the main course.

Pizza/Burger Restaurants

Vaguely American inspiration; can be quite good, and with a range of other types of food as well — may have excellent serve-yourself salad bars, and pizza restaurants have meatless and fishless pizzas.

Pubs

Every pub (short for Public House) has its own atmosphere and character, and caters for its own style of clientele. Customers are usually 'regulars', and may treat the place almost as a social club. Pubs manage to combine conviviality with intimacy, serve predominantly the different sorts of draught and bottled British beers (tourists asking for 'a beer' will be met with uncomprehending expressions) and many also have food which they call bar snacks, bar food or, with real delicacy, pub grub. Typically there are cheese and ham sandwiches, soup (may be acceptable), quiche (OK if not 'Lorraine'), salad, Ploughman's Lunch (vegetarian), as well as hot meat dishes. A few serve coffee at lunchtime.

Sandwich Bars

Mostly confined to city centres and open during office hours only, providing a wide range of sandwiches — mostly to take away — and some of the usual café fare.

Snackbar, 'Coffee Shop', 'Coffee House', 'Coffee Bar and Restaurant'

These slightly smarter versions of the café have added a few more salads and cakes to their selection and are often self-service; serve tea, coffee, soft drinks, and a few have wine by the glass.

Tea Shop

Serves pots of tea or cups of coffee; scones, muffins, teacakes or similar; also cakes. Occasionally, hot snacks on toast or sandwiches.

Wine Bar

Considers itself up-market from a pub. Serves wine rather than beer. Has some food, especially salads.

DISHES TO LOOK OUT FOR

Bubble & Squeak

boiled cabbage mixed into mashed potato, and fried

Cheese Salad

an uninspired mixed salad with grated Cheddar cheese; Cottage Cheese Salad replaces the Cheddar with low-fat cottage cheese, and Egg Salad has sliced hard-boiled eggs instead

Egg & Chips (& Beans)

fried eggs, french fries and optional baked beans. The baked beans are purchased ready-cooked and are haricots in a sweet tomato sauce.

Jacket potatoes

potatoes baked in their skins, cut open and served with butter (and optional other toppings)

Laverbread

cakes made of seaweed

Muslin Kale

a Scottish vegetable soup, should be made without meat stock

Omelette

the commonest are Plain, Cheese, Mushroom and Spanish, this last

	being filled with peas, onions, tomatoes and potato (not eaten by Spaniards)
Pease Pudding	dried peas boiled into a purée, enriched with added egg and butter, and baked
Ploughman's Lunch	found in pubs only: a disappointing salad with cheese, pickle and bread, all on one plate (not eaten by ploughmen)
Quiche	egg and cheese flan, often accompanied by salad; beware Quiche Lorraine — contains ham
Rumbledethumps	Scottish: potato and cabbage mashed together
Toasted sandwiches and hot snacks 'on toast'	the commonest are mushrooms on toast, tomatoes on toast, egg on toast, (baked) beans on toast and toasted cheese sandwich
Welsh Rarebit (or Rabbit)	another snack 'on toast': melted cheese mixture grilled on toast. Buck Rarebit (or Rabbit) is Welsh Rarebit with a poached egg on top.

BEST OF BRITISH PUDDINGS

Plenty of sugar and carbohydrate — often protein too. Try hard to get home-made, they can be delicious. In cafés they may be submerged in bright yellow instant custard unless you ask to the contrary, though if the custard is good it can make a fitting accompaniment. Avoid other puddings made with suet, jelly/gelatine, junket/rennet (all animal products).

Apple Charlotte	baked apple-and-bread pudding
Apple Crumble	pieces of apple covered with 'crumbly' mixture of flour and

	butter, and baked. Can be made with any other fruit
Bread & Butter Pudding	weighty . . . baked layers of buttered bread with currants and raisins
Cabinet Pudding	a baked mixture of sponge cakes, ratafia (almond) biscuits, dried fruit, candied fruit and custard
Christmas Pudding (or Plum Pudding)	Christmas and New Year only: one of the best — a dense, dark cake baked into a circular shape, made with dried fruits, spices, flour, sugar, treacle, and more. Usually also contains suet but health-food shops sell suet-free Christmas Pudding. A whole pudding should be served *flambé* and ideally eaten with brandy-butter
Custard	a real home-made custard is exquisite: a pale, quite liquid mixture of butter, flour, milk, sugar and egg yolks
(Fruit) Fool	any fruit blended with cream to make a firm mixture
Poor Knights of Windsor	bread soaked in sherry, milk and egg yolks, and then fried
Rice Pudding	rice slowly baked in plenty of milk with sugar and butter until thick and creamy
Sherry Trifle	a cold dessert made in layers of sponge cake soaked in sherry, sliced fruit, ratafia biscuits and custard. Sometimes delicious, sometimes awful — it should have a distinct sherry tang and liquidy custard
Summer Pudding	stewed berries and slices of bread marinaded for many hours in the

fruit's juice until the bread loses its form

Syllabub   a near-liquid dessert of an alcoholic drink blended with cream and sugar until stiff

SELF-CATERING

In my part of London, not just every supermarket but every ordinary grocer's shop sells brown rice, dried beans, lentils, wholewheat bread, free-range eggs, vegetarian cheese, ewe's milk yogurt, soya milk, decaffeinated coffees and herb teas, and keeps in its refrigerator a wide choice of packaged vegetarian meals. One of the supermarkets has, besides packs of commercially-produced vegetarian 'cheddar', two sorts of English farm-made cheeses made with vegetable rennet. Within a mile radius there are a dozen excellent health food shops, some with organic vegetables, besides the delicatessens, Chinese food stores, shops producing fresh pasta, cheese specialists, and many more. Yet in other parts of the capital, particularly the more resolutely English working-class neighbourhoods, none of these are available at all except the health-food shop.

The same contrast exists throughout the country. Prosperous or cosmopolitan, usually very urban, areas have a selection of foods to satisfy all tastes, including vegetarian and wholefood. Rural areas usually offer conventional British food at its worst and most limited. Country towns may be enlivened by attractive markets each week, but when it comes to shopping the paucity of choice and quality is striking. Much of the produce has already lost its freshness — or is still far from ripe. This apparently does not concern the customers, whose interest is more with appearance than quality or taste. On many a market stall you will see the evidence for this in the form of signs declaring, for example, 'Tomatoes — Rock Hard' as if this were an inducement to buy. And indeed, people are buying!

Nevertheless a few foods are worth looking out for. The

pasteurized milk, which the milkman delivers to the door each morning, is fresh and rich. There are many sorts of fresh cream too — particularly good are 'double' and 'clotted'. Matured English Cheddar, easy to find, is one of the world's best cheeses. And search out other traditional cheeses from around the country. Home-grown apples — notably the variety called Cox's Orange Pippin — can be exceptionally good. And ordinary bakers' shops, for all that their bread may not have been baked on the premises, sell some fine white and wholemeal loaves.

Information

Advertisements for the hundreds of vegan and vegetarian hotels, guesthouses, restaurants and shops around the country fill several pages of *The Vegetarian* and similar magazines sold in main newsagents. In addition, *The Vegetarian* carries restaurant reviews and recommendations, local vegetarian society addresses, feature articles about eating out in various parts of the country and plenty of other information. The *International Vegetarian Handbook* is another good source (though phone establishments listed to confirm they are still in business). For more information contact The Vegetarian Society, 53 Marloes Road, London W8 [phone: (01) 937 7739/1714]; or The Vegan Society, 33–35 George Street, Oxford OX1 2AY [phone: (0865) 722166].

A couple of restaurant guides (although some entries may be out of date): Lesley Nelson, *Vegetarian Restaurants in England* (Penguin); and Annabel Whittet, *Where To Eat If You Don't Eat Meat* (Papermac).

Vegetarian Cuisine, edited by Jenny Mann (Fontana/Collins), a collection of recipes from vegetarian restaurants in Britain, is useful as a list of good eating places throughout the country. The Scottish Tourist Board, 23 Ravelstone Terrace, Edinburgh, publishes a free booklet, *A Taste of Scotland*, listing hotels and restaurants with a particular interest in food; most, according to the details given, are happy to provide vegetarian meals.

— *Germany and Austria* —

Europe's German-speaking countries have a long-established preoccupation with health. Fit, glowing, 'love to go a-wandering' types hold a special place in the German heart. There's an abiding love of outdoor activity which gets confused with a love of nature. However, a more useful concern for nature also exists, expressed in the powerful Ecology movement which now plays so crucial a part in West German party politics. Frankly, the interest in the Great Outdoors and health has little or nothing to do with caring for animals. It has, rather, an ascetic, puritanical streak not dissimilar from the legendary Prussian enthusiasm for cold showers; and interestingly, most vegetarian establishments proclaim themselves 'alcohol-free'.

WEST GERMANY

Vegetarianism had many followers in the German states even before the beginning of the nineteenth century. A big vegetarian restaurant (the Vegetarische Gaststätte) started in Hamburg in 1865, in the midst of a period of intense political and idealistic upheaval, and is still going strong — today, a lovely old-fashioned place. A similar flourishing of ideas took place in this century in the turmoil of the 'twenties and 'thirties, and once again vegetarianism gained new ground. However, this period also gave birth to the Nazi party which in the general elections of 1933 was everywhere swept to victory. Although Hitler himself was a vegetarian, he set out to destroy all independent schools of thought — including the vegetarian movement. Instead, through his Youth Movement, he revitalized an earlier ideal of the German as Spartan. Nevertheless, vegetarianism continued to thrive, and now in West Germany it is more popular than ever before.

The traditional focus of this 'alternative' approach to food has been the *Reformhaus*, basically just a health food shop with all the same type of products as its British equivalent. Prices are high, and they have a middle-class image: most towns have at least one. More and more nowadays, there will also be, in larger towns, either a vegetarian restaurant or an ordinary restaurant which can offer a vegetarian menu on request. There is no 'capital' city in the sense that London is the capital of Britain, or Paris of France. Germany's population spreads itself fairly evenly across the country, so facilities do not collect all in one place. Obviously though, cities like Hanover, Bremen or Munich have more to offer than smaller towns.

The normal German diet has a justified reputation for blandness and stodginess. German recipe books mention many meatless dishes, but few of these ever appear on the dining tables either of restaurants or people's homes. Great big thick slices of pork and a heap of boiled potatoes or dumplings are the commonest items, appearing at almost every meal. Ham and sausages are tremendously popular too. Potatoes are prepared in dozens of different ways. Breads are heavy, dark and filling. One distinctive dietary feature is that main courses may include a sweet flavour, especially apples, which are treated as much as a vegetable as a fruit. Unfortunately it seems that the emphasis is firmly on quantity rather than quality. Portions are gigantic. Another traditional custom, now apparently dying out, is that there is no course structure to a German meal — everything comes together. Filling, gassy beers are the usual accompaniment to food, though numerous types of wine (some surprisingly dry, considering the sugariness of the exported varieties), as well as bottled mineral waters and fruit juices, are readily available.

Vegetarian meals have many of the same faults: vast quantities of plain boiled stodge. In vegetarian restaurants I have visited, overdone rice, too many potatoes and great blobs of sticky pasta were dished up with mounds of overboiled vegetables. Attempts at seasoning lacked all delicacy. At times, packet foods from health food shops were used instead of cooking on the premises.

The real division in Germany is not the political line separating East from West, but a cultural divide between North and South. Northerners, much admired as the embodiment of the nation's most sterling characteristics, tend to be more disciplined, stiff-necked and militaristic and their diet contains much more meat. In northern towns vegetarians may at times experience problems finding a hot meal more interesting than a plate of boiled potatoes. In the South, sweeter flavours, potatoes or potato dumplings, other carbohydrates and substantial cakes form a larger part of the diet. Most ordinary restaurants in this part do have something meatless on the menu, and even the classiest places will not be astonished by a request for vegetarian food. However, things are more difficult than they look. It is hard to be 100 per cent certain that you have ever really escaped the German obsession with eating *Fleisch*. The basic cooking fat, used for almost everything, is lard. And even the ubiquitous, inno-cent-sounding *Gemüseplatte*, a plate of boiled vegetables, is some-times boiled in meat stock rather than plain water. *Sauerkraut* (fermented chopped salted cabbage — tasty and nutritious) often includes onions fried in lard, or may be served with sausage chopped into it. Some of the foreign restaurants, including pizzerias and the salad counters of hamburger places, have reliable meatless opportunities. As well as being proud of their 1,450 varieties of sausage, Germans also think of themselves as a cheese-producing nation, although in fact many of their cheeses, such as Brie, Emmental or Camembert, are copies of foreign cheeses; even the two best-loved and most typically German of all — Romadur and Limburger — are actually both Flemish cheeses properly belonging to neighbouring Belgium. Yet even cheese dishes cannot be trusted: minced meat may be concealed in 'cauliflower cheese', and slices of sausage in 'tomatoes stuffed with cheese'. The enticing Emmentaler soup of cheese and vegetables is made with chicken stock. Note though that the various curd cheeses are rennet-free.

Caution is the watchword in Germany. It will be no easy matter to eliminate all trace of lard or meat stock from your food unless eating exclusively in vegetarian restaurants (or self-catering). For the rest, learn how to say 'I am a vegetarian — no meat — and no meat stock', repeat this incantation to the waiter, and hope for the best.

Breakfast and snacks

Considering the vast quantities consumed at each sitting, Germans eat with surprising frequency. Breakfast at home tends to be a relatively simple affair of eggs, bread and coffee, followed in mid-morning by a second breakfast which is much more substantial. Typical hotel or guesthouse breakfasts are a cross between the two, with boiled egg, rolls and butter, jam, processed cheese and coffee with cream. Both tea and coffee are remarkably bad, sometimes almost undrinkable, not just in hotels, but also in cafés and snackbars. Only more expensive *Konditorei* (coffee-and-cake shops) offer a reasonable cup.

The menu of an ordinary *Gasthof* consists of a long list of dishes, some large, but others small enough to suffice if all that's wanted is a snack. There is no obligation to order a full meal in such places. *Schnitten*, light dishes, may be listed on the menu under their own heading. *Käseschnitte*, the most widely available, resembles a heavier and more filling Welsh Rarebit. For something even less formal, inside a *Bäckerei*, bakery, there may be chairs and tables where you can sit to eat a breadroll or pastry and drink a coffee, or in a *Milchbar* or a *Molkerei*, dairy shop, sometimes milk and cheese can be bought to consume on the premises. The numerous *Kaffeehäuser* and *Konditorei* are pastry and cake shops serving tea and coffee: here, in general, everything is delicious. Note that although cakes might conceivably contain lard, and some recipes call for gelatine — another animal product — normally butter is the only fat used in cake-making.

Beer is extremely popular and there are many varieties. It is drunk with food, including second-breakfast, as well as in bars called *Bierstube* or *Schnellimbis* or in more rumbustious halls called *Bierhalle* which capture much German character. Snacks are usually available with the mugs of beer, but these are the least likely places to discover anything without meat.

Lunch and dinner

A *Gasthof* or *Gasthaus* is an inexpensive ordinary eating place. *Schnellimbis* means a snack bar. A *Gaststätte*, a proper restaurant, has more style, or at least more pretension. All exhibit a long printed menu, the *Speisekarte*, with a handwritten or typed menu of the day, the *Tageskarte*, attached to it. The menu of the day, a three-course meal at a modest price, would be the thing to choose if one ate meat. Despite Germany's regional variations, the *Speisekarte* lists the same limited vegetarian possibilities throughout the country.

Almost any menu includes the following meatless items: a vegetable soup, brown bread, a plate of assorted vegetables (*Gemüseplatte*), with or without fried eggs (*Spiegelei*), omelette, a plate of assorted cheeses (*Käseplatte*), salad (*Saladplatte*), chips (*Pommes frites*), or one of the 'snacks' (*Schnitte*) listed under a separate heading, particularly melted cheese on toast (*Käseschnitte*). Although there is no meat or fish in them, these are not truly intended as vegetarian dishes, so there's no guarantee that they are free of meat products. The soup probably has a meat stock, and occasionally (though I have never personally known this to be the case) the *Gemüse* might have been boiled in meat stock rather than water.

Typically, *Gemüseplatte* consists of boiled carrots, cauliflower with a white sauce, peas, french beans, plus one sauce jug of meat gravy and another of melted butter. Every once in a while, with luck, the menu includes something much more interesting, like potato pancakes with mashed apples, *Falafel* (fried chick-pea balls), light fluffy *Knödel* (dumplings) with, say, blueberries and cinnamon, or *Kaiserschmarrn*, which falls somewhere between scrambled egg, omelette and pancake and is a delicious sweet dish, sometimes eaten as a part of a main course.

Some vegetable concoctions intended to accompany meat could be served on their own if your German is good enough to make such a request. For example, *Himmel und Erde*, Heaven and Earth, a purée of mixed apples and potatoes; *Sauerkraut*, salted and fermented white cabbage cooked with other vegetables; or *Apfelrotkohl*, a mixed stew of apples and red cabbage. Among the imported dishes which occasionally find their way on to German menus is the Swiss favourite *Rösti*, fried grated potatoes.

To finish, you could be offered anything from a fruit or some ice cream (often with hot sauce) to substantial layered gateaux or filling egg desserts.

Self-catering and picnics

By far the best way to enjoy eating in Germany is self-catering, because although restaurants make such a poor showing there is nevertheless a wonderful diversity of interesting and tasty food available in the shops. Dairy produce particularly excels, with all sorts of sour cream, buttermilk, both full-cream or low-fat yogurt with or without fruit, as well as the other delicious cultured milk products, such as *Kefir*, which is a tangy yogurt-like liquid, *Handkäse*, moulded curd cheeses, and *Quark*, a thick sharp soft curd cheese also resembling yogurt. *Quark*, aside from being delicious, nutritious and low in calories, has amazing versatility. Eaten straight from the pot, it's all the better for a little honey or fruit, and is often sold that way. Other versions can be bought containing herbs or vegetables. *Magerquark* has a very low fat content, less than 1 per cent, while tastier *Speisequark* has 5 per cent (still considered low) fat. Full fat quark has as much as 12 per cent butterfat. Numerous recipes call for the addition of *quark*, and it is much used in baking and cake-making. Together with the displays of foreign and domestic cheeses, you'll discover several mild cream varieties, processed cheeses and *Frischkäse* (same as French *fromage blanc*), a cool white almost-liquid cheese.

But one thing to be wary of is yogurt which has been set by adding gelatine — a slaughterhouse product.

For brown rice, wholemeal pasta, soya milk, and other grains you may have to seek out a *Reformhaus*, which sells all the familiar 'health foods' — at high prices. Any ordinary grocer or supermarket, though, stocks wholemeal flour, lentils, split peas and potato flour which is for cakes, soups and sauces. Bakers' shops display a superb array of tempting dark breads made of rye and wheat in different combinations. Germany has not only devised the largest number of sausages of any nation, but also the largest variety of breads — a much more worthwhile distinction! *Schwarzbrot* ('black bread'), containing a dense rye and wheat mixture, and *Pumpernickel*, very heavy sourdough with a strong rye flavour, which takes up to twenty-four hours to bake, are two of the best known from the two dozen or more types commonly seen. Altogether there are over 200 sorts, some lovely white breads among them, and such is the range of tastes that sometimes you'll even see someone eating a 'bread sandwich' — a slice of pumpernickel on a piece of buttered white bread. *Landbrot* ('country bread'), a lighter rye bread, comes in round, flattish loaves; *Kümmelbrot* is a heavy, coarse wholemeal mix with caraway seeds; *Leinsamenbrot* has seeds of the linseed plant instead of caraway, which gives it an oily texture; *Vollkornbrot* is 100 per cent whole rye. And there are dry, biscuity bakes too, *Knäckebrot* ('crisp bread') and the stick-shaped *Pretzels*. Bakers sell cakes too, for example orange-flavoured madeira with chocolate covering.

A selection of fruit and vegetables is always available, though not quite as wide a choice as might be expected or hoped. Brassicas, the diverse cousins of the cabbage, are among the most popular. Other useful items on the food-shop shelves are the multitude of coffees, including *entcoffeiniert*, decaffeinated; herb teas; hazelnut butters (and others); honeys; muesli; canned vegetable dishes, especially *Sauerkraut*; and an extraordinary range of vegetable pickles.

From this considerable choice, picnics of bread, milk products, salad and fruit are easy to put together, and if you happen to notice a Nordsee shop, this is a chain of take-away fish snack places which also does handy take-away salads (check they have no fish in them — herrings get put into lots of German snacks).

EAST GERMANY

It's not much fun for vegetarians in East Germany, but then it's not much fun for anyone. Low population density and lack of investment coupled with wartime devastation have resulted in a country beset by shortages and inefficiency: Soviet domination is everywhere oppressively apparent. Not surprisingly, East Germans have much the same diet as West Germans, and are broadly in the more northern meat-and-potato area. There has been some East European influence, but this too leans heavily towards meat. To some extent, this has been modified by the shortage of meat, but fruit and vegetables are in short supply as well. Fortunately, wholemeal bread and curd cheeses are quite plentiful.

Reformhaus shops are rare, but do exist. Until 1961, when the population drift was halted, every year many East Germans would leave for the West. Inevitably vegetarians took part in this exodus, and very few remain. Those that do, the East German Vegetarian Society tells me, are mostly over fifty years old. Eating out is difficult. The state-run *Interhotels* and *Interrestaurants*, intended exclusively for foreign visitors, claim in principle to have one meatless meal available on their menus — in practice, a rather depleted *Gemüseplatte* with a fried egg.

The typical East German breakfast is white rolls with coffee or tea, plus an egg occasionally. The mid-morning 'second breakfast' is exactly the same as the first, perhaps with cake instead of bread. Lunch is the main three-course meal, while dinner in the evening tends to be little more than bread and cheese or fried potatoes, with a glass of beer. The afternoon snack and all other between-meal breaks are generally exactly the same as breakfast.

AUSTRIA

It hardly does justice to the beautiful Alpine country and the traditional, rather jolly way of life of Austria to include it with Germany. Yet it is, and not just from the vegetarian point of view, clearly part of South German culture. Not only is the language the same, but the Deutschmark is readily accepted in payment for all goods instead of Austria's own currency, the Schilling, and the eating habits of the two countries are almost identical.

At mealtimes, there are few non-meat dishes, but again, the *Gemüseplatte* is a possibility. So too could be one of the creamy vegetable soups, pea, lentil or onion, though these should be viewed with some suspicion. A popular Austrian salad is *Gurkesalat*, cucumbers with cream and paprika. Some rustic peasant dishes traditionally have no meat in them, but these make few appearances on restaurant menus, though they might be encountered in unpretentious eating places in country areas. One type would be *Spätzle* dishes, based on big noodles of egg-dough; *Kas Spätzle*, for example, has the noodles baked with onions, cheese and eggs. A Tyrolean speciality called *Gröschtl* is made of potatoes, big milky dumplings and onions, all roasted together until crispy — nowadays this might have bacon in it, but ask to have it made without — a hearty, simple meal, satisfying when eaten with salad.

Unlike Germany, Austria does have a real, living capital city: Vienna, one of Europe's most cosmopolitan, cultured, and historically fascinating towns. Today it has restaurants representing many foreign cuisines, including excellent crêperies, as well as some establishments offering specifically vegetarian meals. The other main towns each have one or two vegetarian places. And, of course, there are *Reformhäuser* in Austria too: self-catering has all the advantages that it has in Germany. Ordinary food shops are extremely well supplied, and the cheese counters have a number of tangy cow's-milk specialities from the mountain villages.

One cannot live on cakes alone, at least not for long unfortunately, but the fact is that Austria's very best cooking is found in the realm of *Mehlspeisen*, 'flour dishes'.

Mehlspeisen includes nearly everything from delicate pastries to rich layered gateaux, and even creamy puddings. In fact, some of the most delicious *Mehlspeisen* have no flour in them at all, but are held together by using ground walnuts, hazelnuts, almonds or chocolate. In summer, fresh fruit pastries add to the abundance. One type of fresh fruit cake, in practically every restaurant and patisserie, is called *Obstschnitte* or *Obstkuchen* according to whether it is sold in slices or whole: this is a rich sponge covered with fresh fruit which sinks into the cake, making it moist and succulent. It makes its annual debut with the first cherries of spring, is made with wild strawberries in high summer, and carries on to the last of the autumn plums. Morello cherries form the basis of many pastries and are mixed with cinnamon, cloves and walnuts to make strudel. The nicest strudel though is still the old favourite, *Apfelstrudel*. Walnuts, ground and fried in butter, are often used instead of breadcrumbs in baking.

Desserts are likely to be the most substantial course in a meal — omelettes filled with strawberries and cream, for example, or rich dark chocolate puddings submerged in iced whipped cream and hot chocolate sauce. Another dessert, sometimes eaten as a main course in people's homes though not in restaurants, is small *Knödel*, dumplings, filled with fruit and fried in butter. The dumplings are made of flour, water, egg and *Topfen*, a soft tangy cheese just like quark.

Not only cakes, but coffee-making has also been developed into a fine art in Austria. Vienna's old coffee houses retain a wonderful character and charm. They are almost like clubs, in a sense, each appealing to a particular type of person. There is never any rush to leave — once someone has installed themselves, perhaps reading the newspapers which are supplied for patrons, they may stay forever and will never be asked to move on. Coffee is prepared in numerous different ways, each appropriate to a time of day, and all equally delicious. The best I ever tried was a large cup of strong black coffee, with a generous head of whipped cream which floated lightly on the surface, topped with a tot of rum. It's quite amazing that Austria does not have a particularly bad record for heart problems!

What to say
Pronounce W as V, and make all Gs hard.

The Essentials

Do you speak English?	Sprechen Sie Englisch?
Hello	Guten Tag (daytime), Guten Abend (evening). In south Germany and Austria, Grüssgott.
Goodbye	Auf Wiedersehen. Much less formal is Servus.
Menu	Speisekarte. Menu of the Day is Tageskarte. A set meal is a Menü or Gedeck.
Have you got . . .	Haben Sie . . .
Please	Bitte. The waiter will also say this before taking the order and when bringing the food, in the sense of 'at your service'.
Thank you (very much)	Danke (schön)
Is this seat free?	Ist hier frei? People sit at occupied tables even in quite smart restaurants.
Eat, drink	Essen, trinken
I am (we are) vegetarian	Ich bin (wir sind) Vegetarier
I don't want meat/fish	Ich möchte keinen Fleisch/Fisch essen.
Is there a vegetarian restaurant near here?	Gibt's ein vegetarisches Restaurant in dieser Gegend?
No } meat/fish/ Without } cheese/egg	Keine Ohne Fleisch/Fisch/Käse/Ei

No meat stock	Keine Fleischbrühe
Is there meat in this?	Gibt es Fleisch darin?
Yes/No	Ja/nein
(Very) good	(Sehr) gut
And/with	Und/mit
Cheers!	Prost!
The bill . . . how much?	Die Rechnung . . . Wieviel?
That/this	Jener/dieser
100, 200, 500 grams . . .	Hundert, zwei Hundert, fünf Hundert Gram . . .
Breakfast, lunch, dinner	Frühstück, Mittagessen, Abendessen
Bread, flour	Brot, Mehl
Rye, wheat, barley, oats	Roggen, Weizen, Gerste, Haferflocken
Rice, brown rice	Reis, braun Reis
Honey, sugar	Honig, Zucker
Yogurt, cheese	Yogurt, Käse. A thick soft curd cheese, eaten on its own or used in cooking is called Quark.
Moulded curd cheeses	Handkäse
Processed cheese	Schmelzkäse
Milk, butter	Milch, Butter. There is a liquid cultured milk called Kefir.
Cream	Rahm or Sahne
Whipped cream	Schlagsahne. In Austria, Schlagobers
Buttermilk	Buttermilch
Egg(s)	Ei(er)
Oil, salt, pepper	Öl, Salz, Pfeffer
Cocoa, coffee, tea	Kakao, Kaffee, Tee
Decaffeinated	Koffeinfrei. Or sometimes, Entcoffeiniert
With milk/cream	A white coffee is Milchkaffee. 'With cream' is mit Sahne. For tea with milk, ask for it mit Milch.

Water	Wasser
-juice	– saft
Beer (large/small/stein)	Bier (grosses/kleines/mass)
Wine (red/white)	Wein (rot/weiss)
Bottle, glass, carafe	Flasche, Glas, Carafe
Quarter-litre of house wine	Schoppen
Health food shop	Reformhaus
Baker	Bäckerei
Dairy shop, milkbar	Molkerei, Milchbar
Grocer	Lebensmittelhandlung
Supermarket	Supermarkt
Cake shop	Konditorei (very often with tables and chairs for tea or coffee).
Places for a drink and a snack	Weinstube, Bierstube, Schnellimbis, Heuriger (Austrian).
Basic restaurants	Gasthof, Gasthaus, Beisel
More stylish restaurant	Gaststätte, Restaurant
Roadside pull-ups	Raststätte, Rasthof
Places selling cakes and coffee	Café, Kaffeehaus

On the menu

-art	in the style of . . .
Beilagen	side dishes
Eierspeisen	egg dishes
Früchte	fruit
Gebackene	baked
Gemischte	mixed
Gemüse	vegetables
Gemüseplatte	plate of cooked vegetables
Gemüsesalat	vegetable salad
Hauptgerichte	main dishes
Hausgemacht	home-made
Kalt	cold

Kartoffel(n)	potato(es). Also known as Erdapfel(n)
Bratkartoffeln	fried
Kartoffelbrei	mashed
Kartoffelpuffer	potato pancakes
Kartoffelklösse	potato dumplings
Kartoffelknödeln	more potato dumplings
Kartoffelsalat	potato salad
Pellkartoffeln	potatoes boiled in their skins
Reibkuchen	potato cake
Rösti	a Swiss speciality: potatoes grated, seasoned, and fried
Röstkartoffeln	roast potatoes
Schwemmkartoffeln	boiled potatoes

but avoid:
Speckkartoffeln and Stampfkartoffeln, which are both potatoes cooked with bacon.

Käse	cheese
Mehlspeisen	'flour dishes'
Nachspeisen	dessert
Nockerln	dumplings
Nuderln	noodles
Pfannengerichte	'frying pan dishes'
Quark mit . . .	. . . in quark
Rohkost	raw vegetables
Rührei	scrambled egg
Salat	salad
Schnitten	small or light dishes; or literally, slices
Sosse	sauce
Spätzle	big noodles (in Swabian style)
Speisen	dishes
Specialitäten	specialities
(zwei) Spiegelei, Spetzei	(two) fried eggs
Stück	a portion
Suppe	soup
Beetensuppe	beetroot soup

Bier-	beer soup, served hot or cold, usually with eggs and spices
Blumenkohl-	cauliflower
Bohnen-	bean (check no meat)
Brot-	bread soup, with bread, apples, wine, and raisins; but don't order if it's von Metzelsuppe, which has meat stock
Erbsen-	split pea
Fruchtkalt-	cold fruit soup
Kartoffel-	potato; check other ingredients — could include leeks, noodles, bacon or sausage
Kerbel-	chervil
Kraut-	cabbage
Linsen-	lentil (but this usually contains meat stock or pieces of pork).
Stoss-	soup of sour milk and potatoes
Tomaten-	tomato
Zwiebel-	onion
Süssspeisen	dessert
Vorspeisen	starters
Warm	hot

Other vegetables

Artischoken (Herzen) — artichoke (hearts); *Auberginen* — aubergine; *Blumenkohl* — cauliflower; *Bohnen* — beans; *Champignons* — mushrooms (there are many kinds); *Chicorée* — endive, chicory; *Erbsen* — general term for all sorts of peas and beans; *Grüne Erbsen* — peas (literally, green peas); *Grünkohl* — curly kale; *Gurke(n)* — cucumber; *Karotten* — carrots; *Knoblauch* — garlic; *Kohl* — cabbage; *Kopfsalat* — lettuce; *Kohlrabi* — a bit like a turnip; *Kraut* — cabbage; *Lauch* — leeks; *Linsen* — lentils; *Mais* — sweetcorn; *Möhren, Möhrruben* — less common words for carrots; *Pilzen* — mushrooms; *Röhnen* — beetroot; *Rosenkohl* — brussel sprouts;

Rotkohl — red cabbage; *Rüben* — turnips; *Sellerie* — celery: *Spargel* — asparagus; *Spinat* — spinach; *Schwammerl* — a kind of mushroom; *Tomaten* — tomatoes; *Truffeln* — truffles; *Zwiebel* — onion; *Zwiebelgrüne* — spring onion.

Fruit and desserts

Apfel — apple: *Bratapfel* — baked, *Apfelkuchen* — delicious apple tart or cake, *Apfelpfannkuchen* — apple-filled pancake, *Apfelreis* — rice pudding with apples; *Apfelsinen* — oranges; *Aprikosen* — apricots; *Arme Ritter* — fried bread with sugar, cinnamon and applesauce; *Backpflaume* — prunes; *Baiser* — meringue; *Banane* — banana; *Birnen* — pears; *Blaubeeren* — bilberries; *Brombeeren* — blackberries; *Erdbeeren* — strawberries; *Feigen* — figs; *Fruchte* — fruit; *Gebäck* — pastry; *Haselnusscreme* — hazelnut butter; *Kastanien* — chestnuts; *Kirschen* — cherries; *-Kranz* means *-cake*; *-Kuchen* means tart or cake; *Mandeln* — almonds; *Mohr im Hemd* — steamed chocolate pudding; *Obst* — fruit; *Orangen* — oranges; *Nuss* — nut; *Pampelmuse* — grapefruit; *Pfannkuchen* — pancakes; *Pfirsich* — peach; *Pflaumen* — plums; *Rosinen* — raisins; *Rumtopf* — fruit soaked in rum; *Schokolade* — chocolate; *Schwarzwalder Kirschtorte* — Black Forest Gateau; *-Torte* means cake, as in *Käsetorte*, cheesecake, or *Nusstorte*, walnut cake; *Topfen* — curd cheese (much used in desserts); *Trauben* — grapes; *Walnuss* — walnut; *Zitrone* — lemon.

Dishes to look out for

As well as things like *Omelette*, *Pizza*, and *Salat*, or *Gemüseplatte*, you may come across:

Apfelrotkohl	apple and cabbage stew, usually supposed to be a side dish for pork
Blinder Huhn	fruit, vegetable and bean stew (check no meat)
Bratkartoffeln, Pommes Frites	fried potatoes

Dresdener Eierschecke	little curd-cheese rolls with nuts and raisins
Falafel	seasoned and fried balls of chick-pea paste
Gebackene Schwammerl	breaded baked mushrooms
Himmel und Erde	purée of apples and potatoes, intended to be served with sausages
Kartoffelpuffer, Reibe-kuchen, Reibtaschen	all potato pancakes
Knödel	bread, potato, or rice dumplings, with or without fillings (usually fruit)
Langos	refried garlic pancake
Leipziger Allerei	mixed vegetable dish (but ask if any meat)
Palatschinken	large baked crêpes with either curd cheese or fruit
Rösti	fried grated potatoes
Sauerkraut	fermented salted grated white cabbage, served with other vegetables (check no sausage)
Weinkraut	Sauerkraut cooked in wine

But beware of

Brühe	(meat) stock
Heringe	herrings (they get everywhere)
Speck	lard, bacon fat — very much used
Schmalz	More accurate word for lard, or dripping
Frühlingsuppe	a vegetable soup with meat stock
Knödelsuppe	dumplings in meat stock
Rotkohlsalat	red cabbage salad, but usually with bacon
Schinken	ham

. . . and anything ending in – Wurst is a sausage

Information

West German and German-Swiss organizations and publications are relevant for all Europe's German-speaking areas.

West Germany: The main vegetarian organization is Vegetarier-Bund Deutschlands, contactable through Rudolf Meyer, Munzeler Str. 18b, 3000-Hannover 91, West Germany (phone: 0511-42.46.47). They publish *Der Vegetarier*, plus many factsheets, booklists, and a useful restaurant and guesthouse list which is accurate and up-to-date for Germany itself but not so good for foreign countries.

Institution Ganymed is a holiday company and tour operator which organizes social and sporting events, classes and seminars, leisure activities and foreign holidays, all on an exclusively no-meat, no-smoking, and no-alcohol basis. Their address is Niddagaustrasse 18, 6000-Frankfurt/Main 90, West Germany (phone 069-78.47.54/78.39.70).

West German tourist offices abroad (in UK: 61 Conduit Street, London W1 [phone (01) 734 5853] issue a list of vegetarian restaurants, but this is now over five years old.

East Germany: The small and helpful vegetarian society is Arbeitsgemeinschaft DDR-Vegetarierfreunde, Konigsberger Weg 13, 6238 Hofhein/Ts, East Germany (phone 06192-26333).

Austria: Local tourist offices have up-to-date restaurant lists including details of vegetarian restaurants. The National Tourist Offices abroad (in UK: 30 St George Street, London W1 [phone: (01) 629 0461] have lists for Vienna and other main towns. The Austrian Vegetarian Society is Osterreichische Vegetarier Union, Dipl. Ing. Julius Fleischanderl, Leechgasse 2, 8010-Graz, Austria (phone: 316-358714).

See also: 'Switzerland' (page 95).

Holland

The Dutch like filling food and plenty of it. Big pieces of meat and heaps of potatoes dominate the diet. Anything extremely high in cholesterol will be particularly favoured as a side-dish or between-meals snack: chips covered with mayonnaise are top favourite. Shops and cafés selling cakes, pastries, filled rolls, sandwiches and waffles trade busily all day long. For a hearty bowl of soup people pop into what the Dutch call a café — a charming, relaxed place close in atmosphere to an English pub. Having to guard against meat obviously inhibits a full participation in this free-and-easy approach to food.

Fortunately, vegetarians, vegans and macrobiotics are all numerous in Holland and have amply provided themselves with restaurants. In addition, many conventional snackbars and restaurants make a point of offering vegetarian dishes. Particularly in Amsterdam, that strange, enchanting city both decadent and civilized, besides having several specifically vegetarian establishments, almost any type of eating place from a humble café to a high-class French restaurant is likely to have either some traditional meatless dish or else some specially devised vegetarian alternative. Always look on menus (displayed outside premises) for the words *Vegetarische Schotel*, vegetarian dish.

The Dutch like foreign food; main towns have all sorts of ethnic restaurants. Thanks to Holland's colonial history, Indonesian restaurants can be found in every part of the country, even in small towns and villages. These can usually accommodate vegetarians without much difficulty and may have meatless dishes on the menu. Nowadays Indonesian cuisine overlaps with Dutch, so that any ordinary eating place may include an oriental plate or two on its menu, and something like spicy peanut sauce could turn up with otherwise completely Dutch food.

Whether the restaurant is Indonesian, Dutch or otherwise, it's best to say that you want vegetarian food rather than merely leaving things to chance — the waiter can help you choose something suitable, and may reveal meatless options not listed on the menu.

Light meals and snacks

Bread rolls with butter and a cup of good strong coffee with cream is the usual start to the day, perhaps with a few slices of cheese or a bowl of muesli. Hotels add ham and hard-boiled eggs. No sooner has breakfast finished than people start making use of the multitude of places selling pancakes, sandwiches and rolls, pastries, pies, bowls of soup, chips and the rest.

A *Lunchroom*, despite the name, has coffee, tea, and light meals or snacks at any time of day. *Broodjeswinkel* means a sandwich bar, popular for a light lunch or quick bite. *Patatshop* is a down-to-earth chip shop or stall: chips will be covered with mayonnaise unless you especially ask for them not to be. There are several other sauces instead — try *pindersaus*, spiced peanut-butter sauce. Anything called a *Snackbar* is just that, but again would do nicely for a light lunch. More high-class, a *Tearoom* comes into its own in mid-afternoon: a tea shop and coffee house with a fine selection of pastries and cakes. *Pannekoeken*, pancakes, are widely available, often from places that sell nothing else. Variations include *flensjes*, crêpes, and *poffertjes*, smaller, thicker pancakes like doughnuts. There's a proliferation of foreign-style fast foods, not just hamburgers but pizzas, crêperies, and the up-and-coming croissanteries.

The Dutch café, affectionately known as *bruine kroegen*, or brown café, is open all day with alcoholic drinks and hot beverages at bar or table, toasted sandwiches and freshly-made soup, a warm subdued atmosphere, and newspapers to read. Those with a fair selection of 'hot and cold bar snacks', as they would be called in English, are known as *Eetcafes*.

Lunch and dinner

Lunch is from 12 noon till 2 p.m. and dinner at about 6 p.m. The normal formula for a Dutch meal is soup; meat, potatoes and one other vegetable; maybe a side dish of salad or another vegetable; and dessert. Not many people want all that twice a day, so at lunchtime restaurants offer what they call a *koffietafel*, a light set lunch of bread and perhaps cheese and/or cold meat or soup, maybe a salad, and a cup of coffee (or tea or a glass of milk). It's often possible to have this without meat.

Low-priced set meals feature in most restaurants, and are the standard way of eating. At dinner time, this can make life harder rather than easier for the vegetarian. One way to deal with a set meal can be to substitute an omelette for the meat.

Vegetables are prepared and presented with a certain flair. To give but one instance, green beans are always served with butter and nutmeg. If proper vegetable dishes have been made, rather than mere boiled vegetables, these can turn out to be filling: a meal could prove quite sufficient (unless your appetite is of Dutch proportions) even with the meat left out. When choosing à la carte, ask the waiter if things have meat in them: for example, both *Tomatensoep* (tomatosoup) and *Erwtensoep* (pea soup) probably do contain meat, or at least meat stock. Waiters generally have proved sympathetic and helpful, and often propose things which are not listed on the *menukarte*, the written menu. Some side dishes make excellent vegetarian food: apple purée and grated cucumber are two commonly seen.

Useful resources for those in search of a meatless dinner include all the Indonesian and other foreign restaurants, pizzerias and self-service cafeterias. Obviously the number of vegetarian restaurants varies from place to place. Some towns have none, others have just one or two, and others — like Amsterdam — dozens. Among the many places which offer a vegetarian alternative meal are the railway station buffets. Remember too that many Dutch snacks could serve as a full meal for those with modest appetites.

Self-catering and picnics

Dutch supermarkets have as good a range of fresh and frozen foods, ready-to-cook meals, canned foods, muesli and 'health foods', grains, pastas, cooking oils, coffees and other drinks, as any in Europe. Vegetarian produce is stocked as a matter of course in most towns. The dairy section holds a magnificent store of good rich milk, excellent yogurts, buttermilk, *kwark*, cream (which is liberally used in coffee and on desserts), butter and cheeses. Specialist cheese shops and delicatessens sell cheese and dairy produce of course, but also ready-to-eat take-away snacks.

For centuries, though such a small country, The Netherlands has been the world's largest exporter of cheese, although hardly more than two dozen varieties in total are produced. Those which travel to all four corners of the globe tend to be creamy, firm, and bland, Edam and Gouda being the best known. Those which stay in Holland have more bite and more flavour. Caraway flavoured Leidse or Leiden is particularly good. Look out for cheeses labelled *Boerenkaas*, for these are farm-made as opposed to the more usual factory-produced cheeses. Note that Edam in Holland does not have the red waxy skin which makes the exported version so familiar.

Bakers and cake shops have an impressive choice of good breads, rye, wholemeal, tasty bread rolls *(broodjes)*, waffles and take-away snacks.

What to say

Though not quite universal, English is very widely spoken in The Netherlands, and with a remarkable fluency in many cases. Nevertheless a few basic Dutch phrases could prove invaluable. Pronunciation is tricky: G and CH are both guttural, like the *ch* in Scottish *loch* — G is the softer, closer to *h*; the diphthong IJ sounds rather like *ay*; J sounds as *y*; R must be trilled; V sounds like *f*; and where the letters CHTJ appear together it makes a sound like a Dutch CH followed by a Dutch J.

I am (we are) vegetarian   Ik ben (wij zijn) vegetariër — pro-
                                    nounced *vayhutarier*

I (we) don't eat meat	Ik (wij) ate geen vlees — last two words pronounced *hain flais*
No ⎱ meat/fish/ Without ⎰ animal fat	Geen ⎱ vlees/vis/dierlijk vet Zonder ⎰
Is there meat in it?	Is er vlees in?
Is there something we can eat?	Is dit iets dat wij kunnen eten?
Please/thank you (very much)	Als't u blief/Dank u (wel)
Yes/no	Ja/nee
And/with	En/met
Breakfast/light set lunch/dinner	Ontbijt/koffietafel/avondeten, diner
The bill . . . how much (is it)?	De rekening . . . hoeveel (is het)?
That/this	Dat/dit
100, 200, 500 grams	Honderd/twee honderd/vijf honderd grams
(Brown) rice/wholemeal bread	(Bruine) rijst/(volkoren) brood
Rye, wheat, lentils	Rogge, tarwe, linze
Beans, fruit, vegetables	Bonen, vrucht, groenten
Honey, sugar	Honing, suiker
Yogurt, buttermilk	Yogurt, kernemelke
Milk, butter	Melk, boter
Cheese, egg(s)	Kaas, ei(eren)
Cream, whipped cream	Room, slagroom
Oil, salt, pepper	Olie, zout, peper
Tea, coffee	Thee, koffie. (With milk = met melk; With cream = met room; With whipped cream = met slagroom; Half milk, half coffee = verkeerd; Black = zwarte; Decaffeinated = cafeïnevrije)

Water, wine, beer	Water, wijn, bier
(Fruit) juice	(Vruchte) sap

The other popular Dutch drink is *jenever*,gin.

Baker	Bakker
Greengrocer	Groenteboer
Grocer	Kruidenierswinkel
Health food shop	Reformawinkel
Supermarket	Supermarkt

Bistro, Café, Cafeteria, Eetcafe, Koffieshop, Lunchroom, Restaurant, Snackbar, Tearoom are all places with snacks or meals.

Dishes to look out for

Bami	Indonesian noodles and vegetables (check no meat)
Bitterballsen	potato croquettes often served with peanut sauce (check not made of meat instead of potato)
Brood Pudding	bread-and-butter pudding with egg and cinnamon
Caramelva	caramel custard
Drie-In-De-Pan	sugared pancakes filled with fruit
Huzarensalade	an hors d'oeuvres of boiled potatoes with mayonnaise, egg and pickle (check no meat)
Kaassouffle	cheese soufflé
Nassi	Indonesian rice and vegetables (check no meat)
Omelet	omelette
Roereiren	scrambled egg
Salade	salad
Sla	simple green salad
Spiegelei	fried egg
Vlaai	large fruit tart served with cream. A speciality in Limburg (the south east) where it's known as 'Lim-

	burgse Vlaai'. A popular snack.
Witlof met kaassaus	chicory in cheese sauce
Zuurkool	sauerkraut (check no ham mixed into it)

But beware of

Tosti — it sounds like toast, but in fact it's grilled cheese and ham on toast: you could try asking for it *'zonder ham'* (without ham). *Russian salad* — usually includes shrimps.

And avoid altogether

Anything whose name begins or ends with *-speck*: it means bacon.

Information

The Dutch vegetarian society, called De Nederlandse Vege-tariersbond, Duinweg 14, 9479 TM Noordlaren, The Nether-lands [phone: (05905) 1329]. They publish a magazine, *Leven & Laten Leven.*

Local tourist offices, clearly marked with a sign saying 'VVV', are knowledgeable and helpful; they have addresses of vegetarian restaurants in their area.

The National Reservations Centre, in The Hague, can tell you what vegetarian and other restaurants exist (and reserve a table) in every town in Holland [phone: (070) 202500].

Netherlands Board of Tourism offices in foreign countries (in UK at: 143 New Bond Street, London W1 [phone: (01) 499 9367]) have no written documentation to hand out but do have a complete list of their own, which they are happy to consult for you, of vegetarian and other restaurants throughout Holland.

Ireland

It would be quite wrong to suppose that Ireland is just like Britain in food or anything else. Despite centuries of domination by its powerful neighbour, Ireland retains much that is purely its own. Even Ulster, for the visitor, is far more obviously Irish than British. Ireland has enormous attractions and interest — it is the most rustic and unmodern society in the English-speaking world; its people seem genuinely kind-hearted and uncontrived; there's often a feeling that everything is thirty years behind the times (in places, they still have phone boxes where you have to 'Press Button B'!); and, both inland and on the coast, there is astonishingly beautiful scenery. In the Republic, despite the IRA's long and bitter (and eventually successful) struggle for independence, curiously there is today no ill-feeling at all towards the British, though this is not true in the six northern counties which remain in the UK. Ireland has all the advantages of a foreign country, with none of the hassle; British citizens don't even need a passport to go there.

Although one of the most eminent of all vegetarians was Irish — George Bernard Shaw — he neither sprang from nor gave rise to any tradition of vegetarianism. In country areas many people have never so much as heard the word and certainly cannot imagine what it means. Not surprisingly, the Irish attitude to eating is coloured by the still-unhealed wounds of the nineteenth-century Famine, in which one million died and another million emigrated (often merely to die of hunger in another part of the world). The gypsy-like tinkers who roam the byways of western Ireland with their caravans, or nowadays more usually live in huge camps on the edge of Dublin, are believed to be descendants of displaced Famine survivors.

There is much to understand about Ireland. The Famine,

terrible in itself, had an aspect which worsened it considerably: throughout the period of the mass starvation, large cargoes of food were being exported from Ireland by the English landlords from whom the peasants rented their land. At the height of the Famine, Irish meat was reckoned among the very best by gourmets at London's restaurant tables. The Irish peasantry, on small, much-subdivided holdings, were themselves surviving largely on potatoes, which had originally been attractively easy and cheap to grow, versatile, requiring little land. As overpopulation and shortages increased, potatoes (eaten half-cooked for longer digestion) became the whole diet. Famine resulted inevitably from the mid-nineteenth century potato blight and bad harvests. Even before these years, historians record*, the peasant family had lived for centuries on milk, butter and cakey bread, as well as potatoes, and rarely, if ever, ate any meat.

All this probably explains why the Irish today like plain, hearty meals with plenty of meat. Cured or processed meats, rich French sauces or subtle foreign delicacies have no following in Ireland. Even cheese is not popular — local varieties have all but died out. What's preferred here is a big slab of meat with a generous helping of straightforward no-nonsense vegetables like potatoes and cabbage. Most Irish dishes revolve around various parts of the pig, while a few places specialize in freshly-caught fish. There are some exceptions, for cheap at-home eating: fry-ups of potatoes and onions ('champ'), Colcannon — a mushy vegetable stew, and dried seaweed called dulse. All these are typically Irish, but they do not find their way on to restaurant menus and I have never encountered any of them when eating out. (Beware of Laver soup, a traditional vegetable and seaweed stew: it has a fish stock). At home or in cafés, with food or between meals, enormous quantities of terribly strong 'stewed' tea perk up the day.

Rustic and pastoral, Ireland depends more on the meat industry than most other nations. Vegetarianism might almost be a

*Mary Daly, *Social and Economic History of Ireland since 1800*, (Educational Co., Dublin); K. H. Connell, *The Population of Ireland 1750–1845*, (Clarendon Press, Oxford).

dirty word here, and two or three times local people have challenged me to explain 'What on earth would happen to Ireland if everyone was a vegetarian? To which the answer is, of course, that it would be very different. And a lot fewer animals would be slaughtered. At town and city markets, meat is the main 'product' on sale, and none of it imported.

Where and what to eat

Travelling around as a vegetarian is not impossible. Cafés can offer egg, beans and chips, sandwiches, or big pieces of wholemeal bread with butter. Freshly made wholemeal breads, cakes, buns, scones and pies are everywhere available. Some of the breads weigh extremely heavy . . . a couple of slices should fill you up for hours! With this abundance of bakery, tea-time is a moment to enjoy.

Pubs have a particular role in Irish life. It is true that the Irish drink a good deal of beer, but more than that, the public house, usually with no other name than that of its proprietor (for example Murphy's, or Paddy O'Reilly's), is a place for men and women to meet their friends and neighbours, relax, and talk. They have a warm, intimate atmosphere into which, nevertheless, strangers are warmly welcomed. In the evenings as likely as not a group of local musicians will come in and exuberantly play Irish folk songs on fiddle and flute. Pub food includes little for vegetarians beyond a cheese sandwich, though the beer — rich, heavy stouts are the most popular — could practically stand as a meal in itself.

Simple bed and breakfasts and guesthouses may also find themselves stumped for meatless dinner ideas. Macaroni cheese, omelette or salad, if you suggest them, can usually be made. At the other end of the market, Ireland has a remarkable number of superb top-quality restaurants and hotels worthy to compete with Europe's best. These establishments prove unexpectedly capable of providing a meal without meat. The acclaimed Arbutus Lodge at Cork was only too happy to have a couple of vegetarians to feed. While we sipped our drinks by the fire in the lounge, waiting to be called to our table, the chef sent out a handwritten list of suggestions. It was especially impressive that he remembered *not* to include the vegetable soup, which, he told us later, had a chicken stock. The meal and wine list were outstanding, but not, of course, cheap. This was among the best meals I have eaten to date anywhere, having that touch of what vegetarian restaurants lack — *haute cuisine* (the *patron/chef* was trained by the brothers Troisgros, famous throughout France for their restaurant at Roanne). And 20 miles east of Cork, the unique and celebrated hotel-restaurant Ballymaloe House produced an interesting vegetarian menu (not *haute cuisine*, however!) without fuss as soon as we made our needs known.

Dublin, though a capital city, and one with an exceptional literary and intellectual tradition, preserves a pleasant provincial air, and in few provincial cities in Britain is it so easy for a vegetarian to find something to eat. At lunchtime, certainly, particularly in the University area north of the Liffey, there are studenty pizzerias, restaurants and cafés where a complete and wholesome meal without meat can be found. Things are not quite so simple in the evening, when fewer suitable places are open. Some are, including (at the time of writing) at least one wholefood restaurant with both meat and meatless main courses. It's worth checking the tourist office in Dublin, at 14 Upper O'Connell Steet. They produce a useful handbook, the *Dublin Official Guide*, with listings for health food shops, wholefood restaurants and the vegetarian society.

Ulster

The 'six counties' of Northern Ireland follow a similar pattern. Potatoes appear at every meal; apart from that, few vegetables are eaten except the home-grown staples of carrots, onions and cabbage. Others, like courgettes or peppers, can be found but are expensive and are even now considered exotically foreign. Restaurants and cafés have little, if anything at all, without meat. The best hope is a salad. Unlike the Republic, fish is rarely eaten in the North — most of their fish is exported — and the diet is consequently even more meaty. Pubs usually offer lunches of Irish stew or similar; the Ploughman's is unknown. As in the South, filling breads and cakes are the one redeeming feature: potato bread has more in common with potato than with bread; soda bread is white and powdery; wheaten bread has a grey colour, is dry in the mouth, and has plenty of body — one slice is generally enough.

Despite the obstacles vegetarianism is a little more common in Ulster than in the Republic. Good quality health-food shops provide, at a price, all that's needed. But meatless eating has to be confined to home because, even in Belfast, eating out presents difficulties. It is not totally impossible though; one vegetarian restaurant (Zero) has been established for several years, and among the restaurants along Great Victoria Street, the city's main thoroughfare, one or two exist where a meatless meal could be put together.

Self-catering

Irish Tourist Board offices abroad have information on renting country cottages. This popular type of holiday provides peace and quiet and close contact with the uncomplicated way of life of rural Ireland. Remember though that outside principal urban areas few health food shops exist, and the stock in an ordinary grocer's looks bleakly unrewarding for a vegetarian. Take with you enough brown rice and other essentials to last, and for the rest it's a case of making do with what the village shop provides.

Information

The UK Vegetarian Society treats Eire (the Republic of Ireland) as part of Britain and their handbook lists addresses of the Vegetarian Society of Ireland, the Ulster Vegetarian Society, and health food shops in several towns. The Northern Ireland Animal Rights Movement is at 3 Donegall Street, Belfast [phone: (0232) 240671].

Russia and Eastern Europe

RUSSIA

Before starting work on this book I wrote a letter to *The Vegetarian* magazine asking readers to contact me with any suggestions or advice. Amazingly, well over half the replies were from vegetarians who had recently visited the USSR. What can be the particular appeal of the Soviet Union to vegetarians? The ballet, the architecture, or the way of life perhaps; but certainly it can't be the food. According to the Russian folk saying:

> Shchi da kasha
> Pishcha nasha.

(*Cabbage stew and buckwheat, That's all we eat*) . . . which isn't true any more. Unfortunately though, a considerable gap still separates the Russian cuisine of cookery books from the food actually available in the USSR. Both provide substantial, solid fare designed, one feels, mainly to ward off the effects of a rigorous climate. Eating with Russian emigrés in various parts of the world gives an impression of a rich and varied diet, full of interesting dishes, lovely vegetable soups, pies and pastries, and lashings of delicious sour cream.

Intourist, the USSR's state-owned tour operator, has this reassuring message for visitors in search of meatless food: 'Tourists can request vegetarian meals in hotels in the USSR, and there is no difficulty ordering vegetarian meals in restaurants. Traditional Russian meals often feature vegetable soups and salads as well as savoury and sweet pancakes which do not always include meat or fish.'

However some of those who have actually been tell a different story. Maria Mann, of Nottingham:

'In the USSR, I stayed at hotels in Leningrad, Minsk, and Moscow.

The hotels were informed that I was vegetarian. It became clear that vegetarianism and knowledge of vegetarian food is not very widespread in the Soviet Union. It is impossible for a vegetarian to eat healthily in Russia. I was given 'vegetable' soups that had shreds of meat in. In any case, Russians use meat broth to make their soups. The average meal provided for me was rice, chips, and gherkins, or pickled cabbage, carrots, and tinned peas, sometimes with white sauce on top. Occasionally I was given protein in the form of hard-boiled eggs, cottage cheese mixed with sour cream and sugar, or slices of cheese. All too often the hard-boiled eggs were topped with caviar. I ate a great deal of black bread and butter to keep me going, and took vitamins and mineral supplements with me.

Rosemary Stevens, of Cheltenham, summed up her food in Russia like this:

'Canned orange juice/greasy cheese (origin very doubtful)/rye bread. There's no food available in the shops although I did see some people joining very long queues in order to purchase a cabbage.' She too advises 'take your own food or decide to go on a stringent diet.'

Unlike most visitors to the USSR, Barry Gray travelled by road, usually self-catering and sometimes eating out. He reports:

'It's not easy to buy food. The problem is lack of variety. Most of the time people eat only meat, bread, potatoes, and sometimes cabbage. When other vegetables are in season, for example cucumbers or tomatoes, they suddenly become abundant — but not in restaurants. The bread is interesting, either white, or else heavy, rough, and dark. Shops also have milk, cream, and fruit in season. In restaurants I had poached eggs, bread, and salad nearly every time, while other customers had a meaty set meal with not much choice. No English is spoken, but some German. In one place I told the waitress I don't eat meat. She laughed and asked "Are you a man?" At tourist sites and in Moscow there are "hard currency bars" and self-service buffet restaurants with more variety. One thing that's always readily available is drink: yeasty beer, revolting wine which dyes the teeth, incredibly cheap "champagne", and rough brandy and vodka.'

Russians, incidentally, always drink vodka neat, in one gulp, and always eat *zakuski*, little snacks, to go with it.

A well-travelled friend, Hilary Munt, seems to have had better experiences than the average, though she too found it hard as a vegetarian. She tells me:

'Package tour hotels in Moscow and Leningrad give three fairly hefty meals a day. The food, on the whole, is lukewarm but rather interesting.

'Breakfast is often lovely hot eggy dishes, gorgeous savoury baked custards, something like warm cheesecake. There's always solid good-tasting bread and Russian tea as well.

'Lunch is my favourite meal with hors d'oeuvres like grated carrot topped with sour cream, Russian salad (like our vegetable salad), and coleslaws in nice mayonnaise sauces. Evening meals, difficult for vegetarians, often start with a hot soup — for example *Borsht*, the famous beetroot and cabbage soup, but here it has slivers of meat in it. The main courses are usually casseroles with a few vegetables, beans, carrots, and potatoes. Concessions seem to have been made to the Westerner's taste with chips appearing occasionally, although not very successfully. Eggs can usually be had on request.

'Ice-cream with fruit conserves in syrup is a popular dessert even with temperatures well below freezing. A street ice-cream seller I saw was doing a roaring trade when temperatures rose to $-3°C$. The only variation for dessert is a nice range of sticky buns and cakes.

'Eating out is expensive and unusual for the 'package' visitor. Restaurants on the whole want hard currency. One could choose salads and vegetables from an à la carte menu — rather un-Russian.

'Having a glass of coffee and a little plain cake is a must to sample Russian life, fitted in between touring the Kremlin and dashing off to the 'Berioshka' for tourist shopping. Food shops (*Gastronom*) are not really suitable for the picnicker. An organized system of queueing makes shopping a lengthy process with the final purchase artfully wrapped in brown paper and string.'

As well as self-service cafés and ordinary bars with snacks, I have heard tell of curious 'ice cream bars' where the proper drink to have with ice cream is Russian champagne. Most visitors head to Moscow, and perhaps take in a visit to Leningrad. Further south though, approaching the Balkans and the Middle East, fruit and vegetables become more plentiful, and the style of cooking more varied and enjoyable. The diet changes still more as you head east, out of European Russia into Asia.

What to Say

Russian language uses the Cyrillic alphabet. For the most part I have changed this to our familiar Roman letters and spelt the words as pronounced (None of the letters are silent. Sound J's as in 'Taj Mahal').

The Essentials

Do you speak English/ French/German?	Gavareéte lee vy pa angleéskee/ frantsoóeskoi/nemetskoi?
Good day/evening	Dobre den/vécher
Hello/goodbye	Zdráhstvooite/do svidanie
Please/thank you	Pazhahlsta/spasibo
Menu	Menoo, meniu. It's quite normal for hotel restaurants and many others to have no written menu — just a set meal. Cafés and bars with food likewise may have no written list.
I am (we are) vegetarian	Ya (my) vegetarianets (vegetar-iantsi)
I (we) cannot eat meat or fish	Ya (my) ne mogu (ne mojem) yest myaso i ribu
No meat/fish/caviar	Myaso/riba/ikra net
Without meat/fish/caviar	Bez myasa/ribi/ikri
Is there meat in this?	Yest myaso v etom?
Animal fat, meat stock	Jir, boolón
Yes/no	Da/niet
And/with	Ee (or da)/S
Cheers!	Na Zdorovie
The bill	Schyot
Fruit, vegetables	Frookty, ovashchi

Rice, buckwheat (uncooked)	Ris, grechikha
Black (rye) bread/white bread	Chornoye khleb/beloye khleb
Cheese, eggs	Syr, yaitsa
Milk, sour cream	Moloko, smetana
Ice cream, yogurt	Morojenoye, prostokvasha
Butter, (vegetable) oil	Másla, rastityelnoye máslo
Salt, pepper	Sol, pyeryets
(Mineral) water, juice	(Mineralniye) vodi, soki
Beer, wine, vodka	Piva, vino, vodka
Bottle, glass	Butilka, stakáhn
Coffee	Kofe. Russian coffee is not much good, and an ordinary jar of instant brought from the West can be sold for a fortune!
Tea	Chai — nearly as important to Russians as vodka. In cafés, trains and anywhere that people gather you'll see the *samovar*, a big urn of boiling water used to make very strong black tea served in glasses and sweetened either with sugar or with jam.
Food shop	Gastronom, Гастроно́м
Grocer	Bakaleya, Бакале́я
Baker	Bóolachnaya, Бу́лочная

On the menu
Aubergine — *Baklajan*; Beans — *Fasol*; Beetroot — *Svyokla*; Cabbage — *Kapusta*; Cucumber — *Ogurtzi*; Gherkins — *Kornishon*; Mushrooms — *Gribi*; Onion — *Luk*; Tomatoes — *Pomidori*; (Fried) Potatoes — *Kartoshki*, *Kartofel (Fri)*.

Borshch, Борш	beetroot soup containing other vegetables — and usually meat too
Free, Фри	chips, French fries

Galushki, Галушкн	doughy fritters, served with sour cream
Kiessel, Кисель	thick tangy fruit purée
Kvass, Квас	a drink (also used as a cooking stock) made from fermented rye bread
Omelette, Омлет	probably with lard
Ovoshchi, Овоши	vegetables
Piroshki, Пирожки	small stuffed pies or pastries filled with meat, fish, cabbage or soft cheese
Salati, Салатı	salad — many varieties
Sous, Соус	sauce
Sladkoye, Сладкое	desserts, puddings
Smetana, Сметана	sour cream
Torti, Тортı	cakes
Tvorog, Творог	soft cheese something like a smooth cottage cheese, used in cooking
Vtoroye, Второе	main course
Zakuski, Закуски	starters, hors d'oeuvres, canapés, nibbles to have with vodka

Dishes to look out for

Always check whether or not these contain meat, even though in principle they should not. Vegetable soups, like the classic cabbage-based *Shchi*, are usually made with meat stock. Note that lard is used to cook many of the vegetable dishes.

Abrikosovi Sup, Абрикосовыı Суп	sweetened apricot soup, served cold with rice and sour cream
Baklajannaya Ikra, Баклажанная Икра	'aubergine caviar' — no fish used: a purée of aubergine, onion, tomato, olive oil and lemon juice
Blinchiki, Блинчики	crêpes or pancakes with savoury or sweet fillings

Bliny, Блины	hot yeasted buckwheat pancakes served with portions of sour cream, caviar, melted butter. You can leave the caviar
Chorniye Olivi, Черные Оливи	salad of olives, hard-boiled eggs, onions and garlic
Farshirovaniye Petzi, Фаршированные Перцы	stuffed peppers, usually with vegetables only
Gribnaya Ikra, Грибная Икра	'mushroom caviar': no fish
Kabachkovaya Ikra, Кабачковая Икра	'courgette caviar': no fish
Kartofelni Salat, Картофельный Салат	potato salad including onion, egg, and sour cream
Kasha, Каша	buckwheat porridge
Khachapuri, Хачапури	a sort of pie or bread with ewe's cheese and yogurt
Ogurtzi v Smetana, Огурцы в Сметане	cucumbers, sometimes stuffed with vegetables, in sour cream
Rediska v Smetana, Редиска в Сметане	diced radishes in sour cream
Syrniki, Сырники	fried cottage cheese and potato pastries, eaten with sour cream
Tvorojniki, Творожники	boiled cream cheese balls
Varyeniki, Вареники	tasty pastries filled with fruit, vegetables, cheese or meat
Vatroushki, Ватрушки	cottage cheese pastries
Vishnovi Sup, Вищневый Суп	cherry soup, served cold
Yablochni Sup, Яблочный Суп	sweetened apple soup, served cold
Yagodni Sup, Ягодный Суп	sweetened soup of wild berries, cream and egg yolk

EASTERN EUROPE

Under this broad heading have been ranked all the so-called Communist countries in Europe. Not because they have anything in common — although there are certainly similarities between them — but rather because in all of them it's difficult for foreign visitors to find a meal without meat. Officials of the small State-controlled tourist industries, anxious though they may be to attract visitors (or rather, their money), have little idea how to respond to individual needs. Yugoslavia, which has resisted the Soviet domination which has stamped the character of the other East European nations, has been given a section of its own (see page 107), while its tiny neighbour Albania, another exception to the rule, instead discovers itself — which would make its ideological blood boil! — listed here with the East European states.

Albania

Not part of the Soviet bloc, Albania has pursued a path of bizarre isolation for thirty-five years. However, it is not impenetrable: organized groups of tourists are permitted to enter the country, which remains fascinatingly rustic and old-fashioned. The 70-mile Mediterranean coast has no modern development at all. Visitors stay, and are fed, at run-down hotels where they are unlikely to meet any Albanians. This is a poor country, and there's not much variety in the food. However, lunch and dinner are always four courses, with boiled vegetables, especially potatoes, served in generous portions, and sticky cakes to finish. Vegetarians are not well catered for, and should take muesli and/or other foods to keep themselves properly fed. At mealtimes they'll generally be offered a plate of boiled vegetables, perhaps with white rice or chips. Breakfast is always eggs and toast. For more information, contact The Albanian Society, 26 Cambridge Road, Ilford, Essex IG7 8LU.

Bulgaria

In the Balkans — say an area taking in Bulgaria, Albania, Greece, southern Yugoslavia and western Turkey — the three styles of eating represented by the three sections of this book come together to form an intriguing transitional style of their own. Greece, Yugoslavia and Turkey have each been dealt with separately, and among Bulgarian dishes you will find much that resembles their food. As in those countries, particularly Yugoslavia, the range of meatless dishes in restaurants is limited, but can be supplemented with fresh fruit, salad vegetables, and bread bought in the markets. Bulgaria's greatest edible asset must surely be yogurt. Rich, tangy, and made of full-fat ewe's milk, it's often eaten as a snack, from a bowl or saucer, with a sprinkle of sugar (though you may agree that it's better still without the sugar).

There are useful milkbar/cafés with delicious milk puddings, yogurt, and *banitsa*, small pastries filled with soft cheese and/or yogurt and egg. Plain and simple eating places have 'Shopska salad' with feta-like *sirene* (cheese) on a bowl of tomatoes, cucumbers, onion and peppers. There's a thick mixed vegetable soup called *Gradinarska Chorba* (though perhaps with lard), and other oily mixed vegetable stews (a stew is *chorba)*. *Fasoul* is a mixed bean and vegetable stew served cold, and another cold dish is *Tarator*, a soup of cucumber and yogurt with nuts and herbs. One meatless dish often available, its very name a reminder of Moslem rule, is *Imam Bayeldi*, aubergines stuffed with vegetables. Indeed peppers, tomatoes and aubergines are all baked stuffed with meat or egg and cheese or vegetables. Among the desserts, typical of this region and another legacy of the Turks, is the wonderful cold creamy rice pudding sprinkled with cinnamon: in Bulgaria it's called *mliako s oris*. Other Turkish-style sweets much liked in Bulgaria include *baklava*, syrupy layers of filo pastry; coffee too is taken the Turkish way, thick, strong and black, in tiny cups. Bottled fruit juices, by the way, tend to be 100 per cent juice, without added sugar.

The language is similar to Russian.

A few useful words

I am (we are)vegetarian	Az sam (nie sme) vegetariantsi
I (we) cannot eat meat or fish	Az (nie) ne jadem meso i riba
Butter	Maslo
Cheese/eggs	Sirene/jaitsa
Fruit/vegetables	Plodove/zelentsutzi
Milk	Mliako
Rice/bread	Oriz/hliab
Vegetable oil	Olio
Yogurt	Kiselo mliako

Czechoslovakia

Scarcity restrains Czech eating habits, which in their true nature are said to be hearty and adventurous. Cafés and restaurants (mostly closed by 9 p.m.) have long lists of dishes, some meatless, nearly all of which turn out to be unavailable. Wine, beer and coffee bars do have a few little snacks though, and the self-service snackbars provide an invaluable resource. Supermarket shelves are startlingly empty. Hotels and restaurants give their customers dull set meals with no vegetarian possibilities at all. Unexpectedly, there is one useful 'Vegetarian' restaurant in Prague, open for midday meals only, but (this gives some idea of the enthusiasm for vegetarianism in Czechoslovakia) it serves meat and fish dishes.

However, according to Čedok, the State-run tour operator, 'There is an enormous variety of restaurants, bars and other eating places. Some hotels are world-renowned for their cuisine.' Quite.

Czech dishes you may come across include potato soup (meat stock), potato salad, and scores of dumplings made of various flours, including that of the essential potato. Fried (in oil) and seasoned potatoes are sold as a snack from street stalls. Dumplings can form the basis of a meatless meal, eaten with *bryndza* (creamy ewe's milk cheese) and salad or vegetables. Pickles and sour cream feature in a wide range of little starters, but it's hard to isolate them from the meat and fish. *Michana Zelenina* means mixed vegetables, and there are some good salads and plenty of substantial cakes, pies, pastries, pancakes and other desserts.

The language and pronunciation are similar to Serbo-Croatian (Yugoslav, see page 112).

A few useful words

I am (we are) vegetarian	Já jsem (my jsme) vegetarián(i)
I (we) cannot eat meat or fish	Nejím(e) maso nebo ryby
Butter	Máslo
Cheese/eggs	Sýr/vejce
Fruit/vegetables	Ovoce/zelenina
Rice/bread	Rýže/chléb
Vegetable oil	Rostlinný olej
Yogurt	Jogurt

Hungary

Spiced stews, goulash being the best known, form the basis of Hungarian cookery, which, to be fair, has far more character than that encountered in most of Eastern Europe. There's no shortage of ingredients either: supermarkets are packed with fruit, vegetables, grains and other food. Street markets too are well supplied. Nevertheless any request for a meal without meat leaves hotels and restaurants completely at a loss. They expect all diners to choose one of the set meals, called a *menü*, and hardly know how to cope with any individual preferences and requests outside this framework. Rosemary Stevens (see Russia) writes:

'The chef where I was staying was told that I was a vegetarian. He produced a very artistic platter of cooked vegetables. Unfortunately most dishes in Hungary are covered with melted lard and this was no exception. As I couldn't eat it, and didn't like to leave it on the table after all the effort he'd put into it, I parked it underneath the breakfast trolley and didn't dare go back for any further meals.'

At typical snackbars — *ételbar* or *büfé* — the set meal problem may arise again. You're almost certainly better off at one of the self-service places called *önkiszolgáló etterem*. Before the original Russian invasion Budapest was one of the intellectual centres of Europe, with an active social world based on large old-fashioned coffee houses. They have all gone, but there are still many little coffee bars and cake shops, called *cukrászda*, with an intriguing selection of pastries.

As part of set meals, you'll see some of Hungary's many soups. Several of the traditional favourites are vegetable (for example beetroot; asparagus; mushroom), often with cream and egg. It is not possible to be certain whether or not meat stock has been used, but I suspect in many cases it has not. Anything ending in *-leves* is a soup; some are interesting: *Borleves* is a wine soup almost like hot punch except that there's an egg in it; *Kaporleves* is a soup of dill, milk, cream and egg yolk; *Saláteves* is lettuce soup; and there are quite a few sweet fruit soups, served cold. Soups often have dumplings in them for added bulk.

Be aware that bacon and/or lard creep into a good many 'vegetable' dishes. Vegetable salads and dips, usually being no more than one or two vegetables and some sour cream, pose no problems and are enjoyable. One of the very best vegetable dishes, lard-free as far as I know, is *Tökfőzelék*, sautéed marrow with sour cream and dill. When all else fails, as it often does, it's generally worth asking for eggs. Various meatless egg dishes do form part of the national cuisine. *Rántotta* is an omelette, but do be careful about what is in it. *Rántotta Zöldpaprikával* is a green pepper omelette. Finally, as in other East European countries, there are plenty of filling cakey desserts.

A few useful words

I am (we are) vegetarian	Én (Mi) vegetáriánus vagyok
I (we) cannot eat meat or fish	Nem ehetek (ehetünk) húst és halat
Butter	Vaj
Cheese/eggs	Sajt/Tojás

Fruit/vegetables	Gyümölcs/Zöldség
Milk	Tej
Rice/bread	Rizs/Kenyér
Sour cream	Tejföl
Vegetable oil	Olaj. *Napraforgó* is sunflower oil. Another type of vegetable oil is called *Repce olaj*.
Yogurt	Joghurt

Poland

Much 'Russian' cuisine is actually Polish. However, the second world war wrought an economic destruction from which Poland never recovered. If anything, its problems get steadily worse rather than better. Today food is scarce and the quality of life meagre and oppressive. Most hotels and restaurants put together extremely dull, stodgy meals. Lunch is the main meal; dinner may be small, sometimes just a cold snack. However, eggs are a definite vegetarian alternative at mealtimes, and excellent cheesecake helps to fill the gaps. As well as proper restaurants there are self-service snackbars and, out of town, cheap transport cafés.

Dishes to look out for are mainly the same selection as in Russia, *bliny*, for example; the names of some are spelt a little differently, such as *Kasza* (still pronounced kasha) or *kisiel* (kiessel). A few are called by another name altogether, as with *mizeria* (the same as Russia's *ogurtzi v smetana*). In theory at least, Polish food includes a few meatless possibilities, such as *buraki* (hot beetroot and apple with sour cream), *nalesniki* (pancakes with cheese or fruit fillings), or dumplings called *pieroge leniwe* which are made of curd cheese, egg and flour, or others called *kluski slaski* made of potato and egg. There are sweet dumplings too; *knedle z wisniami* have a filling of cherries; and there's no lack of other sweet dishes. Cafés, *kawiarna*, remain popular meeting places and offer a tempting range of these delicious cakes and pastries. *Mazurek* are sweet fruit or nut pastries; *torte makowy* is poppy seed cake; *sernik*, a creamy cheesecake with sultanas;

paczki, curious highly flavoured jam doughnuts.

Hors d'oeuvres could turn up something meatless, but bear in mind that lard is used to prepare the vegetable dishes. Vegetable soups can be substantial and filling and are a standard feature of the typical Polish meal, but again, lard is much used, as is suet. *Chlodnick*, a cold vegetable soup, sounds nice but includes crayfish. One supposed to be entirely free of meat or fish is the traditional *barsczcz* (pronounced 'borschch', and indeed it is the prototype of the Russian soup of the same name), a stew of beetroot and mushrooms, which you'll probably only taste if you visit Poland at Christmas or Easter. Meals are preceded, accompanied and followed by vodka, while between meals lemon tea *(herbata)* is as popular as coffee *(kawa)*.

A few useful words

J sounds like y. SZ sounds like j. W sounds like v, and Ł like w.

I am vegetarian	I jestem jaroszem
We are vegetarian	My jesteśmy jaroszami
I cannot eat meat or fish	I nie mogę, jeść mięsa i ryb
We cannot eat meat or fish	Mi nie mozemy jeść mięsa i ryb
Lard, animal fat	Lard (for cooking); Smalec (for eating as it is)
Butter	Masło
Cheese/eggs	Ser/jajka
Fruit/vegetables	Owoce/warzywa
Milk	mleko
Rice/bread	Ryz/chleb
Sour cream	Śmietana
Vegetable oil	Oliwa, ólej

Romania

Visas, pre-paid vouchers, shortages of food, lack of information for visitors, besides such inconveniences as intermittent hot water supplies, make Romania a difficult country to enjoy visiting, despite a fascinating culture and impressive landscapes.

Hotels and tourist restaurants confine themselves to bland and boring set meals accompanied by oily fried potatoes. Instead, if you can, find a *lacto bar*, a type of cheap traditional snackbar which specializes in meatless dishes. These places are quite numerous. Another alternative is a counter-service *bufet-express*. Most Hungarians eat as much meat as they can get (not very much, in some areas), yet a substantial part of the diet is made up of vegetables and milk products. Among the popular snacks and hors d'oeuvres are several types of cheeses, cheese pastries (*plăcintă cu brinza*), completely vegetable purées and dips (*ardei copt romănese* — cold green peppers in spicy sauce; *pătlăgele vinete tocate* — aubergine pâté), salads, and other meatless dishes like eggs stuffed with spinach. The Hungarian's basic 'filler' is *mămăligă*, boiled corn meal, similar to polenta. *Balmos* is *mămăligă* mixed with sour cream and ewe's milk.

Romania has an interesting style of cooking, featuring a number of vegetable stews. Unfortunately meat stock is normally used to make them, as is the case with *ghiveci (cu zarzavaturi)*, an excellent vegetable casserole; some, like *supa de cartofi*, literally 'potato soup', actually contain pieces of bacon. One which seems meat-free is a simple *ciorbă*, a strange sour fermented liquid made of bran (but beware variations, *'ciorbă de . . .'*, which are almost invariable made with meat). As usual in this part of the world you can fill up on rich cakes, many of them based on cheese. There are pies and puddings based on apples too, and – a good example of Romania's strong historical and cultural links with the Mediterranean — syrupy Middle Eastern desserts like *baklava* and *kataifi*. Cakes and coffees are best enjoyed in a *cofeteria*, a proper coffee house, though in fact while the cakes remain available the coffee itself is sometimes in short supply and cannot be had, not even for ready hard-currency!

The language has little in common with others in this part of Europe. If anything, in pronunciation, it has a closer resemblance to Italian. T = *ts*; S = *sh*; Î comes somewhere between *ah* and *eh*.

A few useful words

The words *cu carne* in the name of a dish mean 'with meat'.

I am (we are) vegetarian	Eu (noi) sint(em) vegetarian(i)
I (we) cannot eat meat or fish	Eu (Noi) nu pot (putem) minca carne sau peste
No meat (literally, 'don't want meat')	Nu vreau carne
Butter/vegetable oil	Unt/Untdelemn (Lard = *Untură*).
Cheese/eggs	Brînzá/Ová
Fruit/vegetables	Fructe/Legume, Vegetale
Milk	Lapte
Rice/bread	Orez/Pîine

Scandinavia

It hardly does justice to the quite separate histories, cultures and peoples of the Scandinavian countries to class them together under a single heading. Yet the truth remains that in matters of food they have much in common. First, all consume an enormous amount of fish, and at times it becomes impossible to find anything to eat which doesn't have herring, tuna, anchovy, cod or eel mixed into it. Secondly, when not eating fish, they're eating meat. For this part of the world lends itself more readily to raising animals than growing vegetables. However this does allow for dairy farming, so there's no lack of milk products. In all the Scandinavian countries open sandwiches play a big part in the eating habits. And all of them go in for a large buffet of small dishes, many of these indeed being open sandwiches, to start a meal, and sometimes eat so many of them that there's no room for anything else. Everywhere in the world such a spread is known by its Swedish title, *Smörgåsbord*. In few other places though can it be done so well: invariably Scandinavian food is of high quality and beautifully presented.

The more pity then that so few of the *smörgåsbord* items are free of meat and fish. The best chance lies with some good cheese, or vegetable or egg salads with mayonnaise. Sometimes there are boiled potatoes or other hot items, especially in Sweden. Apart from these buffets, restaurants make 'ordinary' meals, normally meat or fish accompanied by a couple of plain boiled vegetables, or an undressed salad of raw vegetables. Where more complicated vegetable dishes have been prepared, it's likely that meat or fish stock has been used.

Iceland and Norway, most ruled by the sea, are the most consistently fishy. Finland, unexpectedly, has a good deal of dairy produce, Denmark and Sweden, looking more towards the rest of

Europe, have a more varied diet and they can also offer the consolation of an active vegetarian movement and quite a large number of vegetarian restaurants. In none of the countries would it be impossible to travel as a vegetarian: almost any restaurant can provide a plate of boiled vegetables, a salad, chips, omelette or fried eggs, bread and cheese. There are not many foreigners living in Scandinavia, hence not many foreign restaurants; the occasional Italian place generally has one meatless pizza and one meatless pasta sauce on its menu.

Far better would be to steer clear of hotels and restaurants altogether and concentrate instead on self-catering — something which is very much part of the tourist industry in these countries. In Sweden and Denmark, most supermarkets have a health food/vegetarian section with brown rice, muesli, soya products, ready-to-cook meatless package foods, savoury spreads, in short, most of the same products familiar in British health food stores. Cynthia Boskett, of Devon, who wrote to me about vegetarian eating in Scandinavia, resolutely continues to holiday in these countries despite the difficulties; the secret of her success is having several Scandinavian friends – and clearly getting to know people is to be recommended, for she says, 'they excel themselves in providing a vegetarian meal when we visit them.'

DENMARK

'The fare was the worst I have ever encountered, and we sat at the table for a very long time.'
Robert Sidney, after dining with the King of Denmark in 1632.

Danish food has undoubtedly improved since that remark was made, although for those in need of a meatless dinner it still leaves much to be desired. Most cosmopolitan of the Scandinavians, the Danes are a wonderfully civilised and good-natured people. They are also scrupulously polite, and the most important word for any foreigner to learn is *tak*, which means thank you. After eating, whether at home or at a friend's house or in public, it is usual to say *Tak for mad*, thanks for the meal, no matter how dissatisfied you were.

The day starts early, and for breakfast Danes have coffee and *krydder* (like rusks) or fresh white bread, with cheese, and maybe an egg or cereal, although one third of the population, a survey shows, still start the day with the traditional bowl of porridge. Lunch, eaten at noon, might well be open sandwiches and a glass of milk. The working day ends at about 4 or 5 p.m., and at 6 o'clock people sit down to a two-course hot meal, eating again later in the evening, at say 9 or 10 o'clock, to have a last cup of coffee and another open sandwich or a pastry. Those who started the day with porridge may well finish it the same way — or perhaps with *øllebrød*, 'beer bread', a porridge-like brew of stale bread boiled in non-alcoholic beer. *Kager* means cakes and pastries. *Weinerbrød*, 'Viennese bread', is what Danes call the famous Danish pastries. Done properly, this is a rich yeasted pastry, often spiced, baked into various shapes with or without a filling of, for example, almond paste, chocolate, jam, cheese or vanilla. No lard should be used to make these tasty snacks, sold in coffee houses, tea shops and bakeries.

For centuries, the Church in Denmark dictated that there should be four meatless days each week. On those days, fish was to be eaten. Royal Edict laid down which class of people could eat what food, and how much. Ordinary labouring people were permitted one meal of three courses, the final one to be porridge on both meat and fish days. As in Britain, plates were not used until the sixteenth century: people ate from a slice of bread, ending the meal by eating the bread itself. Perhaps from this comes the all-important custom of the *smørrebrød*, or open sandwich.

Smørrebrød, (not to be confused with *smörgåsbord*) literally means 'buttered bread', but that's only the beginning of the story. The thinly sliced pumpernickel, thickly spread with butter (or lard), typically has a piece of lettuce on one corner; meat, fish or cheese laid across the bread; then a covering of vegetable or fish salad or both; and finally a little decoration of herbs or pickles.

The impromptu flinging of pieces of food on to bread certainly does *not* constitute a *smørrebrød*: there are traditional toppings, and these almost take the form of recipes, which must be followed to the letter. There are said to be over 1,000 varieties of *smørrebrød*, and in restaurants sometimes well over 100 sorts are displayed. In principle, they should be eaten in a specific order — fish first, then meat or other savouries, and finally cheese — and they should be eaten with knife and fork, not fingers.

Where *smørrebrød* are not a meal in themselves but only a starter or hors d'oeuvre, the meal which follows, principally meat or fish, may have vegetable side dishes made without meat, for example *champignons med fløde*, mushrooms in cream. The usual cooking fat is butter, but it's never possible to be sure if lard or meat or fish stock have been used to make vegetable dishes or sauces. In general, vegetables are simply boiled and lightly covered with melted butter. Vegetable soufflés *(Grønsagsgratin)* are not uncommon. *Frikadeller* normally means meatballs; their meatless alternative, sometimes seen, can be made of breaded balls of mixed egg and vegetable purée fried in butter – they're called *Grønsags-frikadeller*. Soups should be assumed to have meat or fish stock, except in the case of *Urtesuppe*, a plain vegetable soup, or one of Denmark's sweet soupy curiosities like Chocolate Soup, Fruit Soup and the popular Buttermilk Soup which can either begin or end a meal.

Cheese helps to provide meatless dishes from time to time. *Osteaeg* are fried breaded balls of mixed cheese and egg; *Ostekager* is baked egg and cheese mixture.

Self-caterers can try out not only well-known Danish cheeses like Samsoe or Danablu but many other milk products – there's excellent butter, fresh cream, sour cream, yogurt, buttermilk and *ymer*, a thick milk culture similar to yogurt.

Further afield, the Faroes, an autonomous Danish possession, would no doubt be fascinating to explore. Take your own muesli: a leaflet sent by their tourist office describes the diet of the Faroe Islanders as 'wind-dried whale, mutton, fish and birds.'

Danish language – or rather, the pronunciation – takes some

effort to learn. Ø sounds like the u in fur. Luckily, English is widely spoken throughout the country.

A few useful words

I am (we are) vegetarian	Jeg (Vi) er vegetar(er)
I (we) cannot eat any meat or fish	Jeg (Vi) kan ikke spise køod eller fisk
No	Ingen
Without } meat-fish	Uden } køod/fisk
Health-food Shop	Helsekost
Buttermilk	Kaernemaelk
Egg/Cheese	Aeg/ost
Rice/bread	Ris/brøod
Fruit/vegetables	frugt/grøontsager

Cheers! = Skål! A toast is a very formal, solemn business in Denmark. Eyes must meet, glasses be on the same level when raised, and the *snaps* knocked back in one.

Information

For all information, the people to contact are: Vegetarisk Information, Valkyriegade 14, 2200 København N, Denmark.

The Danish Tourist Board in Copenhagen issues a list of vegetarian restaurants, currently showing ten in Copenhagen and seventeen in the rest of the country. Some of these do not officially qualify as restaurants, but they are, nevertheless, eating places open to the public. Contact Danmarks Turistråd, Vester-brogade 6D, 1620 København V, Denmark (phone (01) 11 14 15).

FINLAND

Finns call an open sandwich *Voileipä*, and their word for a *smörgåsbord* is *Voileipäpöytä*. Apart from the meat of reindeer, elk and the like, and of course fish, they make and eat a lot of cheese. I hear there's even a sort made of reindeer milk, which it would be intriguing to try. Munajuusto cheese has eggs mixed into the milk and is made without rennet. Cultivated fruits and vegetables, other than the potato, are rare; wild fruits and berries provide an important part of the diet. These appear as sweets, savouries and even soups.

Dishes to look out for include *Kaalikeitto* — soup of cabbage and other vegetables cooked in milk; *Karjalanpiirakka* — rye-flour pastries filled with rice; *Kesäkeitto* — soup of vegetables in milk; *Kiisseli* — fruit soup; *Munakas* — omelette; *Pinaattalaatikko* — a sort of rice pudding containing spinach; *Viili* — cultured-milk dessert powdered with cinnamon. Finns drink buttermilk with their food.

The language is wonderfully unlearnable. No matter how many As, Is, Ks or Ts come in a row, every letter must be pronounced.

A few useful words

I am (we are) vegetarian	Olen (Olemme) kassvissyöjä (kassvissyöjiä)
I (we) cannot eat any meat or fish	En (Emme) voi syödä lihaa enkâ (emmekä) kalaa
No / Without } meat/fish	Ei / Ilman } lihaa/kalaa
Egg/cheese	Muna/juustoa
Bread/rice	Leipää/riisiä
Fruit/vegetables	Hedelmiä/vihanneksia

ICELAND

Iceland is noted more for its volcanoes, hot springs and spectacular scenery than its cuisine. Indeed, Icelanders seem little interested in food, probably because there's hardly anything to eat except fish, birds and sheep. That aside, Iceland has much charm, a neat clean country, with a touch of formality. Milk and cheese of both cows' and ewes' milk are produced on the island. Most important of the milk products is *Skyr*, like a skimmed-milk quark. The bread can be good, and brown bread is available.

Buffet meals are as popular here as elsewhere in Scandinavia, and particularly enjoyable are the afternoon coffee buffets of cakes and pastry.

NORWAY

Porridge has fed more people than it has killed
(Norwegian proverb)

This cryptic understatement about Norway's national dish perhaps reveals something of the Norwegian respect for bland nononsense home-cooking. Here too the open sandwich, *Smørbrød* in Norwegian, and the cold buffet, called *Koldt Bord*, have a primary importance. Indeed the buttered-bread-with — toppings *Smørbrød* are eaten at every meal, either by themselves at breakfast and lunch or as a starter for the evening meal.

Bread with cheese or fish is the usual breakfast, often with a goat's cheese callet *Gjetost*. Lunch is bread with meat or fish, and dinner a more substantial meat or fish meal with a boiled vegetable or salad. Anything more adventurous than a potato has probably just emerged from a packet in the freezer. A few more complicated vegetable dishes occasionally put in an appearance, though it's never possible to be sure whether meat or fish stock have been used to make them. Salads, too, should be inspected carefully: most contain fish. Meat or fish stock almost without exception forms the basis of soup, although not in the case of such oddities as fruit soup or *ølmsuppe*, made of beer.

For the most part, vegetarian possibilities in restaurants, even at their best, do not extend beyond salad, plain boiled vegetables, maybe chips, bread, cheese and perhaps eggs. If you want a plate of mixed vegetables ask for *Blandede Grønnsaker*. Indeed, desserts can prove the most filling, tasty and nutritious part of the meal, for example *Himmelsk Lapskaus*, fruit and nuts covered with egg sauce laced with rum.

Norway has a small homogenous population with a uniform

diet. There are no foreign tastes to cater for. Shops are well stocked within the limits of what Norwegians themselves eat, which does include some useful milk-culture products, especially yogurt, and another, *filmyölk*, thicker and firmer than yogurt. In the south, health food shops are not unknown and are called (take a deep breath) *Helsekostforretninger*. Anywhere further north than Norway's south coast, towns often are little more than basic mining or fishing communities, with no restaurants and certainly no vegetarians.

A few useful words:

I am (we are) vegetarian	Jeg (Vi) er vegetarianer
I (we) cannot eat any meat or fish	Jeg (Vi) kan ikke spise noe kjøtt eller fisk
No ⎫ meat/fish Without ⎭	Ikke noe ⎫ kjøtt/fisk Uten ⎭

SWEDEN

Smörgåsbord is a Swedish word and in Sweden this type of buffet meal, or hors d'oeuvres if other dishes are to follow, is at its best. *Smörgåsar* are open sandwiches, in other words pieces of buttered bread with food artistically arranged on top, and although *smörgåsbord* no longer consists only of *smörgåsar* (singular: *smörgås*) they do still play an important part. There will also be herring dishes; cheeses; egg dishes; salmon, other fish and smoked meats, each with a traditional sauce; pickles; salads, shellfish; and quite often hot food too: omelettes, vegetable soufflés, vegetables with cheese; and to complete the selection, milky eggy desserts and cakes. Custom dictates the order in which everything must be eaten, but this hardly applies for vegetarians, whose choice is limited. Nevertheless, a good *smörgåsbord* can provide an excellent meatless and, what's harder to achieve, fishless meal. A good *smörgåsbord* will be found in tourist haunts and expensive restaurants — it won't be featured by cheap eating places. *Smörgåsbord* is essentially an informal, lunchtime way of eating, hardly ever used for the evening meal.

Swedish breakfast can be substantial, with bread, cheese, eggs, yogurts and/or *kefir*, *filmyölk* or *yuma*, other naturally-occurring milk products on the theme of yogurt. The main meal of the day is eaten at around 6 p.m. Milk or beer is drunk with meals. The least expensive way to sample Swedish restaurant food would be to order the set meals, but this is not an option for vegetarians. Instead we have to make do with what were intended as side dishes. There's always a wide variety of fresh vegetables — carrots, courgettes, green peppers, cauliflower, alfalfa sprouts — often eaten raw, with neither dressing nor seasoning. *Råkosttallrik* is a raw vegetable salad. Waiters usually bring vegetarians a plate of boiled vegetables, served with a dressing of melted butter and sugar. Other possibilities worth looking out for would be *Raggmunkar* — grated potatoes, mixed with egg and milk, fried; *Ris a la Malta* — rice with cream and fruit; *Fruktsoppa* — fruit soup: *Saftsoppa* is a thinner fruit soup, without pieces of fruit. A lot of coffee is drunk in Sweden, with rich cakes, at *Konditorier*, cafés or cake shops.

Three different types of vegetarianism have a large following in Sweden: lacto-vegetarians, vegans, and the 'green people' who eat only raw food. Several vegetarian restaurants can be found in the capital Stockholm. Health food shops are called *Hälsokost* or *Hälsocentrallen*. Swedish vegetarianism seems infected with a streak of puritanism: Claire Milne, a British Telecom executive, travelled as a business guest to Sweden, and one might expect that in the circumstances she must have been given the best that could be offered to a vegetarian. She remembers that 'everywhere I was given plain boiled vegetables and salads without dressing. And it was always assumed that a vegetarian would drink no coffee or alcohol'.

A few useful words:

I am (we are) vegetarian	Jag är (vi är) vegitarianer
I (we) cannot eat any meat or fish	Jag (vi) kan inte äta något kött eller någon fisk

No
Without } meat/fish

Nej
Utan } kött/fisk

Bread/rice

Bröd/ris

Egg/cheese

Ägg/ost

Fruit/vegetables

Frukt/grönsaker

Information

For more information contact: Svenska Vegetariska Föreningen, Rådmansgatan 88, 113 29 Stockholm, Sweden (phone: 32 49 29).

Switzerland

The single theme which unites Switzerland is, of course, the Alps. Nearly every part of the country has dramatic, extraordinary scenery: magnificent lakes bordered by soaring hills, neatly cultivated green valleys dwarfed by distant summits, flower-filled mountain meadows and, most awe-inspiring of all, the massive enduring grandeur of the snow-covered peaks. Despite this, Switzerland is not so much one country as four; or rather, three parts of other countries (Germany, France, and Italy), plus one high mountain district with nothing in common with anywhere (the Romansh-speaking Grischun, also known as Grisons or Graubunden in the east). In addition, the minuscule Alpine principality of Lichtenstein has become to all intents and purposes part of Switzerland. Each region has its own language, and astonishingly, a large proportion of the Swiss know only their mother tongue and rarely travel, if they can avoid it, into areas where another language is spoken. When they learn a second language it is most likely to be English.

Swiss food borrows freely from the surrounding nations, but also has much that is purely its own. Although there are many cheese or vegetable dishes and meatless soups, the typical Swiss meal places the emphasis firmly on meat, and served in generous portions. For some reason though, vegetarianism flourishes in Switzerland, especially in the German-speaking sector. As in Germany itself, many middle-class German Swiss take a great interest in health and food, and *Reformhäuser*, or health food shops, abound. Many of the foods familiar in British health food shops have been imported from Switzerland: muesli, vegetable pâtés and spreads, vegetarian baby foods, meatless stock cubes, and many other products. In Switzerland, many of these are so accepted that they hardly qualify as 'health foods' at all. Any pavement café serves muesli, for example — and remarkably good it is too.

In non-German areas too, while the number of vegetarians may be smaller, it is still not difficult to find health food shops and meatless snacks in restaurants. Always remember though, throughout the country, that non-vegetarians tend to be very meat-orientated. One should take great care when eating out, especially in rural districts or in ordinary workingmen's café-restaurants, as I discovered one day after venturing into a cheap transport café. We told the serving girl we were vegetarians and asked if there was something with no meat or fish. She was happy to point out suitable dishes on the menu. The soup of the day was vegetable soup. 'No meat?' we asked.' 'No meat'. To follow, what about *Käseschnitte* (normally like Welsh Rarebit)? 'That's a cheese dish', she said. It was listed on the menu as *Käseschnitte Valaisanne*, a variety which, at the time, I had not heard of. When it arrived, the soup turned out to be a few pieces of vegetable floating in a meat stock, while the *Käseschnitte* had a layer of ham beneath the cheese! With qualms of appetite and of conscience, we laboriously picked out all the ham and ate the rest. As a meat-eater the girl simply hadn't remembered the ham nor thought it important. 'Oh sorry!' she smiled with embarrassment on discovering her mistake.

However, treat menus with caution and there's every chance of finding something meatless, even though the choice may be limited in any Swiss eating establishment. Because portions are large, a simple snacky order often proves sufficient for a main course. In any case it's likely that almost any Swiss town will have at least one vegetarian restaurant (or macrobiotic, in the French sector). These serve traditional Swiss meatless dishes as well as omelettes and egg dishes and the more 'international' style of vegetarian cuisine — rice and vegetables, nut cutlets and so on. At times it may be necessary to specify brown rice or wholewheat flour, as whole grains are not always used. In general, it must be said, Swiss restaurant cooking, while perfectly adequate and digestible, lacks inspiration and style. The same criticism applies equally to the vegetarian restaurants in which, however, the tastiest items on the menu are usually the traditional Swiss dishes.

Breakfast and snacks

Most Swiss people start the day with bread and butter with jam or honey, and a cup of hot milky coffee or some other milky drink like *'Ovomaltine'* or hot chocolate. A few prefer tea, considered rather a refined drink. Those who like a larger breakfast eat a few slices of cheese with their bread, or have a bowl of muesli. Many cafés serve *Caffé* (or *Thè*) *Complet*, meaning rolls, butter, jam, perhaps orange juice, and a cup (or jug) of coffee or tea.

Muesli, known here as *Birchermüesli*, or just *Bircher* (after Dr Bircher, the dietician who first promoted the idea of eating raw cereals), is widely available at cafés and snackbars all day long. The popular version comes close to being a dessert, succulent and tasty, with loads of fruit and even (optional) cream. Indeed in restaurants it may be offered as such, while in cafés it is sometimes served with a slice of brown bread and butter.

Cafés and bars amount to much the same thing, both selling alcoholic drinks as well as coffee, which comes black or with cream or with whipped cream (the Germans, it seems, refer to this as cappuccino). Good quality decaffeinated coffee is nearly always available, as are hot chocolate, tea and herb teas, and again some unexpected beverages such as Ovaltine. They generally serve a range of snacks, rolls, cakes, heavy doughnuty pastries with fillings, and — especially in Ticino, the Italian area — ice cream. The commonest rolls are called *Weggli*, *Gipfel* and *Mutschli*; and anything whose name ends in *-torte* is not necessarily a tart but more likely a cake: most are delicious and go well with a creamy coffee. Among the savoury snacks are cheese pastries and slices of pizza. Hot cheese tarts can be bought from bakers and street stalls. Many cafés have a range of cooked snacks too, verging on being complete meals, such as salads, *Rösti* (fried potatoes — see page 105) and fried eggs, omelettes, pizza, pasta and vegetable-plates with grated cheese.

Lunch and dinner

Lunch, eaten at about 12.30 p.m., is called *diner* if it's the main meal of the day (which is usual), or *lunch* if it's something light. The evening meal is called *souper*. Both normally start with soup, and have a main dish of meat or fish with one or two vegetable side dishes.

Restaurants offer a *menu*, or a choice of *menus*, these being fixed-price set meals. These are not usually suitable for vegetarians, except where the *entrée* (the course between the starter and the main course) is a vegetable or egg dish which would do as a main dish. You could then ask to leave out the meat or fish course. It's best to explain to the waiter that you cannot eat meat: all but the most out-of-the-way restaurants have met with vegetarians before and have something suitable to offer them. Be cautious about their recommendations however; double check that they really contain no meat or fish.

Aside from the set menus, there will be a *carte*, from which you may choose with more freedom. Eating *à la carte* in this way, the individual dishes do cost more, but servings are generous and a relatively small order may suffice. Upmarket restaurants are more French in style, and more meaty than simple places, and sometimes pose problems for vegetarians; yet even at quite a posh place recently I noted on the *carte* omelettes, salads, fondue, vegetable soups and two side dishes — rice and mixed vegetables — which could be comfortably combined.

A word of warning: oil and butter predominate in Swiss cooking, but it is hard ever to be completely sure of having escaped from lard, which sometimes substitutes for butter in both savoury and sweet dishes. Tempting vegetable dishes may turn out to have been made with animal fat. Even when asking for a salad it can be a wise precaution to specify 'no meat, no fish'. Cheese soups, that curious speciality of Switzerland, normally consist only of grated cheese, milk, butter, flour, water and seasoning. *Früchtensuppe*, by the way, are hot fruit soups; these, and other sweet soups, put in appearances at either end of a meal.

Desserts, often not included in the price of a set *menu*, are amazingly rich and filling, with fresh cream and chocolate liberally employed. Heavy cakes and tarts, eggy desserts and fruit fritters are popular, and almost everything comes with the offer of *rahm*, cream.

Other tips: some hamburger places have good eat-all-you-want salad bars; and the nationwide supermarket chain Migros (and others) have cheap cafeterias attached to their shops (look for those with the sign 'MM' or 'MMM'. Migros stores with a single 'M' are small and have no restaurant). Remember too that in Switzerland it's always well worth asking if there's a vegetarian restaurant in the locality.

The menu on page 100 with such a huge list in three languages including English is typical of popular eating places in the main towns, with the surprising exception that on this one neither *Rösti* and fried eggs nor *Rösti* and salad appear, though no doubt it would be all right to ask for them. Some of the English translations may bring a smile to your lips, but nevertheless they make it clear enough that — starting in the top left-hand corner of the menu — there are ample meatless opportunities among the salads, soups (though not no. 220 or 216, and perhaps not 215), cheese dishes, Italian specialities (no. 304 only), Quick-Lunch dishes (nos. 280 and 281), the suggestions 'For Not Very Hungry' (nos. 286, 287) and desserts. Incidentally, the dessert cryptically rendered into English as 'Williams Sherbet' is actually a delicious water-ice made of pears and laced with a dash of the pear brandy called Poire Williams!

Self-catering and picnics

Though the range of foods stocked by supermarkets and grocers varies from region to region, everywhere it provides a very adequate selection of fresh and frozen vegetables, good quality canned and frozen ready-to-eat dishes, beans, lentils, pasta (not wholewheat), rice (not brown), olive oil and other cooking oils, brown sugar and honeys, muesli, coffees, teas, and plenty of dairy foods — yogurts, kefir (a drinkable milk culture like yogurt),

Salati · Salades · Salads

223	*Grüner Salat	3.50
	*Salade verte	3.50
	*Green salad	3.50
224	*Salat assortiert	5.–
	*Salade mêlée	5.–
	*Mixed salad	5.–
225	*Grosser Salatteller	7.50
	*Grande salade mêlée	7.50
	*Large mixed salad	7.50

Salatsauce nach Ihrer Wahl
Sauce aux choix
Sauces at jour choice

Täglich Salatbuffet im Restaurant
Jaque jour Salades Buffet au Restaurant
Daily salad buffet in the restaurant

Suppen · Potages · Soups

215	Tagessuppe	2.50
	Potage du jour	2.50
	Today's soup	2.50
216	Kraftbrühe mit Mark	4.50
	Consommé à la möelle	4.50
	Clear soup with beef marrow	4.50
217	Spargelcrèmesuppe	4.50
	Crème d'aspèrges	4.50
	Cream of aspargus soup	4.50
218	Tomatencrèmesuppe	4.50
	Crème de Tomate	4.50
	Cream of tomato soup	4.50
219	Erbsensuppe	4.50
	Potage pois jaunes	4.50
	Soup of yellow beans	4.50
220	*Gulaschsuppe	6.–
	*Potage goulache	6.–
	*Brouwn stew soup	6.–

Kalte Küche · Plats froid · Cold plats

230	*Bündnerfleischteller	12.–
	*Viande des Grisons	12.–
	*Air cured beef of the Grisons	12.–
232	*Wurstsalat garniert	7.50
	*Salade saucisse garnie	7.50
	*Sausage salad garnished	7.50
233	*Wurstsalat einfach	4.50
	*Salade saucisse simple	4.50
	*Sausage salad simple	4.50
234	*Wurst und Käsesalat	8.50
	*Salade saucisse et fromage	8.50
	*Sausage and cheese salad	8.50
235	*Kalte Platte gemischt pro Pers.	10.–
	*Plat froid mélangé, par pers.	10.–
	*Cold plat mixed, p. pers.	10.
236	*Ankerteller	9.
	*Assiette Anker	
	(viande froide & salades)	9
	*Anker plat (cold meat and salad)	9
237	*Schinkenbrot	4
	*Sandwich au Jambon	4
	*Ham sandwich	4
238	*Salamibrot	4
	*Sandwich au Salami	4
	...	

Käseecke · Fromage · Cheese

245	*Käse assortiert	7.50
	*Fromage assortie	7.50
	*Mixed cheese plate	7.50
246	*Käse Dessertportion	4.50
	*Fromage, petit portion	4.50
	*Small portion of cheese	4.50
247	*Käsesalat garniert	7.50
	*Salade de fromage garnie	7.50
	*Cheese salad garnished	7.50
248	Käsefondue mit Morcheln und Kompottbirnen (Spezialität) ab 2 Pers. pro Pers.	14.50
	Fondue au fromage au morilles et poire, par pers.	14.50
	Cheese fondue with morels and a pear	14.50
248	Schweizer Käsefondue ab 2 Pers. pro Pers.	12.–
	Fondue au fromage Suisse par pers.	12.–
	Swiss cheese fondue per pers.	12.–

* ganzer Tag erhältlich
serve toute la journée
we serve them all day round

Aus der Pfanne · A la poêle · From the pen

316	Kalbsschnitzel, Morchelrahmsauce, Kroketten und Gemüsebouquet	24.50
	Escalope de veau, Sc. Morilles, Pommes croquettes, bouquet de légumes	24.50
	Veal cutlet with morels sauce croquette potatoes and vegetable dish	24.50
317	Currygeschnetzeltes «Madras Style» Reis, Früchte, Salat assortiert	16.50
	Emincé au curry «Madras Style» (avec du riz et garniture de fruits) avec une salade mêlée	16.50
	Shredded Currymeat «Madras Style» (with rice and fruit garnished) with a mixed salad	16.50
318	Schweinssteak an Rahmsauce, Pfirsich, Ananas, Kroketten	16.–
	Steak de porc à la crème avec pêche et ananas, pommes croquettes	16.–
	Porc steak on a cream sauce with peach and pineapple, croquette potatoes	16.–
319	Ratsherrenteller, Rinds Kalbs Schweins Medaillons, Rösti, überbacken	18.50
	Les trois Médaillons sur Rösti (boeuf, veau, porc) gratinée	18.50
	Three medaillons with Swisspotatoes (beef, veal, porc) over baked	18.50
298	Gemüsebouquet als Beilage	4.50
	Bouquet de légumes comme garniture	4.50
	Vegetable dish as garnishing	4.50

Specifità italiana · Specialités italiennes · Italian Specialties

303	Lasagne verde el Forno	12.–
	Nouilles verte à l'Italienne	12.–
	Green noodles oven-backed	12.–
304	Risotto con Funghi	9.50
	Risotto ai Funghi	9.50
	Risotto with mushrooms and cheese	9.50
305	Schweinsfiletspiess «Vercelli» mit Safranrisotto	18.–
	Brochette Filet de porc «Vercelli» Safranrisotto	18.–
	Skewer of porc-filet «Vercelli» with Safranrisotto	18.–
306	Piccata milanaise (Schw.) Spaghetti und Sugo, ger. Käse	12.50
	Escalope Piccata, Spaghetti, Sc. Tomate	12.50
	Pork cutlet Piccata with spaghetti and tomate sauce	12.50

Vom Grill · Les grillades · Grilled meat

312	Kalbsschnitzel	18.50
	Escalope de veau	18.50
	Veal cutlet	18.50
313	Schweinssteak	15.–
	Steak de porc	15.–
	Porc steak	15.–
314	Rumpsteak	17.50
	Rumpsteak	17.50
	Rumpsteak	17.50
315	Entrecôte	22.–
	Entrecôte	22.–
	Sirloin Steak	22.–

– zu diesen Grilladen servieren wir unsere hausgemachte Sauce Café de Paris und Kartoffelkroketten
– avec Café de Paris et Pommes croquettes
– with har-butter and croquette potatoes

Montag bis Samstag · Lundi au Samedi · Monday till Saturday

276	Menu 1 mit Suppe oder Jus	9.–
	Menu 1 potage ou jus	9.–
	Menu 1 soup or jus	9.–
277	Menu 2 mit Suppe oder Jus	11.50
	Menu 2 potage ou jus	11.50
	Menu 2 soup or jus	11.50

Regardez la vitrine
Look at the glass case

Unser ausgebildetes Fachpersonal verwendet ausschliesslich Frischprodukte für die Herstellung dieser köstlichen Speisen
Nous prenons seulement des produits frais
We take only very fresh products.

Menuänderungen vorbehalten.
Changement du menu possible
Changes ...

Schnell Gut Preiswert · Pars chaud vite servie · Quick Lunch

280	Champignontoast	8.–
	Crôute aux champignons	8.–
	Mushrooms on toast	8.–
281	Gemüseteller	8.–
	Assiette de légumes	8.–
	Vegetable dish	8.–
282	Schnitzel paniert (Schw.), pommes frites	11.–
	Escalope panée (porc), frites	11.–
	Breaded cutlet (porc) fried-potatoes	11.–
293	Rahmschnitzel (Schw.) mit Champignons und Butternüdeli	12.–
	Escalope à la crème Sce Champignons et nouilles	12.–
	Creamed cutlet, mushroomsauce and noodles	12.–
284	*Spezialschweinswürstli mit Kartoffelsalat	7.50
	*Saucisses de porc, salade pommes de terre	7.50
	*Porc sausages and potatoe salad	7.50

Typisch schweizerisch · Suissa spécialités · Swiss specials

292	Alpler Maggrone, Zungenwurst	9.50
	Nouilles avec pommes de terre, oignons et Saucisse Bernoise	9.50
	White noodles with potatoes, onions and bernese sausage	9.50
293	Schweinsleberli geschn. Marsala, Rösti	11.–
	Emincé foie de porc, Sce Marsala et Rösti	11.–
	Sliced porc liver, Marsalasauce and Rösti	11.–
294	Bauernbratwurst, Zwiebelsauce und Rösti	9.50
	Saucisse paysan, Sce oignons, Rösti	9.50
	Grilled sausage with an onion sauce and swiss potatoes	9.50
295	Bauernbratwurst, Zwiebelsauce, Brot	6.50
	Saucisse du paysan, Sce aux oignons, avec du pain	6.50
	Grilled sausage with an onion sauce and bread	6.50
296	Innerschwyzer Nydel geschnetzeltes (Schw.) mit Rösti	12.
	Emincé de porc, Sce au Vin blanc, Chantilly et Rösti	12.
	Sliced porc meat on a swiss cream sauce, swiss potatoes	12.
297	Luzerner Kügelipasteti Erbsli und Pommes frites	10.50
	Bouchée Lucernoise avec petits pois et pommes frites	10.50
	Paste pie, call boules on a white wine sauce, green peas and fried potatoes	10.50

*** HOTEL RESTAURANT

Für den kleinen Hunger / Pour le petit faim / For not very hungry

285	*Schinken und Käse Toast	4.50
	*Toast au jambon et fromage	4.50
	*Ham and cheese Toast	4.50
286	Spaghetti al Sugo	7.50
	Spaghetti napolitaine	7.50
	Spaghetti with tomato-sauce	7.50
287	Portion Pommes frites	4.50
	Pommes frites, portion	4.50
	Fried potatoes, portion	4.50
220	*Gulaschsuppe	6.–
	*Potage goulache	6.–
	*Brown stew soup	6.–

Spezialitäten des Hauses / Les spécialités du maison / Specialities

323	Rindsfilet auf Schiferplatte Café de Paris, Kroketten, Gemüsebouquet	29.–
	Filet de boeuf sur plat ardoise, beurre aux herbes, pommes croquettes et légumes	29.–
	Tenderloin of beef served on a slate plate with herbbutter, croquettes, vegetables	29.–
324	Châteaubriand (ab 2 Pers.) Béarnaise, Kroketten, Gemüsebouquet, p. Pers.	30.–
	Châteaubriand, Sce Béarnaise à part. de 2 pers. pommes croquettes et légumes p. pers.	30.–
	Châteaubriand, bearnaise-sauce, from 2 pers. potatoe-croquettes, vegetables p. pers.	30.–
325	Entrecôte Schiferplatte (ab 2 Pers.) Béarnaise, Kroketten, Gemüsebouquet, p. Pers.	27.–
	Entrecôte sur plat ardoise Sce Béarnaise, croquettes, légumes	27.–
	Sirloin Steak on a slate plat Bearnaise sce, croquettes, vegetables	27.–
326	Fondue Bourguignonne mit Rindfleisch Salat assortiert ab 2 Pers. pro Pers.	30.–
	Fondue bourguignonne avec viande de boeuf Salade mêlée à partir de 2 pers.	30.–
	Fondue bourguignonne with beef meat, Mixed salad from 2 persons p. pers.	30.–
327	Fondue Bacchus mit Kalbfleisch Salat assortiert ab 2 Pers. pro Pers.	30.–
	Fondue Bacchus avec viande de veau, Salade mêlée à partir de 2 pers.	30.–
	Fondue Bacchus with calf meat, Mixed salad from 2 persons p. pers.	30.–

Aktuell / Actualitées / Actualitees

299	Sechs Burgunderschnecken überbacken	7.50
	6 Escargots au gratin	7.50
	6 snail's with herb-butter	7.50
300	Kalbswienerschnitzel Pommes frites und Gemüsebouquet	23.–
	Escalope de veau Viennoise pommes frites, bouquet de légumes	23.–
	Breaded veal cutlet, fried potatoes, vegetable dish	23.–
311	Beefsteak Tartar klein	12.50
	Beefsteak Tartar, petit	12.50
	Beefsteak Tartar, small portion	12.50
310	Beefsteak Tartar gross	18.50
	Beefsteak Tartar, grand	18.50
	Beefsteak Tartar, large portion	18.50
	mit Cognac verfeinert dazu Toast und Butter	
	avec Cognac Toast et beurre with Cognac Toast and butter	
	*** Mild – Mittel – Feurig	
	*** doux moyen épicé	
	*** mild middle spicy	

Beilagen zu Bourguignonne und Bacchus / Fondue garniture / Fondue garnishing

	– Hausgemachte Saucen	
	– Sauces de la maison	
	– Home-made sauces	
	– Senffrüchte, Essiggemüse	
	– Fruits de moutarde, légumes vinaigrette	
	– Mustard fruits, vinaigre vegetables	
	– Früchte	
	– Fruits	
	– Fruits	
	– Soufflé Kartoffeln	
	– Pommes soufflé	
	– Soufflé potatoes	

Vom Fischmarkt / Au marché du poisson / From the fish market

336	Crevettencocktail «Calypso» Toast und Butter	9.50
	Cocktail de Crevettes, Toast et beurre	9.50
	Shrimps Cocktail with Toast and butter	9.50
337	Meeresfrüchte an Weisswein-sauce und Kräuter, serviert im Reisring	17.50
	Fruits de mer, Sce au vin blanc à l'herbes, servie avec du riz	17.50
	Sea fruits on a white win sauce with herbes with rice	17.50
338	Forelle filetiert in Butter gebraten dazu Dillkartoffeln	16.–
	Filet de truite frit au beurre Pommes au Dill	16.–
	Troutfillet fried in butter Dill potatoes	16.–
339	Eglifilet gebacken, Sce Tartare Dillkartoffeln und grüner Salat	22.–
	Filets de perches frite Sce Tartare, Pommes au Dill et salade verte	22.–
	Perch fillet baked with tartaresauce, Dill potatoes and green salad	22.–

Desserts / Desserts / Desserts

252	Coupe Danemark	6.50
253	Birnensorbet	6.–
	Sorbet au poire	6.–
	Pear Sherbet	6.–
254	Nougat Eistorte	5.–
	Ice tart Nougat	5.–
	Torta glacée nougat	5.–
255	Café glacé	5.50
	Café glacé	5.50
	Coffee ice cream	5.50
256	Bananensplit	6.50
258	Frappées Vanille, Erdbeere, Mocca	4.50
	Frappées vanille, fraise, mocca	4.50
	Milk Shakes Vanille, Strawberry, Mocca	4.50
259	Meringue glacé	6.50

260	Gemischtes Eis mit Rahm	4.–
	Glace panachée avec crème chantilly	4.60
	Mixed ice cream with whipped cream	4.60
261	Gemischtes Eis ohne Rahm	4.–
	Glacé panachée sans crème chantilly	4.–
	Mixed ice cream without whipped cream	4.–
262	Zitronensorbet	6.–
	Sorbet au Citron	6.–
	Lemon Sherbet	6.–
263	Wodkasorbet	8.–
	Sorbet au Vodka	8.–
	Sherbet with Vodka	8.–
265	Schwyzer Meringue	5.50
266	Caramelköpfli im Töpfli	3.20
	Crème caramel	3.20
	Caramel custard	3.20

Fruchtsalat immer frisch zubereitet
Macedoine de fruits toujours servie fraiche
Mixed fruit salad – always freshly prepared
von 11.00 – 14.00 und 17.00 – 22.00
à partir 11.00 h. – 14.00 h. et 17.00 h. – 22.00 h.
from 11 a.m. to 2 p.m. and 5 p.m. to 10 p.m.

268	Fruchtsalat nature	5.50
	Macedoine de fruits nature	5.50
	Plain fruit salad	5.50
272	Fruchtsalat mit Rahm	6.30
	Macedoine de fruits avec crème chantilly	6.30
	Fruit salad with whipped cream	6.30
267	Fruchtsalat mit Kirsch	7.–
	Macedoine de fruits avec Kirsch	7.–
	Fruit salad with Kirsch	7.–
270	Glacé mit Rahm für Kinder	3.50
	Glacé avec crème chantilly pour enfants	3.50
	Ice cream with whipped cream for children	3.50
271	Schlagrahm Garniture	.80
	Crème chantilly comme garniture	.80
	Whipped cream for garnishing	.80
246	Dessertportion Käse	4.50
	Portion de fromage comme dessert	4.50
	Cheese plate as dessert	4.50

Unsere Dessert Hits / Nos spécialités de dessert / Our dessert highlights

257	Coupe Waldmeister heisse Beeren über Vanille-Eis	7.–
	Coupe Waldmeister baie chaudes sur glace vanille	7.–
	Coupe Waldmeister hot berries on Vanille ice cream	7.–
264	Sorbet Williams Birnensorbet mit Williamine	8.–
	Sorbet Williams Sorbet de poire avec Williaminal	8.–
	Williams Sherbet	8.–
269	Zabaione al Marsala idie feine italienische Wein-schaumcrème mit Marsala	8.–
	Zabaione al Marsala	8.–
	Sabeyon Marsala	8.–
273	Irish Ice Coffee iein Glacetraum mit Mokkaglace, Espresso, Whiskyliqueur und Schlagrahm	8.–
	Irish Ice Coffee	8.–
	Irish Ice Coffee	8.–

Tägliche Angebote aus der Vitrine.

quark (thick white unset sour 'cheese'), butter, creams and cheeses. You'll probably notice the 'M', 'MM', 'MMM' signs of the well-stocked and bargain-priced nationwide supermarket chain Migros: the number of 'M's indicates the size of the store. Supermarkets and bakers sell a magnificent selection of breads, mostly brown (and rye), as well as rolls, cakes, and take-away savoury cheese snacks. Many towns have regular open-air markets with fresh farm produce brought in from the surrounding countryside. For wholewheat flour, brown rice and soya products you may have to make a trip to a *Reformhaus* or *Magasin Diététique*.

Cheese shops sell butter, milk and enticing items such as *Kwarktorte*, a quark cheesecake, as well as Swiss and French cheeses. Most Swiss cheeses are firm and pale and riddled with holes, and are made of unpasteurized cow's milk; they tend to be clean-tasting with a sweetish tang. The most widely available, all worth seeking out, are Appenzellar, Emmentaler, Gruyère (also called Greyerzer or Groviera), Raclette (particularly used to make *raclette*, obviously!), Tilsit, Vacherin Mont d'Or (an almost liquid cheese contained in a firm crust; it has a rich, sharp tang and is sold in wooden boxes). Another interesting cheese is Piorn, made of mixed cow's and goat's milk. Sbrinz is a very hard cheese like Italian Parmesan. Toggenburger Ploderkäse is mild low-fat soft cheese made without rennet.

What to say and where to eat

The German area takes up most of the country — 65 per cent of Swiss speak German; 18 per cent are French-speakers, mainly in the south-west, around Geneva; 12 per cent speak Italian, and live in Ticino, the area south of the high Alps. Just 5 per cent speak the curious Latin dialect called Romansh, one of Switzerland's official languages but confined to the Grisons and Engadine, a large but sparsely-populated region in the south-east.

Despite pronunciation and spelling differences, the German, French and Italian spoken in Switzerland are broadly the same as in Germany (see page 49, France (see page 141), and Italy (see page 188). There are just a few vocabulary differences.

A glass of beer or wine	deci (decilitre)
Café, Salon de Thé	café, bar or tea room with a quiet civilized atmosphere and serving cakes and maybe other snacks
Imbiss, Snack	cheap simple restaurant or cafeteria
Restaurant	can be anything — a bar or café without food; a modest snackbar; or a luxury restaurant. *Speise-Restaurant* clarifies that food is served
Wirtschaft	a simple bar
Pension	accommodation with meals
Zimmer, Camere, Chambres	'Rooms', i.e. Bed & Breakfast, sometimes with evening meal if required
Café, Garni, Hotel Garni, Gasthaus, Meublé	all possible names for a hotel *without* a restaurant

Dishes to look out for

Birchermüesli, Müsli, Bircher	muesli: mixed oats, other grains, dried fruits and nuts, soaked and then served with fresh fruit and yogurt or cream
Ramequins (de fromage) Chäschüechli	small hot cheese pastries
Croûte aux champignons, Champignontoast	mushrooms on toast (better than it sounds!)
Emmentaler Soufflé	light but actually very filling cheese soufflé
Fondue	a pot of hot cheese, flavoured with garlic, pepper, white wine, kirsch

(cherry liqueur) and lemon juice, kept simmering at the table and eaten on cubes of bread which are dipped into the cheese mixture on long forks. More of a festive occasion than just a meal, and not something to eat on your own. By tradition, only dry white wine or kirsch should be drunk with fondue, and the custom is that anyone losing a bread cube in the cheese must buy another bottle. Don't drink water or beer with fondue: they go badly together.

Gemüseteller	a plate of vegetables (usually boiled; sometimes in meat stock rather than water)
Gnocchi	(pronounced Nyoki) small light dumplings made of corn, wheat or potato flour
(Schwyzer) Käsekuchen	a filling tart of cheese, egg and mashed potato. Käsekuchen can also refer to a sweet cheesecake
Käseschnitte, Chäseschnitte, Croûte (au fromage)	something along the lines of Welsh Rarebit: a lot of melted cheese on (sometimes fried) bread. But don't order Käseschnitte Oberlander Art, Käseschnitte Valaisanne, or others which include a slice of meat
Käsesuppe, Kässuppe	cheese soup. Recipes vary, a popular sort includes bread, but in general there's neither meat nor meat stock, though it's wise to check
Käseteller	plate of cheeses (usually with bread and butter)

Käsewahe, Quiche au fromage	large cheese tart
Pitz	cheese and tomato pastry, like pizza
Polenta	(Ticino) maize flour boiled until very firm and sliceable; eaten as it is, with butter or cheese, or fried, or baked with cheese
Pommes (de terre) au gratin	baked slices of potato with garlic, butter, pepper, milk and grated cheese
Raclette	like fondue, this is something of a party dish. A whole cheese cut in half is heated before a fire and as the cheese melts it is scraped off and eaten at once with potatoes boiled in their skins and pickled onions
Risotto mit Gemüse	mixed (white) rice and vegetables (maybe meat stock)
Rösti, Röschti	potatoes — first boiled, then grated, and fried in butter until they turn into a crispy golden 'pancake'. Oily, delicious, popular. Worth asking for even if not on menu, though sometimes made with lard instead of butter.
Spaetzli, Spätzli, Spätzler	boiled batter balls, often served with a covering of butter and cheese (check no meat). *Knopflis* is spaetzli made with spinach mixed into the batter.
Spiegelei	fried egg
Tomates farcies	baked tomatoes stuffed with mixed vegetables, egg and cheese (check no meat)

Desserts

Aargauer Rüeblitorte, Aargauer Kuchen — carrot and almond cake; *Apfelwähe* — creamy apple tart; *Clafoutis* — a cakey cherry pie; *Compote* — stewed fruit; *Käsekuchen* — a substantial cheesecake; *Leckerli* — spicy honey and almond bread; *Mont Blanc* — cone-shaped chestnut pudding with a covering of whipped cream; *Rote Grutze* — 'Red Pudding': a sweet stew of cherries, redcurrants and raspberries; *Schaffhauserzungen* — dessert made of biscuits and cream; *Zuckerwähe* — a sweet custard pie with cinnamon.

Information

Overseas offices of the Swiss National Tourist Office, an impressively efficient and well-informed organization (in UK: Swiss Tourist Office, Swiss Centre, New Coventry Street, London W1 [phone: (01) 734 1921]), distribute a short list of some of the country's principal vegetarian establishments. The copy they gave me was already over eighteen months old but still proved accurate and useful, despite some conspicuous omissions. Local tourist offices inside Switzerland can supply more up-to-date and complete information.

There are several Swiss vegetarian organizations and publications, all of them catering only to German-speakers. The leading magazine, widely read in Germany too, is *Regeneration*, which contains adverts for health cure/vegetarian hotels and restaurants, booklists, and much useful information — it even reviews English publications. It is produced by the organization called Arbeitkreis für Lebensneuerung (address: Schwarzenbachweg 16, 8049 Zurich), whose president Edwin Heller is helpful and can be reached by phone on 01/56.88.47.

Yugoslavia

Despite a growing tourist popularity, Yugoslavia remains extremely rustic and unspoiled. It's a large country with a great variety of landscapes, almost entirely unexplored by foreign visitors. The coast is remarkable not for sandy beaches but for really lovely views, with rocky bays and fjord-like inlets enclosing exquisitely blue water. Offshore runs a string of appealing little islands, some now developed for camping holidays.

For many years Yugoslavia has successfully accomplished what one would guess to be a difficult balancing act, poised between the Eastern and Western blocs. It is, definitely, a socialist country, but without restraints either on political discussion or on the opposition parties. By comparison with Western Europeans, Yugoslavs (except Party officials) have a very modest standard of living indeed. Yet basic needs are all fulfilled, and the mood of egalitarianism together with the Government's all-embracing care for its citizens has made the people very content with their system and rather proud of it.

In reality, Yugoslavia is hardly one country at all, but six semi-autonomous regions, each using its own language as well as the national composite Serbo-Croatian. Slowly regional differences are diminishing, but there's a long way to go before they vanish altogether. Certainly food varies from one part of the country to another. In the South more sunflower oil is used, in the North more animal fat and butter; in the West and North there is more diversity of food and more sophisticated cuisine (and more vegetarians too, though nowhere are there very many), while in the South the food is simpler, more Oriental or Turkish, and has stronger flavours. Whichever country happens to be the nearest neighbour has an important influence: in the South, for example, there are similarities to Greece, and Greek-style cheeses —

Kefalotir and Feta — are made. But taken as a whole, Yugoslavia is most decidedly a meat-eating, and especially a fish-eating, country with animal fat or meat stock used in the preparation of almost everything.

From place to place, meatless dishes can be found, often served as a starter, such as stuffed peppers, vegetable dips and a variety of *pitas*, light pastries with all sorts of sweet or savoury fillings. There's a good selection of salads too, made with sumptuous fresh vegetables. Most salads contain just a single vegetable by itself, say tomato, but there are others like *Šopska Salata*, which is slices of green peppers and tomatoes with soft salty cheese — with bread or potatoes it makes an excellent light meal.

Omelettes sometimes feature on restaurant menus, especially in the South — and in any case can be specially made on request — while in touristy areas, particularly Istria, which borders Italy, the world-famous Italian impressarios Pizza and Pasta make their inevitable appearance. But above all it's the *Mlečni Restoran* (milk restaurant) which saves the day, at least for lacto-vegetarians. With an old-fashioned rustic quality, and appealing mainly to older people, these are snack bars which specialize in yogurts for drinking (*Jogurt*) or eating (*Kisolo Mleko*), milky desserts, snacks made with cheese or *kajmak* (a full-fat soft delicious milk product made from the skin which forms on milk while it is being heated), and a multitude of tasty bread rolls and pastries.

Nevertheless, a suitable restaurant for a proper hot lunch or dinner can be hard to find. In six weeks of hiking around Yugoslavia my food rarely extended beyond the limits of bread, rich tangy yogurt, soft salty cheese, crisp sweet cucumbers and big, juicy and full-flavoured tomatoes — a healthy-enough diet, admittedly. Every time I went to a restaurant there would be absolutely nothing to eat but fishy starters and meaty main dishes, accompanied by a boiled vegetable and a simple salad. The only two hot meals during the whole period were both omelettes. Or there may have been one other — for Yugoslavs are tremendously friendly and hospitable, and early one evening in a dockside bar I met a young returning sea captain and his girlfriend. They invited me to dine back in their village up in the hills behind the coast. As we drove up the steep, winding road, the captain stopped to call in at a bar in every village along the way. In each one he was greeted with great laughs and shouts of delight, like a long lost brother. Plenty of drink would be insisted on all round before we continued on our way. Everything began to melt into a fuzzy glow of camaraderie, and language became less and less important. At our final destination, I am almost sure that we did, as planned, go to a crowded and convivial restaurant — though I remember nothing beyond walking through the door. At the end of the night we were each given a glass of mineral water with a spoonful of honey in it to help us sober up sufficiently to return to our beds — and the crystal clarity of my memory on this one point surely testifies to the efficacy of this treatment!

Breakfast and snacks

Even before breakfast, Yugoslavs take their first of the day's many cups of strong black Turkish coffee. Breakfast itself, which can be had in a *mlečni restoran* or snackbar, consists of fresh bread with a glass of milk or drinking yogurt. In hotels, guests are given the usual bread, butter, jam, and tea or coffee. Throughout the rest of the day snackbars and milk restaurants remain open for all sorts of *peciva* (bread rolls). One of the most popular is *kifler*, a crescent-shaped roll, though not really like a croissant. *Pašteta* are square-shaped rolls which do have the buttery consistency of croissant. *Pogačica* are small round rolls of croissant dough (the ending *-ica* denotes something small). *Lepinja* is another tasty kind of bread made in flat 'loaves', and one of the most delicious snacks of all is *lepinja sa kajmakom*, which is *lepinja* with a layer of *kajmak* inside. There are plenty of other filled breads and pastries too, some with spinach, others with cheese, and many more, savoury or sweet. *Burek*, made of thin layers of filo pastry, is filled either with cheese or meat (with cheese it's called *burek sa sirom*). *Pita* is a general word for pie or pastry, the two commonest sorts being *pita sa* *sirom*, cheese pastry, and *pita sa jabukama*, apple pastry. Sweeter bakery brings in the delectable varieties of *Strudla*, something like strudel, the most popular being filled with poppy seeds, *strudla sa makom*. And almost anywhere that these pies and rolls are being sold, they have been baked on the premises.

In bars and cafés, *meze* — canapés, or small savoury snacks (mostly unsuitable for vegetarians) — are on offer to accompany alcoholic drinks. Besides the ubiquitous *kafa*, Turkish coffee, which comes in a small cup half-full of coffee grounds, it's not hard to find herb teas, especially *kamilica*, camomile, and *lipa*, lime tree blossom. If invited to someone's home between meals, you may be offered a saucer of *slatko*, a preserve made with whole fruits, with just a glass of water.

Another vital resource is the simple type of patisserie, usually run by Albanians, called *poslastičarnica*. They're all over the country, at least one in every town, and they specialize in *Baklava*, *Tulumba*, *Sutlijas* and other Balkan-style sweets (see desserts on page 117).

Lunch and dinner

For Yugoslavs themselves, the big meal of the day is lunch, eaten at about 2–3 p.m. It usually consists of soup or cheese to start; a substantial meat or fish dish with vegetable and salad; finishing with cakes or ice cream, and coffee. Dinner, a much lighter affair, is barely more than breakfast — say, bread with a salad or a plate of cold meat or cheese — and can be eaten at any time of the evening. Foreign visitors, or at least hotel guests, are not expected to conform to these customs, and the tourist-orientated restaurants serve 'international'-type three-course meals at 12–2 p.m. and 7–10 p.m. These generally have little to interest vegetarians: to date, Yugoslav hotel-restaurants have not distinguished themselves in catering for meatless diets. Often the only thing made available is a plate of two or three boiled vegetables and perhaps a salad.

As likely as not, ordinary local restaurants will have just as little to interest a vegetarian, though it is worth studying the menu because there is always a chance of finding one of the dishes to look out for (page 118), or a vegetable soup, or salad and chips with bread, or an omelette. The best bet could be to have two or three starters, if they are suitable, and miss out the main dish: there will be no objection to this, and it's worth explaining that you are a vegetarian — the concept is not unknown in Yugoslavia.

The usual accompaniment to meals is either a locally-brewed beer or a Yugoslav wine. These are inexpensive and tend to imitate foreign varieties, but can be quite excellent. With a not-so-good wine it is normal to cut it with a little water. Mixed wine and water is called *bevanda*.

If 'proper' restaurants cannot provide a meal without meat, it should certainly be possible to find something filling enough for a main meal among the food on offer at a snackbar or milk restaurant; failing that, you may have to do-it-yourself with what you can find in the market.

Self-catering and picnics

With such limitations on eating-out, the ideal way to experience Yugoslavia would be by self-catering, with 'mobile self-catering' — camping or caravanning — perhaps best of all. Fortunately the country's tourist industry is well geared up for this, and low-cost apartment and camping holidays abound. Yugoslavia has also, incidentally, made a special feature of naturist holidays, both self-catering and in hotels, although before booking one of these packages remember that naturism is in any case permitted at all Yugoslav beach resorts.

Supermarkets and grocery shops, except in some resort areas, resemble old-fashioned 'dry goods stores', poorly equipped apart from basics — canned beans, peanuts, rice, flour, coffee, pasta, honey and dairy products. Most people do all their shopping in markets, which take place two or three or more times weekly in most localities, and where vegetables and fruit in season are abundant and cheap. Depending on the time of year, the range may be limited, though some items, potatoes, spinach, huge tomatoes called by a name that sounds like 'Paradise', and cucumbers with tough skins but sweet and juicy insides (better peeled), seem always plentiful.

What to say

Serbo-Croatian may be written in Cyrillic alphabet, but in practice Roman lettering is just as widely used, especially in the North and along the coastal strip, so I have kept to it here. In pronunciation, accents on Cs and Ss are all-important: S sounds like *s*; Š like *sh*; C as *ts*; Č and Ć are both *ch* (Ć is 'softer' and a little further forward in the mouth). Other letters to remember: J is y. Z is like *z*, while Ž is like a soft kind of *j* sound (as in pleasure), and DŽ is a harder and more definite *j* (as in jam). If you come across đ, this is yet another *j* sound. The vowel U is always pronounced *oo*. In general, the emphasis is on the first syllable of a word.

The essentials

Good morning/after-noon/evening	Dobro jutro/dan/veče
Goodbye	Zbogom
Do you speak English?	Govorite li Engleski?
Menu	Cenovnik, jelovnik
Set meal, Table d'hôte	Menia
Have you got . . .?	Imate li . . .?
Can we have . . .?	Možemo li dobiti . . .?
Please	Molim
Thank you (very much)	Hvalah (lepo; but a simple 'thank you' is considered quite enough in all but exceptional circumstances!)
Breakfast/lunch/dinner	Doručak/ručak/večera
Eat/drink	Jesti/piti
I would like (some) . . .	Želeo bih . . .
I am (we are) vegetarian	Ja sam (mi smo) vegetarijanac(i)

Is there something without meat?	Da li imate nešto bez mesa?
I don't want meat/fish	Neču meso
No } meat/fish/ Without } cheese/egg	Bez mesa/ribe/sir/jaja
No meat stock	Ništa mesne juhe
No animal fat	Ništa životinjskih masti
Is there meat in this?	Da li ima mesa u ovom?
Vegetable stock	Biljna osnova (you may have a lot of trouble getting Yugoslavs to understand the concept).
Yes/no	Da/ne
(Very) good	(Vrlo) dobro
And/with	I/sa
Cheers!	Ziveli!
The bill . . . how much?	Račum . . . koliko?
That/this	Ono/to
100, 200, 500 grams	Sto, dvesto, petsto grama
Bread	Hleb. Normally white. Wholewheat is called Crni Hleb literally 'black bread'. Rye bread is Ražani Hleb. Soya bread is Hleb od Soje. You can buy half a loaf of bread — ask for Pola Hleb.
Corn bread	Proja. Used to be the main sort of bread in large areas of the country.
Flour	Brašno
Rye, wheat	Raž, žito. Wheat grains sold in some shops
Oats, maize, soya	Zob, kukuruz, soje. Soya beans in some shops.
Rice	Pirinač. Always white — brown seems unobtainable
Honey, sugar	Med, šećer
Yogurt	several sorts: Kefir is a liquid milk culture; Jogurt is liquid yogurt;

	Kisolo mleko is set yogurt to eat with a spoon
Butter, cream, sour cream	Puter, crem, pavlaka. The cream is thick and heavy.
Eggs	Jaja
Cheese	Sir. There are several types, mostly soft and salty, made of sheeps' or cows' milk
Salt, pepper, oil	So, biber, ulje
Olive oil	Maslinovo ulje
Sunflower oil	Ulje od suncokreta
Garlic	Beli luk
Vegetables	Povrće
Herbs and spices, seasonings	Začini
Fruit juice	Voćni sok
Coffee	Kafa (Turkish coffee. The only other types you may find are Espresso Kafa and Cappuccino).
Decaffeinated	Kafa bez kofeina — very rare
Tea, herb tea	Čaj (pronounced Chai), biljni caj. But the word čaj on its own implies herb tea. Offer tea to a Yugoslav and he'll probably decline, making some comment like 'I'm not ill', thinking no one who's well would drink it.
with Milk	sa mleko. Milk, mleko, is all semi-skimmed and heat-treated
Hot/cold	Vruće/hladno
(Mineral) water	(Mineralnu) vodu
Wine (red/white/rosé)	Vino (crno/belo/ruzica)
Bottle, glass	Flašu, čašu
Half-bottle	Pola flaše

Carafes are not much used, and restaurants do not usually keep a House Wine.

Beer (light/dark)   Pivo (svetlo/crno)

Yugoslavs are fond of strong fruit 'brandies' — best liked is the plum-based Sljivovica

Bakery   Pekara

Dairy shop   Mlekara. You can also buy dairy produce to take away in a *mlečni restoran* (milk restaurant).

Food shop   Prodavnica hrave, Bakalnica

Greengrocer   Piljarnica

Supermarket   Samoposluga. The English word is also used.

And also you will find:

Kafic   a café-bar, not much to eat

Mlečni restoran   dairy restaurant and snackbar

Bife, kafana   both are names for a snackbar, or a café-bar with food

Bar   more of a nightclub than a bar

Ekspres restoran   self-service café/snackbar

Gostiona, krčma   two names for an inn, with food, drink, and possibly lodgings

Poslastičarnica   simple Balkan-style pastry-and-pudding café

Restoran   restaurant – a *riblji restoran* is a restaurant with mainly fish dishes

On the menu

Burek   small savoury pastry

Čorba   thick soup

Čorba od gljiva/paradajze mushroom/tomato soup (beware meat stock)

Čorba od povrca   vegetable soup (beware meat stock)

Dezert   dessert

Dimljena   smoked

Domaća   home-made

Gibanica   cheese-and-egg pastry

Grilovana   grilled

Juha	clear soup — meat stock
Kajmak	a tangy, creamy milk product
Kuvana	poached or stewed
Lepinja	a kind of bread made in flat pieces
Lepinja sa kajmakom	lepinja bread with a layer of kajmek in it (delicious!)
Marinirane	marinaded
Meze	bites of food to go with drinks. Can be quite substantial
Omlet	omelette
Orasima	nuts
Pasirano	creamed
Pita	a pastry, sweet or savoury (or both)
Pommes frites	chips
Praziluk	leeks (much used)
Predjelo	starter, appetizer, hors d'oeuvres
Pržena	fried
Prženi krompir	fried potatoes, chips
Punjene, punjeni	stuffed; e.g. Punjeni masline, stuffed olives
Ruska salata	Russian salad, diced vegetables with mayonnaise
Salata	salad. Many kinds, usually with a single vegetable, often with yogurt added
. . . sa sirom	. . . with cheese
Seckano	diced (pronounced: setzkano)
Sir, sirom	cheese
Šopska salata	salad of peppers, tomatoes and soft cheese
Špargle	asparagus (much used)
Supa	clear soup — meat stock
Topfn (or Belava)	a white soft cheese like low-fat German quark, often used in cooking
Voća	fruit
Voćnu salatu	fruit salad

Fruit, vegetables, nuts, herbs, etc.

Ananas — pineapple; *artičoke* — artichoke; *bademi* — almonds; *beli luk* — garlic; *biber* — pepper; *boranija* — haricot beans; *cvekla* — beetroot; *groždje* — grapes; *gljive* — mushrooms; *gomoljica* — truffles; *grašak* — peas; *jabuke* — apples; *kajsije* — apricots; *karfiol* — cauliflower; *kesteni* — chestnuts; *kozlak* — tarragon; *krastavac* — cucumber; *krompir* — potatoes; *kruške* — pears; *kupine* — blackberries; *kupus* — cabbage; *leće* — lentils; *lešnik* — hazelnuts; *limun* — lemon; *lubenica* — watermelon; *luk* — onions; *majčina dušica* — thyme; *masline* — olives; *mrkva* — carrots; *orasi* — walnuts; *paprike* — green peppers; *paradaiz* — tomatoes; *pasulij* — beans; *patlidžan* — aubergines; *peršun* — parsley; *pomarandža* — oranges; *praziluk* — leeks; *repa* — beet; *šljive* — plums; *smokve* — figs; *spanać* – spinach; *spargle* — asparagus; *suvo groždje* — raisins; *trešnje* — cherries; *začini* — spices; *zelena boranija* — green beans; *zelena salata* — lettuce; *zelje* — herbs; *žutenica* — chicory.

Dessert or between-meals — mostly substantial

Alva — halva, i.e. a hard paste of nuts and sugar; *baklava* — thin layers of pastry with layer(s) of ground-up nuts, the whole thing soaked in syrup; *istarske fritule* — Istrian, spicy sweet fritters made with wine and liqueur; *jabuku u rumu* — whole apples cooked in rum; *kompot* — stewed fruit; *medenjaci* — honey cakes; *palačinke* — crêpes, pancakes, with sweet fillings or toppings; *potica nadevena orasima* — walnut and cream cake; *ratluk* — Turkish Delight; *sladoled (od vanilje)* — (vanilla) ice cream; *slatko* — sugary preserve of whole fruits, can also be made of nuts or even flowers; *strudla (or pita) jabuka* — apple strudel; *strudla sa makom* — poppy seed strudel; *sutlijaš* — cold rice pudding, with a dusting of cocoa or cinnamon on top; *suva pita sa orasima* — walnuts and raisins in filo pastry; *taška sa pekmezom* — ravioli-type pasta filled with jam; *torta (od čokolade/voća)* — (chocolate/fruit) cake; *tulumba* — very sweet, moist cucumber-shaped pastry; *ulutma od oraha* — heavy, syrupy walnut cake.

Dishes to look out for

Although these are all non-meat dishes, it's always wise to ask.

Flekice sa kupusom	square noodles and chopped cabbage
Gibančici	deep fried pastry containing sheep's cheese
Gibanica	cheese and *kajmak* pastry
Jaja sa sirom i pečenim paprikama	egg with cheese and baked peppers
Kačamak	polenta, cooked corn meal
Kisele paprika	pickled peppers
Knedle	dumplings (wheat flour) — as a dessert, too
Knedle od pourća	dumplings made of finely chopped vegetables, flour and eggs (hope for the best concerning whether vegetables were prepared in stock or water)
Kuvani štruklji	little dumplings made with eggs, butter, cream and cheese
(Naravni) omlet	(plain) omelette
Paprike sa sirom	green peppers stuffed with egg and cheese mixture and topped with *kajmak*
Pogača	hot bread, usually with *kajmak*
Priganice	small deep-fried wholewheat pastries served with *kajmak* or cheese
Sauerkraut	not really like German sauerkraut, just a cabbage salad
Srpski ajvar	Serbian, a kind of relish or dip made of chopped aubergines and peppers, served as a side dish
Tarator (od krastavaca)	Macedonian, spicy yogurt and cucumber dip
Taške sa sirom	ravioli pasta filled with cheese, served as a main dish

Zeljanica   spinach-filled pita

and for an interesting drink, try *boza*, a cold sweet drink made by fermenting cornmeal, served all day long in snackbars in Macedonia.

But beware of

Boršč	(borscht) a soup of beetroot or other vegetables mixed with cream and often also with meat
Djuveč	green pepper stew, with or without rice or potatoes. As a vegetable side dish, this generally contains no meat, but when listed as a main dish it normally does include meat
Pašta i fažol	literally, pasta and beans — but usually with meat as well
Punjeni paradaiz/paprike	baked stuffed tomatoes/peppers — the filling can be either vegetable or meat
Punjeni plavi patlidžani	baked aubergines stuffed with rice, herbs and vegetables — may include meat
Tavče	literally, a small casserole; also the name for white beans baked with fried onions and hot peppers and occasionally meat

And avoid altogether

Paštetice od sira-skute	'cottage cheese pastries': they contain pork
Prosciutto, šunka, šunkom	all different names for ham, much used in the west and north-west
. . . sa mesom	means 'with meat'
Sogan dolma	stuffed onions: the filling is meat

Information

The Yugoslav Vegetarian Society can be contacted at: Vegetari-jansko Društvo, Preradovićeva 33, 41000 Zagreb, Yugoslavia (phone: 41/213-803). The long-standing Secretary, Milan Mag-laić, speaks (or at least writes) quite good English.

The Yugoslav National Tourist Office, at 143 Regent Street, London W1 [phone: (01) 734 5243] has no information specifi-cally for vegetarians, but has a supply of the most important brochures for self-catering and other holidays, and when I visited their office they also had details of vegetarian guesthouse holiday accommodation which happened to be on offer just then.

Part Two:

The Olive and The Grape

In southern Europe, in those nations which touch upon the Mediterranean Sea, olive oil, garlic and herbs give their distinct flavour and character to the food. Aubergines, tomatoes and green peppers make a frequent appearance. The usual meal is one in which meat and vegetables, meat and grains, or grains and vegetables have been combined as a single dish. In a larger meal, a piece of meat or fish may be served as an almost ungarnished course on its own. In these countries, vegetarians are helped by the fact that eggs are thought of as a sort of meat, and regarded as a suitable alternative to it. Two other characteristics of this part of the world: the locals eat little or nothing for breakfast; and huge amounts of alcohol are consumed in the form of spirits, aperitifs, liqueurs and of course wine — considered an essential accompaniment to meals.

France

The only European country extending right across the cultural divide between the North and the South, France is the most popular holiday destination for independent 'unpackaged' travellers. No wonder, for it covers an unrivalled wealth of landscapes, climate and civilized living, with thousands of good inexpensive family-run hotels and restaurants. For many people, French food is a major attraction. It is really quite wrong to include France in the Olive and Grape section of this book, because there are whole French provinces (Normandy, for example) where neither of these fruits grow and certainly where olive oil is relatively little used. However, even less does France fit into either of the other two sections! In truth, when it comes to food and drink, France must be looked upon as uncategorizable — unique.

Concern with food has been elevated almost to the status of a religion. It is the main topic of conversation, and takes up the largest proportion of the average household budget. The nation's greatest chefs are revered as stars, and their names become household words. Of course, there is an enormous difference between the refinements of Haute Cuisine and the down-to-earth workaday cooking of ordinary people — yet even in the most typical family home or modest little restaurant, food is usually prepared with the utmost respect and feeling, a touch of refinement too, and presented with simple elegance. True, there are exceptions, most of them around the tourist 'sights' in Paris. But in the real France, in the unpretentious backstreets or in the towns and villages, where there is invariably a cheap restaurant to be found, delicious food is one of life's most accessible delights.

In some ways, vegetarians are at a tremendous disadvantage here. To the French mind, anything edible is fair game. Some of the things they are happy to tuck into might turn the stomachs of more squeamish Anglo-Saxons. Tripe, offal, brains and even more repugnant parts of the body are specialities in some regions, certain butchers deal exclusively in horse flesh and one of the most beloved of gourmet foods — *foie gras* — is made by using machines to force-feed geese. While the English meat-eater is normally struck with affection and sentiment at the sight of, say, new-born lambs in a field, the French (less hypocritically, it must be admitted) would more likely find their mouths watering at such a prospect. Meat is normally very lightly cooked or on occasion eaten raw. Furthermore, the conventional structure of a French meal requires either meat or fish to be its focus: sometimes there may be very few vegetables, or indeed none at all, to accompany the meat dish.

Yet there are advantages too. Firstly, by choosing a restaurant carefully, a vegetarian stands a chance of putting together a better meatless meal than can be found anywhere else in Europe. And secondly, the trump card for vegetarians, the French do understand that when it comes to food you want what you want and nothing else will do. They may think you mad, they may think you foolish, but they still think you entitled to a good dinner.

THE NEW CUISINE

Traditional Haute Cuisine concentrates on robust, substantial dishes and rich sauces. In recent years, urged by the growing interest in healthy eating, a new style has developed. This 'Nouvelle Cuisine' has already established itself as a vital element in the evolution of Haute Cuisine: it demands considerable training and refinement, and in its pure form is the preserve of the richest customers of the most expensive restaurants in the land. The essential qualities of Nouvelle Cuisine are an emphasis on lightness, freshness and visual appeal. The originator of the new style was Fernand Point, chef-proprietor of the famous Restaurant La Pyramide on the outskirts of Vienne, just south of Lyon; among his most eminent followers are the brothers Troisgros, chef-proprietors of the Frères Troisgros restaurant at Roanne, west of Lyon. Certain rules have been laid down by these acknowledged masters of the art: vegetables must be both crisp and tender; in all dishes, precise timing is of the absolute essence; flour must be avoided, especially in sauces, and the taste of a sauce must not conceal, even slightly, the taste of the dish it accompanies; ingredients must be finely cut with exceptionally sharp knives; and ultimate appearance must be kept in mind throughout the preparation.

In reality, only purists adhere strictly to all these principles. For most chefs, and most diners too, Nouvelle Cuisine is more of a tendency, or an influence, than an absolute. And for vegetarians it is an extremely valuable influence. My very best meals to date have been in French restaurants leaning strongly towards the Nouvelle. And even while both Classic and Nouvelle styles continue to vie with each other in their most uncompromising forms, it will be of great benefit to vegetarians if at the more homely levels of cooking the two merge more and more. In the meantime, look out particularly for restaurants which favour Nouvelle Cuisine, or at least include examples of it on their menus. Even if they have no meatless dish listed, they are likely to be imaginative and willing when called upon to prepare something for a vegetarian.

In the wake of Nouvelle Cuisine have flowed several other novel ideas, more or less obscure, but all contributing to the overall scheme of French cooking and eating: Cuisine Minceur ('slimming cuisine', that is, low-calorie ingredients) and Cuisine Naturel (no oil, butter, cream or alcohol, little salt or sugar, and plenty of vegetables), for example, and also, we hope, the first stirrings of a genuine Cuisine Végétarienne.

FRANCE'S REGIONS

Historically, France was never one country until the Revolution, after which Napoleon tried to iron out the immense cultural and linguistic differences between the provinces. To some extent he succeeded, hence the single French nation we see today. Yet huge regional variations remain, not least in the style of cooking. For a vegetarian, this can assume more than mere academic interest. Some regions are popularly regarded as 'gastronomique' — they have a particularly fine tradition of cookery — and while these areas tend to be the most meat-orientated, they can also be the most capable of imaginative variation. The principal gastronomic regions are Périgord (taking in the Limousin and Dordogne), Burgundy (whence originated many of the classic French dishes) and Alsace (where the food has a German quality). Paris too, or at least the surrounding Ile de France, was traditionally a gastronomic centre: nowadays, of course, it attracts both the best and the worst of French — and foreign — food.

Administratively, France is divided into twenty-two regions, some modern and artificial, others following historical boundaries. However, as far as eating habits go, there are roughly sixteen, not including Corsica (see page 162), which in food as in everything else has practically nothing in common with the mainland. The local emphasis of each region is something along these lines:

Alsace-Lorraine — salt and spices; butter and lard; ham and charcuterie, river fish, truffles, pâté. Much German influence: potatoes and cabbage popular, as are heavy cakes — and portions of everything are huge. Wines are good, mainly dry white or rosé, and good beer is brewed here too.

Auvergne/Massif Central — sausage and ham appear in most dishes, lard is used for cooking; potatoes, cabbage, lentils, lots of cheeses, fruit conserves, and liqueurs. Hardly any wine made, but some cider.

Basque Country — butter; fish (stews), delicate seasoning.

Bordeaux and Atlantic — butter; seafood, fish, caviar. Great wines.

Brittany — seafood and more seafood, plus lamb, ham and charcuterie, abundant vegetables; dry white wine from neighbouring Loire valley; butter.

Burgundy & Lyonnais — beef, poultry, ham and charcuterie, strong cheeses, good vegetables sparingly served, snails, quenelles (light dumplings); great wines and wine sauces; butter; fruit puddings and tarts.

Champagne & Ardennes — butter; fish, quenelles, charcuterie, Brie and other soft cheeses, cabbage, beetroot, fruit. And of course, Champagne.

Franche Comté & The Alps — cow's milk cheeses, especially Comté; Fondue, Raclette and other cheese dishes; river fish, pork, ham, sausages; lard and butter; nuts and nut oils. Sweet waffles, tarts, fritters.

Ile de France/Paris — fresh vegetables, mushrooms, potatoes; soups, sauces; butter.

Languedoc — goats' and sheep's cheese (notably Roquefort), fish (stews), beans (in stews with meat), pork and ham, snails, honey, chestnuts; cheap red table wines and sweet muscat wine; lard and olive oil.

Loire & Central France — river fish and stews, pork and charcuterie, meat and fruit prepared together, pâtés, beans, mushrooms, quince, mustard, goats' cheeses; pastries; excellent fresh and fruity dry white wines; butter and lard.

Normandy — omelettes and eggs, cream; butter and lard; tripe; cheeses, from mild to very strong; fish; apples, cider and Calvados (apple brandy); savoury and sweet crêpes.

Périgord & Quercy — this is the region which specializes in the cruellest food — *foie gras*; yet another speciality from the same area is truffle omelette; lots of sausages or black pudding; tripe; cabbage, potatoes, dumplings, truffles; lard.

Picardy & Flanders — sausages, tripe, black pudding; lard stews; pâtés; herrings; beer both for drinking and for use in cooking.

Provence — olive oil; garlic, tomatoes, aubergines, peppers, courgettes, onions; fish and fish stews; pies and pastries. Red wines, mostly of the cheap and cheerful variety.

Roussillon & The Pyrenees — small game, fruits and berries, fish, snails, chestnuts, herb liqueurs; lard and olive oil.

Breakfast and snacks

At home and in many hotels, the day starts with *tartine* (buttered French bread) and a large cup or bowl of strong coffee with hot milk, or some other milky drink such as drinking chocolate or *Ovomaltine*. In café-bars and in some hotels, instead of buttered bread there are croissants, soft flaky crescent-shaped rolls made of thin buttery dough.

In hotels it is quite normal that breakfast be brought to your room on request, this being in my view one of the greatest little luxuries of France. On the other hand, if your hotel cannot provide a satisfactory breakfast it is quite permissible and normal to go out to a nearby bar — hotels in France cannot oblige you to take either breakfast or dinner (though in the case of dinner they sometimes give the impression that they can).

It is perfectly in order, at any time of day, to buy croissants or cakes at a *pâtisserie* (cake shop) or *boulangerie* (baker's) and take them into a café to eat with a hot drink. You may freely do this even at bars which have their own croissants on the counter at breakfast time, but it is not acceptable to take cakes or croissants to a *Salon de Thé* or similar, where cakes and pastries are a special feature and are sold all day long. Broadly, the rule about what food may be taken into a café to eat is that any small item is acceptable provided it needs no cutting, buttering or other preparation. There are some tempting alternatives to ordinary croissants, by the way: *croissants au beurre* have extra butter, and *pains au chocolat* are made of rolled croissant dough with a strip of chocolate inside.

French *pâtisserie*, which literally means pastry-making, has little similarity to cakes and bakery in the English sense. French cakes are indeed mainly made of light pastry with generous fillings of *crème pâtissière*, confectioner's custard. Fresh cream is not used. There are hundreds of varieties, the great favourites being exquisitely delicate and delicious. Those little shops called *pâtisseries*, found in every town and almost every village, are not mere retail outlets but are places where a trained pastrycook bakes his own cakes and pastries on the premises. *Gâteaux* are more like

English or North European cakes (though beware: some savoury dishes are called *gâteaux*), and the word *cake* is also used, referring only to plain fruit cake. Savoury and cheese-filled pastries and tarts can be bought at pâtisseries too.

Apart from pâtisserie, France suffers from a terrible lack of between-meal snacks. Anyone who hasn't filled up at a proper mealtime is regarded as a foolish wretch deserving to suffer. A bar can generally provide a sandwich — a bready and unappetizing half-loaf sliced longways and meanly 'filled' with ham, pâté or cheese. In the South, thanks to an out-of-doors climate and a more casual lifestyle, snacks are a little more in demand and street vendors hawk *pissaladière*, which is a type of pizza, and *pan bagna*, a salad roll, but unfortunately both of these contain fish.

The best exceptions are in those bars called *brasseries*. Literally this means brewery, an old-fashioned title for what are now, from the drinks point of view, bars just like any other. From the food point of view though, brasseries are essentially bars which can provide hot dishes at almost any time of day. Pictures of what's available are often on view in the window, or the word *Casse-Croûte* — snacks — may be displayed. Needless to say, the big favourites are not suitable for vegetarians: *Croque-Monsieur*, like Welsh Rarebit with ham; *Croque-Madame*, same thing with some other meat instead of ham; *Steack-Frites*, steak and chips. However, eggs feature often as well, either fried or as omelettes, and there are soups which may be acceptable, and *crudités* (vegetable salad), which can be pieced together to make a good, though perhaps rather too large, meatless snack or light meal.

Any bar or brasserie sells all alcoholic drinks, tea (weak, black and tepid), hot chocolate (not very good — usually too sweet), herb teas (called *tissanes* or *infusions*) and coffee (excellent). *Un café*, simply enough, means a strong black coffee in a small cup. *Café crème* or *café au lait* are both a strong black coffee topped-up with hot milk (the milk is UHT semi-skimmed. Real cream is not added to coffee). Almost any bar or restaurant can provide *un decaféiné*, decaffeinated coffee, known colloquially as *un deca*. Decaffeinated coffee may be made of real ground coffee beans, just as good as ordinary coffee, or it may be instant. Apart from that, instant coffee is hardly ever served anywhere. The occasionally-used expression *Un Café Complet* means, in effect, a continental breakfast: a *café au lait* with croissant or *tartine*.

Lunch and dinner

Rigid conventions govern French eating habits. It's important to remember the **mealtimes** as it can prove difficult to find something to eat at any other time of day. The lunch break is from 12 noon to 2 p.m. and almost everyone in France is *à table* at 12.30. The one exception is Paris, where some workers are given only one hour for lunch. Lunch is everywhere the main meal of the day. Dinner is slightly more flexible, starting from between 7.30 and 8.30 and continuing until about 9.30 p.m. After that time, restaurants ruthlessly turn away potential customers with a brusque '*C'est terminé*' (finished) or even, despite waiters still rushing about to tables seated with convivial diners, '*Fermé*' (closed). Tourist areas and certain types of restaurants (for example pizzerias) continue until a little later, but even they rarely serve newcomers after about 10.30 p.m.

The next convention is the **meal structure**, every meal having a clearly defined beginning (soup or hors d'oeuvres), middle (meat or fish), and end (cheese or dessert). Within this structure, more courses can be inserted according to certain rules. If there are four courses instead of three, the second (*entrée*) is another meat or fish dish. If both cheese and dessert are served, they must come in that order. Any vegetables or salad to 'accompany' the main course are served as a separate item, with a few commonly agreed exceptions (such as chips) which are eaten together with main dish. The problem posed for vegetarians, and their hosts, is how to fit a meatless meal into this framework. That is why almost any restaurant in France, if presented with a vegetarian, will suggest an omelette — because, according to the rules, in a light meal an omelette can be regarded as the equivalent of meat or fish. By contrast, something like rice and vegetables would be seen merely as side dishes or starters, leaving, for the French mind, a sort of emptiness where the main course should be.

Then there is the importance of **set meals**. The 'correct' way to eat in France is to order a set fixed-price meal, called a *menu*. Each restaurant offers one, two, or usually three alternative *menus* at different prices, for example 50F, 65F and 95F. There is no disgrace attached to choosing the cheapest. They're all such value for money anyway that the assumption is that you are ordering exactly as much as you want to eat The difference between the *menus* is not, or should not be, in the quality of the food served but in the number of courses and the expertise required to make them. As well as the set meals, there is the option of choosing from *la carte*, this being, confusingly, what the English mean by a menu — a list of food on offer, a bill of fare, with the price marked next to each dish. Ordering à la carte allows you the freedom to make eccentric decisions about what to eat but works out vastly more expensive than a set meal. Food cooked to à la carte orders risks being not quite as good, either: often it is stuff from the freezer, while the set meals are being freshly prepared. So avoid, whenever possible, eating à la carte.

Set meals usually have a stern warning that No Substitutions Will Be Permitted, or Any Substitution Will Be Charged Extra. In practice, this is intended as a deterrent to meat-eaters who might want to have a different main dish. It does not apply, at least I have never yet known it to, in the case of a diner who wants to omit the meat altogether (such an eventuality was never dreamed of by the original French menu-writers!). An omelette can usually be substituted for the meat without any extra charge.

Your main problem then becomes **avoiding the omelette**. In France, I count every day without an omelette as an achievement in itself. A French omelette is a delicious affair, light, moist and fluffy, yet filling. But after eating an omelette at three or four consecutive meals, one's liking for them can be much diminished. France has many excellent dishes and salads, quite apart from the fact that individual vegetable side dishes are often cooked to absolute perfection (that is, underdone by average English standards), but these are not intended to be eaten as a main course. Vegetarians must select their meal from among the starters and side dishes: you could order one starter to start, and one or two others as a main course — no one will object, there should be no extra charge, and the meal will probably be adequately large. In reasonably good restaurants it's well worth asking for *une assiette de légumes*, a plate of vegetables, perhaps with *une sauce*. This can yield a remarkably tasty meal, though as always with French food, from the vegetarian point of view, there's a lack of grains, or indeed of any protein other than in the cheese course (and the omelette, if you haven't managed to escape from it).

Before ordering, unless there happens to be a suitable menu, always seek the waiter's advice. Tell him or her that you cannot eat meat or fish. This is sensible, firstly because otherwise your order might look quite absurd to French eyes, and secondly, so that he or she can help you to ensure a completely meat-free meal. With really superior restaurants it's worth contacting them a day or two in advance to discuss your meal and give the chef a chance to think of something suitable. Yet here too, you may have to discourage any proposal to offer 'a delicious omelette'.

Foreign restaurants provide welcome **diversions**. Chinese, Vietnamese and other South East Asian restaurants are all quite common in major towns. Among the other useful alternatives, crêperies and pizzerias invariably spring up in resort areas and university towns. Becoming more and more widespread are self-service cafeteria-style restaurants, often known, in a typically absurd bit of Franglais, as '*Self*'. Make full use of them. Their prices are low and the food surprisingly good (except in motorway service areas and a few of the cafeterias attached to big supermarkets), and you can pick and choose exactly what you want from the range of salads and vegetable dishes. Not unknown, either, are vegetarian restaurants. In my experience they offer a standard of cuisine nowhere near as high as conventional restaurants — but for all that, what a relief it is to come across a plate of brown rice and vegetables.

TACKLING SOME REAL MENUS

At a restaurant in the Limousin

Le repas est absolument complet et comprend:

1°   Apéritifs variés avec amuse-gueule

2°   Un plat d'entrée au choix et son vin de qualité assorti

3°   Un plat de suite au choix et son vin également assorti
    (Le plat de suite comporte toujours deux garnitures).

4°   Salade

5°   Plateau de fromages

6°   Corbeilles de fruits

7°   Dessert glacé ou entremet

8°   Café ou infusion

Grande salle pour lunchs, buffets, mariages,

réunions de travail

jusqu'à 120 personnes

Prix absolument net T.T.C. - Service compris 158F

The menu above is a strange menu because it doesn't actually tell you what dishes are available!

Le repas est absolument complet et comprend tells us the meal is 'as follows' and everything is included in the overall price, given below as 158F. TTC means *Tout Taxes Compris*, taxes included, and *Servis Compris* means service included, so there really is *absolument* nothing else to pay, not even for wine and coffee. The *Plat d'Entrée* turned out to be rice with ham, fish and mushrooms, and the *Plat de Suite* (literally, 'the next course') was *coq au vin* (chicken in wine sauce), but we had phoned in advance to say we were not able to eat meat or fish. It was a lovely day so we sat outside on the terrace for our aperitif of kir (white wine and blackcurrant liqueur), and *amuse-guele* of nuts and olives. At our table inside, we were given an entrée of a huge plate of *crudités* (salad). The main course was a platter covered with several miniature servings of rice, spaghetti napoletana, braised chestnuts, a little cèpes omelette, and green beans. As we had started with a salad, the salad course was replaced by an (enormous) artichoke. There was lots of wine, a selection of cheeses, plus the basket of fruits, and a dessert of *Tarte Tatin*, a sort of upside-down apple cake, with calvados poured over it. A success!

On the outskirts of a Flemish village we tackled an up-market hotel-restaurant with leanings to the classical gastronomy of the region. This menu is 250F per head, or 200F 'sans la 2e entrée', without the second entrée. In either case, an enormous price for a meal in France.

Menu

Délice de foie frais maison, toasts
Petit pâté chaud de truite à l'oseille
Minute de Saumon à l'ancienne.

Médaillon de Lotte à la Julienne de poireau
Feuilleté de ris de Veau aux champignons

Sorbet Hostellerie

Blanc de volaille à la crème d'estragon
Filet de boeuf Marchand de Vin
Gigot d'agneau à l'ail et sa garniture

Plateau de Fromages

Farandole de Patisseries

Créolandt

On the menu (above) there is nothing at all, before the cheese course, which we could eat. We had contacted the management in advance, but they had given no thought to the matter. Perplexed at our obstinacy in not even wanting to eat fish, the restaurant presented us with a vegetable soup, which was delicious but tasted of fish stock, followed by an *omelette fines herbes* and a huge but insubstantial salad. The between-courses sorbet, delicately laced with armagnac, was appreciated though superfluous considering what we were eating. The cheese selection included some of the magnificently malodorous specialities of the region, and having two desserts was a delightful touch. We made the most of the house wines, but even at a discount which knocked a few francs off the price this dinner was no bargain, and no great shakes for an establishment with a 'gastronomic' reputation.

A hotel-restaurant at Bléré in the Loire Valley region.

Menu 70 fr

Brochette de poissons fumé en salade
ou
Melon entier nature
ou
Salade foies de volaille sautés
au vinaigre de xéres

Filet de rascasse au beurre blanc
et petits légumes
ou
faux filet grillé sauce béarnaise
ou
Civet de cuisse de canette
au vin de chinon

Plateau de fromage

Desserts du jour au choix

This 70F four-course menu suggested poor pickings for a couple of epicurean vegetarians. First course: fish, chicken or melon. Second: fish or meat. The restaurant knew we were coming, but had formed the impression that we would 'probably' eat fish. We said fish was not possible, and suggested an *assiette de légumes*. This did not cause any problems at all. Our first course was a superb salad of crisp, cool, sharp tastes, peeled segments of pink grapefruit; two sorts of lettuce, one pale, the other dark; sweet-corn; and wafer-thin slices of avocado. The plate of vegetables could hardly have been more perfect and delectable. With tiny quantities of each, it included courgette, swede, carrot, spinach, cabbage, broccoli, a scoop of vegetable mousse, a tiny leek, a cherry tomato — rarely seen, and even more rare, several mushrooms of the cultivated variety called *pleurotes*. The dessert of *marquise au chocolat avec sauce café* is a favourite in France, rather too rich and filling for some tastes but not for mine. To cut

At a hotel in Dieppe

DINER

POTAGE CRESSONNIERE
OU
ARTICHAUT VINAIGRETTE
—:—
TRUITE AUX AMANDES
OU
EPAULE D'AGNEAU ROTIE
FLAGEOLETS AU BEURRE
—:—
FROMAGES ASSORTIS
—:—
OEUFS A LA NEIGE
OU FRUITS

the richness, this one came with a melon water ice and a few little crisp fruits — a strawberry, grapes, a small piece of melon and some mint leaves. An excellent meal: ingenious, delicious, and not expensive.

More typical than the others, the dinner menu (above) had two acceptable starters — artichoke vinaigrette or watercress soup — but no suitable main course. I asked for an omelette instead, and had it together with the *flageolets au beurre*, buttered beans. *Oeufs à la Neige* is a rather nice dessert of milky meringues in fresh egg custard.

Self-catering and picnics

Shopping and cooking in France are more fun and more rewarding than just about anywhere else in Europe. Part of the reason is the sheer range, availability and quality of products. Part of it too is the charm of lively, bustling, well-stocked markets, where the stallholders are not fast-talking barrow boys but straightforward peasant farmers who grew much of the food they're selling. In the more rustic districts, or in the bigger markets, be prepared though for some distressing sights in the marketplace, such as rabbits and birds — pressed by the dozen into tiny cages — being sold live. Wandering around an ordinary small-town street market in the Dordogne recently, I noted down exactly what was on sale.

There was a big stall loaded with dried fruit, olives, nuts, honey, herbs and spices; another just with medicinal herbs; and one selling honey and nothing else. Two had large, weird-looking sausages and other charcuterie; and there was a stall selling terrified live rabbits. Another sold pigeons (dead) and potted pâtés. One had cakes and biscuits of a plain dry type that I only ever see in markets; and another, cakes, tarts and huge loaves of *pain de campagne* (country-style bread). Three were selling eggs, cheeses and chickens both live and dead; another concentrated solely on goats' cheeses; while another producer was selling honey and cheeses but nothing else. There were four fresh fish merchants, including one specializing in *coquillages*, those curious creatures from the sea. More than a dozen stalls were loaded high with a wide choice of fresh fruits and vegetables, big and glowing with quality. Two stalls dealt only in strings of garlic and onions. A more commercial outfit was selling cheeses, eggs, butter from huge blocks and other milk products from a van — there's always a dairy van at a market — while not ten yards away from it an old woman stood quietly selling eggs from a basket. The market spilled into an adjacent square where most of the non-food stalls had assembled, with their cut flowers, clothes, cassette-tapes, and a multitude of other goods.

Any town or large village has a similar gathering at least once a week. Some are small and homely, perhaps because there's a very good market at a neighbouring village, and others much larger, extending along several streets and squares. Many towns and cities have a permanent covered marketplace, called *les Halles*, open several days a week. Local produce, which dominates the markets, varies from place to place, so in some districts there are more cheeses, in others more eggs, in Normandy, for example, there is an abundance of *crème fraiche*, thick tangy cream, while other areas have, say, more and better tomatoes but fewer cabbages. Goods from other regions have been brought direct — there's no French equivalent to Covent Garden, which is what ruins the vegetables in Britain — so they too are fresh and attractive. Go along late, when the market stalls are ready to pack up, and you can haggle over prices and get some amazing bargains.

Because of the part played by these farmers' markets in the average family's shopping, greengrocer's shops are a rarity. Instead, all types of food with the exception of bread (and meat) are bought under one roof, either at supermarkets or in smaller general shops called *Alimentation*. There seems to be no limit to just how small, dingy, and ill-equipped a backstreet *alimentation* can be. But most that are in business in a more serious way, and almost all supermarkets, whether in village, town, or city, have a tremendous range of foods, much of it well suited to vegetarian tastes.

They stock a selection of fresh vegetables (not as good as in markets), as well as canned and frozen foods of surprisingly high quality; there's milk and French cheeses, though few foreign, and lots of other milk products, including yogurts of various percentages of fat with or without added fruit juice (but never with colouring — not allowed in France). The best yogurt is made of *lait entier* and is described on the packet as *au gout bulgare*, that is, it's whole milk, with Bulgarian culture. And there's pasta (often wholewheat too), all sorts of dried beans and lentils, oats, flour (but not usually wholewheat), good quality fruit juices, mineral waters, brown sugar, good honey, excellent coffees, including several varieties of decaffeinated (the best, to my taste, is 'Nuit et Jour'), and herb teas, ordinary teas, and dozens of other curious drinks along Ovaltine/drinking chocolate lines. There's generally a health food section with muesli, wheat germ and brown rice, and another shelf with South East Asian specialities.

If self-catering, bear in mind that delicious ready-prepared meals can be found in the supermarket freezer, for example (from a supermarket where I recently noted down the contents of the freezer!), cheese and tomato pizzas, cheese crêpes, *feuilletés au Roquefort* (pastry cases with Roquefort cheese filling), *épinards cuisinés à la crème* (spinach cooked with cream), *pommes dauphinés* (sort of sautéed mashed potato). In cans, there's *purée de marrons* (chestnut purée, used in both sweet and savoury dishes), cooked and seasoned tomatoes, ratatouille (just as tasty and as good as home-made) and gazpacho (the cans of this iced vegetable soup may be in the freezer).

It is better not to buy bread at a supermarket or *alimentation*, although they do sell it. Instead go to a *boulangerie*, where baking is done on the premises by a trained baker. They are very numerous, and there's nearly always one open in every neighbourhood on a Sunday morning when other shops are closed. French bread, white and airy, is delicious when very fresh, although it is hardly nutritious. Because the flour has no additives (unlike that used in Britain), it goes stale quickly — within a matter of hours, and as there are usually two bakings daily, many people buy their bread twice a day. It comes in long loaves of varying thickness (in ascending order of thickness they are called Ficelle, Flute, Baguette, Grand Pain), and you can even ask for half a loaf. The price, fixed by law, is reasonably low. As well as this flimsy white stuff, most bakers also make *pain de son*, which has added bran and is therefore not as white, as well as *pain complet*, supposedly made of whole wheat, and *pain de siègle*, rye bread, both of these last two being sometimes rather heavily cut with white flour. Other loaves include *pain de campagne*, 'country bread', a large round unshaped loaf of rough bread made partly with wholemeal flour. Only the white loaves are cheap; other bread can be quite expensive. Bakers make a few brioches (yeasted cakey buns), pastries and croissants, but a better place for these things is the *pâtisserie*, also open on Sunday mornings, when indeed they do most of their business.

Another unexpected vegetarian resource is the *charcuterie*, a specialist in cooked and processed meat, especially pork and sausages. However, apart from meat, the charcutier sells ready-made salads, typically *macedoine*, cous-cous and potato salads, and dozens of others with sweetcorn, beetroot, eggs, mayonnaise or grated carrot. These salads, of which you can buy as much or as little as you want, make ideal picnic fare.

French **cheeses** deserve a special mention. Soft, hard, creamy, skimmed, mild or so strong that some are forbidden to be carried on public transport, and made from cows', sheep's, and goats' milk, over 400 varieties are produced, by far the best and most extensive range produced by any country in the world. Most are farm-made using traditional methods, and many remain strictly local, rarely seen far from their place of origin. The names of several are legally protected and may be used only when made according to certain traditions and within the limits of a certain district. These cheeses are subject to rigorous inspection and only if they come up to a required standard can they be stamped with the name and date. Unfortunately I do not know of any made with non-animal rennet. The occasionally encountered *from-agerie*, cheese shop, may stock an astonishing variety from all over the country, while any ordinary marketplace reveals several of the region's own varieties, and supermarkets sell the dozen or so of the country's top favourites which an assistant will cut from rounds to give you a slice as big or small as required. Among the most popular and available are:

Brie	rich tangy softish cheese (cows'), almost white, in flat discs with an edible white skin
Camembert	small round cheese (cows') sold in little round wooden boxes, soft, slightly pungent; the best still comes from Normandy, though it's made everywhere nowadays
Cantal	hard and cheddar-like (cows' milk), from the Massif Central; can be mild (*doux*), strong (*fort* or *vieux*), or between the two (*entre-deux*)
Chèvre	general name for all goats' milk cheeses, farm-made, sold in small round pats, and tasting strongly of the way a goat smells!
Comté	delicious, firm, sweetish, this is a farm-made Gruyère (cows' milk) from the Alps
Emmental Français	another type of Gruyère, not so interesting and mainly used for cooking; often sold *rapé*, grated
Livarot and Pont l'Éveque	two of the numerous strong-tasting Normandy cheeses (cows') made into flattish round or square shapes
St-Paulin	very mild, full fat cheese (cows')
Roquefort	the greatest of the blue cheeses, creamy, tangy and soft (ewes' milk), it is all made in the caves at Soulzon-sur-Larzac in the southern Massif Central — and cannot be repro-

duced anywhere else (plenty of ef-
forts have been made); sold in foil-
covered rounds. Blue cheeses start
off white but are given blue streaks
and veins by bacteria living in the
cheese. Also in the shops, cheaper
brands of blue cheese such as *Bleu
d'Auvergne* or *Bleu de Bresse*

Fromage frais and   smooth, moist, refreshing unset
Fromage blanc   white curd cheeses sold in little plas-
tic pots. *Petit-Suisse* is a very rich,
high-fat version, often mixed with
fruit or sugar to be eaten as a dessert.

One of the foreign cheeses sold in France is *Edam*, from Holland.
English Cheddar is sometimes seen, and is known, puzzlingly, as
Chester, while factory-made English-style Cheshire is, by the
same logic, called *Cheddar*.

What to say

Most English-speakers have at least a passing familiarity with the
French accent. The important things to remember are that in the
majority of words the final consonant is not pronounced (for
example Mitterand, Petit, Calais) except when the next word
begins with a vowel; and that the conjunction of letters AN, ON,
and EN creates a nasal vowel sound in which — unless followed
by another vowel — the N is not separately audible (for example
La France, Mitterand).

The essentials

Always address men as Monsieur, women as Madame, and girls
as Mademoiselle. The plurals are Messieurs, Mesdames, Mes-
demoiselles.

Do you speak English?   Parlez-vous anglais?
Good morning/good   Bonjour/bonsoir. Much less formal,
evening   for both, is *Salut* — use it only with

friends. When entering shops, cafés, or small business premises, or to greet strangers in the street, say *'Messieurs-Dames'* (unless there are only men or only women, in which case it will be *'Messieurs'* or *'Mesdames'*)

Goodbye   Au revoir
Please/thank you   S'il vous plait/merci
(very much)   (beaucoup)
Menu   what the English call the menu is here *la carte*, while what the English call a set meal is *un menu*. Most restaurants have two or three *menus* at different inclusive prices, as well as the *carte* on which each dish is priced separately. To order, for example, a set meal at 50F, you would ask for *le menu à cinquante francs, s'il vous plait*. Another name for a set meal, especially when there is no choice, normally only in a hotel, is *Table d'hôte*.

Eat/drink   Manger/boire
I am (we are) vegetarian   Je suis (nous sommes) végétarien(s)
What's this?, What is it?   Qu'est-ce que c'est?
I don't want meat or   Je ne veut pas de la viande ou du
fish   poisson
Can I have . . .   Est-ce que je peut avoir . . .
Is there a vegetarian res-   Est-ce qu'il y a un restaurant végétar-
taurant near here?   ien près d'ici?
No   } meat/fish/   Pas de } viande/poisson/
Without   } cheese/egg   Sans   } fromage/oeuf
No meat stock   Pas de bouillon de viande
Is there meat (or fish) in   Est-ce qu'il y a de viande (ou de
it?   poisson) dedans?

Is it made with meat?	C'est fait avec la viande?
Soup/Sauce made with meat/fish stock	Soupe/Sauce à la base de viande/poisson
Lard	Saindoux, Graisse (not the same thing as *Matière Grasse*, fat which includes milk fat)
Yes/no	Oui/non
(very) good	(très) bon
And/with/or	Et/avec/ou
Cheers!	Santé!
The bill . . . how much?	L'addition . . . combien? (in hotels, the bill is *la note*)
That/this	Cela; ça/ceci
100, 200, 500 grams	cent, deux cents, cinq cents grammes. (Note that half a kilo is often called *un livre*)
Breakfast/lunch/dinner/meal	Petit déjeuner/déjeuner/dîner/repas
(Wholewheat) bread	Pain (complet) — see page 139
(Wheat) flour, wholewheat flour	Farine (de blé), farine complète. *Semoule* is semolina or cous-cous (granules of ground wheat). *Semoule de riz* is the same thing made of rice.
Wheatgerm, bran	Germe de blé, son
Rye, barley, buckwheat	Siègle, orge, sarrasin
(Porridge) oats, millet	(Flocons d') avoine, millet
Potato flour	Fécule (de pommes de terre)
Cornflour, polenta	Maïs
(Brown) rice	Riz (complet, brun). Wild rice is called *riz sauvage*
Organic	Biologique, bio
Peanut butter, jam	Pâte d'arachide, confiture
Honey, sugar	Miel, sucre
Brown sugar	Sucre roux, cassonade
Cheese	Fromage — see page 140. Cheeses are marked with their percentage of *Matière Grasse*, fat

(Skimmed, semi-skimmed, whole) milk	Lait (écrémé, demi-écrémé, entier). *Lait frais pasteurisé* is fresh pasteurized milk. *Lait cru* is fresh unpasteurized milk, often sold in country districts
Cream	Crème. *Crème fraiche* is not fresh cream, but a very smooth, rich, slightly soured thick double cream — and none compares with the *crème fraiche* sold in Normandy
Yogurt	Yaourt, Yogurt. *À boire* means 'for drinking'; *Lait Ribot* is thin, drinkable yogurt; *À la pulpe de fruits* contains real fruit; *Sucré* has sugar added; *Non sucré* is unsweetened; *Au gout bulgare* has live Bulgarian culture and a distinctive flavour; *velouté* means creamed, extra smooth.
(Salted/unsalted/slightly salted) butter	Beurre (salé/douce/demi-sel)
Eggs	des oeufs (pronounced: dez uh. The F is silent in the plural)
Salt, pepper, spices, herbs	Sel, poivre, épices, fines herbes. Rock salt and sea salt (*gros sel*, *sel marin*) are widely available
(Olive/groundnut/grapeseed/sunflower/soya) oil	Huile (d'olive/d'arachides/de pepins de raisins/de tournesol/de soja)
Hot chocolate, coffee, tea	Chocolat chaud, café, thé
Ground coffee, coffee beans	Café moulu, café en graines
Herb tea	Tissane, infusion. *Camomile* and *tilleul*, lime blossom, are the most common
Decaffeinated	Decaféiné. Sometimes decaf. and cof-

	fee substitutes are known, rather disparagingly, as *Faux Café*, false coffee
with milk	au lait. For cold milk ask for *lait frais*. Cream is not available in cafés
(Mineral) water	d'eau (minerale). *Gazeuse* means it's carbonated
-juice	Jus de -. But for freshly squeezed orange or lemon juice, available in many bars, ask for *orange* (or *citron*) *pressé*. Beware — this is often served mixed with water and sugar
Beer	Bière, but for a glass of draught beer ask for *un demi*, and for a bottle, ask for the brand name you want
Cider, spirits	Cidre, alcools
(Red/white/rosé/sweet/ sparkling) wine	Vin (rouge/blanc/rosé/doux/ mousseux). No need to ask for dry wine — it's almost all dry and that is the universal preference. Sweet wines are drunk only with dessert or as an aperitif
Bottle, glass, carafe	Bouteille, verre, carafe (or pichet)
Half-bottle, Half-litre	Demi-bouteille, demi-litre
Quarter-litre	un quart (pronounced: uhn carh)
House wine	Vin de maison, ordinaire. For a litre (or half-litre) carafe of house wine, ask for *un litre* (or *un demi-litre*) *de rouge* or *de blanc*

Popular **aperitifs** (drinks before eating) include *pastis*, for example Pernod or Ricard (anis spirit), *kir* or *blanc-cassis* (white wine and blackcurrant liqueur), Noilly Prat (a vermouth), Dubonnet (fortified wine); popular **digestifs** (drinks after eating) include Calvados (apple brandy), Poire William (pear brandy), Cognac (distilled wine brandy), Grand Marnier (orange liqueur) and other fruit liqueurs.

Baker	Boulangerie — bread baked on premises
Bread shop	Depot de Pain — not baked on premises
Cake shop, and often ice cream	Pâtisserie — made on premises
Chocolates, sweets, ice cream	Chocolatier, Confiseur — all made on the premises
Fine foods, delicatessen	Epicerie fine
Grocer	Alimentation, Epicerie — also sells wines etc.
Health food shop	Magasin de diététique
Self-service	Libre-Service — the name adopted by 'mini-supermarkets'
Supermarket	Supermarché
Hypermarket	Hypermarché — vast out-of-town shopping complexes, often with self-service cafeteria attached

Where to eat

Restaurant, Auberge, Buffet, Hôtellerie, Bistro (small, intimate), *Relais, Rotisserie* (for meat), *Pizzeria* (Italian and French food, not only pizzas), are all names used by restaurants. And restaurants in hotels are always open to the public as well.

Restaurant Self, Self, Cafeteria	self-service cafeterias.
Relais Routier	transport café with one cheap set meal — not usually suitable for vegetarians
Salon de Thé	posh little tea rooms serving pâtisserie
Bar, Café-bar	Bar — with all alcoholic drinks, coffee (incl. decaf.), tea, herb tea, fruit juices, hot chocolate, etc. Children welcome. No licensing hours — can open at any time. Often have

| | croissants in the morning |
| Brasserie | Bar as above, but also with a limited range of hot and cold food |

On the menu

There are so many things to be careful of with French food that it would hardly be possible to list them. Always ask, when in doubt, whether food contains meat. A few confusions to avoid are: *Graisse* means animal fat, especially lard, while *Grasse* is any fat and usually refers to butterfat; *Fromage* can mean pressed meats as well as cheese: *Marmite* is not the famous yeast extract, which is not normally available in France, but a type of casserole dish.

Dishes to look out for

Some of these are rarities, and I have not sampled every one of them, but have checked the recipes and they all look OK. A few — those in bold type — are quite commonplace all over the country.

Aigroissade	vegetables and chick peas with aioli
Aïoli, ailloli	garlic mayonnaise
Allumettes du fromage	a sort of cheese pie
Aubergines à l'egyptienne	baked aubergines stuffed with their own flesh mixed with breadcrumbs, tomatoes and garlic
Avocat Fermont	hot avocado halves filled with poached egg and covered with bearnaise sauce
Bouchées aux truffes	truffles cooked in sweet Madeira wine and baked in pastry cases
Bouilli	'boiled'; usually means boiled beef, but in Brittany, buckwheat porridge
Bortsch	a pink-coloured soup of beetroot and other vegetables, cooked with sour cream (sometimes with meat)
Carottes Vichy	steamed carrots

Cèpes marinés	*cèpes* mushrooms marinated in seasoned olive oil
Choucroute	sauerkraut — not a proper sauerkraut, though, because the French style is pickled but not fermented. Do not order *choucroute garnie*, which has meat chopped into it
Choux au fromage	choux pastry filled with cheese
Cousinat	a soup of apples, chestnuts, and cream
Crêpes	(especially in Brittany and Normandy) thin pancakes with either sweet or savoury fillings ranging from chocolate and cream to cheese, peppers and mushrooms. They can be made with *Froment* (white wheatflour) or *Sarrasin* (buckwheat). The correct drink with *crêpes* in Normandy is the local cider.
Crispés de Montignac	egg croquettes in tomato sauce
Croûte au fromage	(Jura, Alps) a pie made of cheese and pieces of bread
Cruchade	fritter or pancake of maize flour
Crudités	a selection of raw vegetables, cut or grated, often including grated carrot, but rarely lettuce. Sometimes there are only one or two vegetables, sometimes several. If it's lettuce you want, ask for *Salade*.*
Duxelles	mushrooms, shallots and herbs cooked in butter and cream
Elzekaria	soup of cabbage, haricot beans, onions and garlic (check no meat)

*On a British television cookery programme, *crudités* was shown being made and was then glazed with chicken stock, but I have never met with, or heard of, this glazing being used in France.

Far	(Brittany) buckwheat porridge cake
Farcidure	(Périgord and Centre) vegetable dumplings; cabbage leaves stuffed with flour and vegetables
Floutes	small potato dumplings
Fonds d'artichauts	artichoke hearts, prepared in lots of nice ways
Fondue	(Alps) melted cheese (the cheese is melted in a pot, mixed with white wine, and the pot is kept over a low flame at the table) served with small pieces of bread to dip in it. But not *Fondue Bourgignonne* or *Fondue Chinoise*, both meat dishes
Friands de Bergerac	(Périgord) sweetened potato 'cakes'
Friands au fromage	cheese pies available at bakeries
Galettes	more substantial *crêpes*, or other flat cakey bread
Gâteau au chou vert	cabbage pastry
Gouerre	(Lyon) like a potato pâté
Gougeas de Quercy	(in Quercy, i.e. SE of Périgord) pumpkin puddings
Gougère	kind of cheese pastry
Gratin Dauphinoise or Gratin de pommes à la Dauphinoise)	thin slices of potato baked with eggs, milk, maybe cream, garlic, pepper, and topped with cheese
Gratin Languedocien	slices of aubergine and tomato, covered with olive oil, topped with parsley and breadcrumbs, and baked
Jardinière de legumes	mixed selection of vegetables
Macédoine (de legumes)	diced vegetables
Mesclun	salad of wild vegetables and herbs
Millier	porridge of rolled rice and maize
Mique	like dumplings, sweet or savoury

Nominoë	soup of chestnut purée and cream (check no meat)
Oeufs Borgia	poached eggs and baked tomatoes, with bearnaise sauce
Oeufs à la coque	not a cock's egg (!) but eggs 'in the shell', i.e. boiled eggs
Oeufs diable	fried eggs with mustard and vinegar
Oeufs Grand Duc	poached eggs, truffles, asparagus tips and mornay sauce
Oeufs Henri IV	poached eggs with artichokes
Oeufs Mireille	truffles, eggs and cream
Oeufs pochés	poached eggs
Oeufs au plat	fried eggs
Omelette (aux fines herbes)	(herb) omelette
Panade	a soup of bread, milk and eggs
Pâté aux pommes de terre	(Central France, Auvergne) Potato pie available at bakeries
Patranque	breadcrumbs boiled with butter, milk and cheese until quite solid; sometimes then fried in slices
Pfluten	(Alsace) dumplings of wheat and potato flour
Polenta	cooked maize flour, usually eaten re-cooked after it has cooled and become fairly solid
Pommes (de terre)	*pommes* are apples, but the name is equally used instead of *pommes de terre*, potatoes, which are prepared in many ways:
Pommes Aligot	fried mixture of Aligot cheese, garlic and mashed potatoes
Pommes Anna	a baked dish of thin slices of potatoes in layers with butter
Pommes Byron	the potatoes are first baked, then mashed, then fried, then toasted

	with a cheese topping
Pommes Dauphine	fried mixture of mashed potato, egg, herbs and flour (not to be confused with *Gratin Dauphinoise*, see above)
Pommes Duchesse	potato mashed with butter and egg yolk
Pommes Frites	chips
Pommes frites allumettes	fried 'matchsticks' of potato, very thin chips
Pommes Lyonnaise	(in Lyon) potatoes fried with onions
Pommes Mont-Dore	(Massif Central) mashed potatoes baked with cream and cheese
Pommes Mousseline	mashed potato, with or without butter, cream and egg yolks
Pommes en robe des champs	Potatoes baked in their jackets
Pommes Sarladaire	(Périgord) potato and truffle pie
Pommes vapeur	steamed potatoes
Potage	a general word for all thick soups, but *potage* itself, from the word *potager*, vegetable garden, is a thick vegetable soup. Many varieties, but sometimes it's not entirely vegetable or is made with meat stock — it's worth asking.
Purée au marrons	(Périgord) chestnut purée combined with purée of vegetables, especially potatoes
Purée de pommes de terre	mashed potato
Quiche	open tart filled with eggy mixture with vegetable (sometimes meat), But *quiche Lorraine* always includes bacon
Raclette	(Alps) melting cheese eaten by scraping at it with pieces of vegetable, usually baked potato

Rapée a la Morvandelle	(Burgundy) grated potatoes baked with cream, cheese and egg
Ratatouille	(Provence) courgettes, tomatoes, peppers, onions and aubergines, all fried separately in garlicky olive oil then stewed together
Rôties Galloises	Welsh Rarebit
Soupe Bergère	soup of onion, garlic and other vegetables
Soupe à l'oignon	onion soup
Soupe à l'oignon gratinée	'French Onion Soup', i.e. onion soup topped with croutons and grated cheese
Soupe Montagnarde	vegetable soup with grated cheese on top (check no meat)
Soupe au Pistou	soup of vegetables, garlic, herbs, cheese, noodles
Tourteaux	(Périgord) pancakes made with maize flour
Vichyssoise	(originally from Vichy) a thick, creamy leek and potato soup, served hot or cold

Vegetables and beans

Ail — garlic; *artichaut* — artichoke; *asperge* — asparagus; *aubergine* — what Americans call eggplant; *batavia* — variety of lettuce; *betterave* — beet, beetroot; *blette* — Swiss chard. Not much seen in Britain but common in France. It's like something between celery and spinach; *bourrache* — the medicinal herb borage, used as a salad vegetable in France; *brocoli(s)* — broccoli; *capres* — capers; *cardon* — a vegetable apparently not known at all in Britain. It is in fact a type of thistle, but resembles an extra-large celery and is eaten cooked; *carotte* — carrot; *céleri* — celery. *Céleri en branche* or *céleri rave* is the stem, as eaten in UK, while *celeriac* is the root, also eaten in France; *cèpe* — common type of wild mushroom;

champignon — general word for mushrooms; *champignon de Paris* — white 'button' mushrooms; *chanterelle* — a type of mushroom; *chayote* — type of sweet marrow; *chevriers verts* — type of bean; *chicorée* — a strong-tasting leafy vegetable eaten cooked or in salads, called 'Curly Endive' in English (but not the same thing as French *Endive*). The root is mixed with ground coffee beans or even drunk by itself to make a cheaper drink than coffee; *chou (rouge)* — (red) cabbage; *choux de Bruxelles* — brussels sprouts; *chou de Chine* — Chinese leaf; *choufleur* — cauliflower; *chou-frise* — kale; *ciboule* — spring onion; *cocos* — type of dried bean, pink (*rose*) or white (*blanc*); *cœur de palmier* — the hearts of palm-tree shoots. Incredibly, these are not only edible but deliciously tender, much used in salads or by themselves as a cold hors d'œuvres; *concombre* — cucumber; *courgette* — courgette, baby marrow; *craterelle* — type of wild mushroom; *cresson* — water cress; *dents-de-lion* — 'Lion's Teeth', one of the names of dandelion leaves; *échalote* — shallots, small onions with strong taste much used in sauces; *endive* — this is a forced variety of *chicorée* (see above) producing the narrow spear-shaped strong-tasting pale leaves, used as a salad vegetable, and known in Britain as chicory; *épinards* — spinach; *fanes* — any edible tops of root vegetables; *faséole* — type of haricot bean; *faviole* — haricot beans in general; *fèves* — broad beans; *flageolets* — type of haricot beans; *girolle* — same as chanterelle; *gombaut* — okra; *haricot* — general name for beans; *haricot blanc, beurre, de lima, d'Espagne, rouge* — varieties of beans: white, butter, lima, runner, red; *haricots verts* — string beans, also called French beans; *laitue* — lettuce; *lentilles* — lentils; *lingots blancs* — type of bean; *mâche* — a tender leaf vegetable eaten raw, supposedly called 'Lamb's Lettuce' in English; *mange-tout* — green pea which can be eaten complete with its pod; *mogette, mougette* — type of haricot; *morille* — variety of mushroom; *navet* — a sort of turnip resembling a pure white carrot; *oignon* — onion; *olive (noir/vert)* — (black/green) olive; *ortie* — stinging nettle, cooked in soups; *panais* — parsnip; *patate* — not potato, but sweet potato or yam; *petit-pois* — peas; *pignons* — pine nuts; *pissenlit* — 'wet the bed', dandelion; *pois cassés* — split peas; *pois chiches* — chick peas;

pois chinois — soya beans; *poivrons* — peppers; *pommes de terre* — potatoes, often abbreviated to *pommes*, which actually means apples; *radis* — radish; *rognons de coq* — 'cock's kidneys', type of dried bean; *salsifis* — salsify; *soja* — soya; *tomate* — tomato; *truffe* — truffle, that expensive underground fungus which is something of an acquired taste by itself but is supposed to enhance the flavour of other ingredients with which it is mixed.

Herbs and spices

Aneth — dill; *anis* — aniseed; *bardane* — burdock leaves; *basilic* — basil; *baume* — lemon balm; *bourrache* — borage; *camomille* — camomile; *cannelle* — cinnamon; *cardamone* — cardamom; *cari* — curry (powder); *(graines de) carvi* — caraway seeds; *cayenne* — cayenne; *cerfeuil* — chervil; *ciboulette* — chives; *girofle* — clove; *coriandre* — coriander; *cumin* — cumin; *curcuma* — turmeric; *estragon* — tarragon; *fenouil* — fennel; *fenugrec* — fenugreek; *macis* — mace; *marjolaine* — marjoram; *menthe* — mint; *mimosa* — the flowers are edible!; *muscade* — nutmeg; *origan* — oregano; *oseille* — sorrel; *paprika* — paprika; *persil* — parsley, often given away free in markets with purchases of vegetables; *piment* or *poivre* — pepper; *poivre de Jamaique* — allspice; *romarin* — rosemary; *safran* — saffron; *sarriette* — savory, a herb resembling thyme; *sauge* — sage; *thym* — thyme (pronounced like the English word 'tan' without the N); *tilleul* — lime-tree blossom, for tea; *tout-épices* — another word for allspice; *vanille* — vanilla; *verveine* — verbena, for herb tea.

Fruit and nuts

Abricot — apricot; *amande* — almond; *ananas* — pineapple; *arachides* — raw peanuts; *avocat* — avocado; *banane* — banana; *barbadine* — passion fruit; *brugnons* — nectarines; *cacahuètes* — roasted or cooked peanuts; *cajou* — cashew; *cantaloup* — cantaloupe melon; *cassis* — blackcurrant; *cerise* — cherry; *châtaigne* — one of the names for chestnuts; *châtaigne d'eau* — water chestnut;

citron — lemon; *citrouille* — pumpkin; *clémentine* — clementine; *coco* — coconut; *coing* — quince; *datte* — date; *figue* — fig; *fraise* — strawberry; *framboise* — raspberry; *goyave* — guava; *grenade* — pomegranate; *groseille* — redcurrant; *kaki* — persimmon; *limon* — not lemon, but lime; *mangue* — mango; *marron* — chestnut; *melon* — general name for several varieties of melon; *mûre (sauvage)* — blackberries; *myrtilles* — bilberries, or blueberries (very popular wild berry); *nectarine* — nectarine; *noisette* — hazelnut; *noix* — walnuts, or nuts in general; *orange* — orange; *pamplemousse* — grapefruit; *pasteque* — watermelon; *pêche* — peach; *pistache* — pistachio; *poire* — pear; *pommes* — apples; *prune* — is not a prune, but a plum. A prune is called *pruneau*; *raisin* — this is not a raisin, but the all-important grape. For raisins, ask for *raisins secs*; *reine claude* — greengage; *rhubarbe* — rhubarb.

Sauces and garnishes

One of the most confusing things can be the multitude of names for sauces and the different ways of preparing food. Among those which usually have no meat or fish in them are:

Sauce à l'ancienne (with wine, cream, mushrooms and shallots); *à l'andalouse* (with green peppers, aubergines and tomatoes); *à l'anglaise* (plain boiled or steamed); *à l'arlésienne* (a sort of Provençal style with added rice or potatoes); *béarnaise* (rich wine sauce with eggs), *béchamel* (plain white sauce), *boulangère* (baked, or with baked potatoes), *bourgignonne* (red wine sauce — usually for meat but it doesn't have to be), *du Barry* (with cauliflower cheese), *hollandaise* (egg, butter and lemon or vinegar), *jardinière* (with sliced vegetables), *à la Lyonnaise* (sautéed with onions), *mornay* (cheese sauce), *parmentier* (with potatoes), *Périgourdine* (with truffles), *printanière* (with spring vegetables), *Provençal* (with olive oil, garlic, herbs and tomatoes), *rémoulade* (a sharp mayonnaise mixed with pickles and mustard — and sometimes anchovy), *sauce Tartare* (mayonnaise made very sharp with added pickles and herbs), *vinaigrette* (oil and vinegar dressing, sometimes with added herbs, pepper and mustard), *pistou* (olive oil, basil and garlic).

Of course there are scores more. If in doubt, ask.

Some to beware of, the commonest with meat or fish ingredients, are:

à l'Alsacienne; *Bercy*; *bordelaise*; *dieppoise*; *financière*; *flamande*; *forestière*; *marinière*; *niçoise*; *normande*; *Mirabeau*, *Richelieu*, *sauce Suprème*.

Other menu words

à la, à l', au, aux	can mean anything from 'in the style of . . .' to 'served with . . .'
Aigre-doux	bitter-sweet, sweet-and-sour
Ail	garlic; do not confuse with *aile*, the wing of a bird, also seen on menus. But *aillé* means 'with garlic'.
Amuse-guele	rather vulgar but in common use: 'mouth delight', appetizers, titbits
Assiette	plate
Assiette anglaise	don't be tempted — it's a plate of cold meats
Assorti	assorted
Boissons; boisson compris	drinks; a drink included
Bouillon	broth, stock
Carte des vins	wine list
Chariot	trolley (of desserts, cheeses or *hors d'œuvres variés*)
Chaud(e)	warm, hot
au choix	of your choice
en cocotte	casserole
Consommé	clear soup, usually a meat stock
Coquillages	shellfish (see *Poisson*)
Corbeille de fruits	basket of fruit
Couvert	cover charge, or a place laid at the table
Crème	creamy sauce or dessert

Croque-Monsieur	grilled ham and cheese on bread; *Croque-Madame* has something else instead of the ham, usually some other sort of meat, though occasionally an egg
Crustade	pastry with meat, vegetable or fish
en croute	in pastry
Croutons	small pieces of bread or toast (usually to put in soup)
Cru	raw
Cuit	cooked
Entremets	sweet dishes
Etuvé	steamed in a sealed pan
Façon	way, style, manner; *à ma façon* means done 'my way'
Farci	stuffed
(aux) fines herbes	with herbs
Flambé	topped with brandy and set alight
au four	baked
Frais, fraîche	fresh, or cool
Frappé	iced
Frites	fried, chips
Froid(e)	cold
(Plateau de) fromage	cheese (board)
Fruits	fruit; but note *fruits de mer*, seafood
Garni, avec garniture	garnished with vegetables
Gauffre	waffle
en gelée	jellied
Glacé	iced. *Glace* is ice cream
Gratin	browned, usually with cheese
Hors d'œuvres	starters, preliminaries
Hors d'œuvres variés	assortment of tiny pickles and salads, mostly fishy
Lard, lardons	not lard (*saindoux*) but pieces of bacon or ham
Légumes	vegetables

Lentils	lentils — usually served with meat or lard
Mariné, marignade	marinaded
Mijoté	simmered
Mousse	airy, frothy preparation of puréed meat, fish or vegetables
Moutarde	mustard
Nouilles	noodles
Panaché	mixed
Pané	breaded
Pâté	pastry, pâté
Pâtes	pasta
Paysanne	peasant-style (could mean anything)
Petits-Fours	miniature sweets and pastries to eat with coffee at the end of a meal
Plat (du jour)	dish (of the day)
à la poêle	'frying-pan style', i.e.: fried
à point	cooked 'to a turn', neither overdone nor underdone
Poisson	fish; names of fish and seafood items include Aiglefin, Alose, Anchois, Anguilles, Bar, Barbue, Bisque, Blanchaille, Bouillabaisse, Brandade, Brochet, Cabillaud, Carpe, Carrelet, Chaudrée, Colin, Coquille, Crabe, Crevette, Crustace, Darne, Daurade, Ecrevisse, Eglefin, Exocet, Flétan, Friture, Fruits de Mer, Goujon, Hareng, Homard, Huître, Lamproie, Langouste, Langoustine, Limande, Maquereau, Matelote, Marlan, Merluche, Moule, Oursin, Palourde, Perche, Raie, Rascasse, Saumon, Thon, Truite
au poivre	prepared with pepper
Prix fixe	fixed price

Quenelles	small light dumplings made of meat, fish, vegetables or flour
Ragout	meat stew
Ramequin	small savoury pastry
Repas	meal
Rissoles	fritters
Riz pilaf	rice boiled in stock
Rôti	roast
Roulade	anything 'rolled' — could be a meat, vegetable or fish pastry, or a swiss roll
en saison	in season
Salade (verte)	(green) salad. Usually nothing but lettuce, though variations include *salade russe*, diced cooked vegetables with mayonnaise, and *salade de tomatoes*, a plate of sliced tomatoes
Salade de fruits	fruit salad
Salé	salted
Sauté	lightly fried in a little oil or fat
Service (non) compris	service (not) included
Soufflé	very light airy dish made with beaten egg — can be sweet or savoury
Soupe	Soup. Hundreds of varieties. If unsure, question the waiter
Specialité (du chef, de la maison)	speciality (of the chef, of the house)
Sucré	with sugar
sur commande	on request
en sus	charged extra (e.g. wine)
Tarte	large open pastry. *Tarte Maison* is the 'tart of the house'. Not the manager's daughter but, almost invariably, *tarte aux pommes*, a large pastry base covered with thin slices of glazed apple.
en timbale	anything at all cooked in a pastry

	shell; or, a stiff mousse of vegetable or fish purée with or without pastry
Tourin	a vegetable soup: many versions, but most with meat fat
Tout Compris	everything included (i.e.: in the stated price)
Tranche	slice
TTC	means *tout taxes compris*, all taxes included
Varié	mixed, assorted
Velouté	anything thick and smooth, especially a soup of creamed vegetable or meat with added butter and flour
Viande	meat; names of meats and meat dishes include Abattis, Abats, Agneau, Agnelet, Agnelle, Aile, Alicot, Aloyaud, Andouillette, Ballotine, Bécasse, Bifteck, Boeuf, Bouchée à la reine, Boudin, Caille, Canard, Carbonnade, Cassoulet, Cervelas, Cervelle, Chapon, Charbonnade, Charcuterie, Chasse, Chateaubriand, Cheval, Chevreuil, Cochon, Contre-Filet, Coq (au vin), Coquelet, Coté, Cotelette, Cuisse de grenouille, Daube, Dinde, Dindon, Dindonneau, Emincé, Entrecôte, Epaule, Escalope, Escargot, Faisan, Filet, Foie, Foie gras, Friand, Fricandeau, Fricassée, Gibier, Gigot, Grasdouble, Grillade, Grive, Hachis, Jambon, Jarret, Langue, Lapin, Levraut, Lièvre, Marcassin, Médaillon, Merguez, Mouton, Oie, Ortolan, Perdreau, Pigeonneau, Pintade, Poitrine, Porc, Pot-au-Feu, Potée, Pou-

larde, Poule, Poulet, Pré-salé, Rillettes, Ris de veau, Rognon, Rosbif (the French nickname for the English), Salmis, Sanglier, Sarcelle, Saucisse, Saucisson, Selle, Steack, Terrine (that's actually the name of the earthenware dish the meat's cooked in), Tête, Tournedos, Tripes, Volaille . . . the list starts to look almost Biblical at times, an anatomy of all the beasts and birds who climbed aboard Noah's Ark. Only Noah himself seems to have escaped being turned into a French dinner

Vin Compris — table wine included

Vol-au-vent — light pastry case, filled with cooked food, usually meat, but not always

Desserts

Cheaper *menus* give the choice of either cheese or dessert, while pricier *menus* offer both. In theory, the range of desserts could be extensive, but in practice restaurants limit their selection, almost invariably, to the near-universal *Tarte Maison* (see above), *Glace* (ice cream — generally good) or *Flan* (crème caramel, caramel custard). You can sometimes have a fruit instead. A few other favourites you might encounter are:

Bavarois — liquid preparation of eggs, milk and sugar, served cold; *Beignets* — fritters, doughnuts; *Bombe* — moulded ice cream; *Charlotte de Pommes* — apple pudding; *Chausson (aux pommes)* — (apple) dumplings; *Clafoutis* — cherries in cakey pastry; *Compote* — stewed fruit; *Crème Anglaise* — custard; *Crème Brulé* — rich egg custard with crisp caramel topping; *Crème Chantilly* — cream whipped with sugar; *Crêpe Suzette* — crêpe with orange sauce and orange liqueur; *Ile Flottante* — egg white, egg custard and almonds; *Madeleines* — small sweet plain cakes; *Millefeuille* —

layers of thin pastry and crème pâtissière; *Parfait* — ice cream dessert; *Paris-Brest* — creamy choux pastry with almonds; *Poire Belle-Hélène* — a cooked pear with vanilla ice cream, covered with chocolate sauce; *Profiterole* — light pastry balls filled with crème pâtissière and covered with hot chocolate sauce; *Sorbet* — water ice; *Tarte Tatin* — upside-down apple cake.

CORSICA

In 1768 France purchased from Italy for hard cash the beautiful Mediterranean island of Corsica. Under the Italians, and then under the French, the islanders fought for their independence but as yet — though the struggle continues — have not succeeded in getting it. Wild and mountainous, an untamed land, Corsica has little in common with the mainland of France. The local language, nowadays not as widely spoken as French, comes from Genoese, an Italian dialect. In food, too, there is but small resemblance to France. Corsica's 'cuisine' consists of an unrefined peasant style of cookery in which the limited local resources are exploited to the full: fish and pigs, sheep and goats, and — for they cover the island — chestnuts.

The pickings are not particularly good for those in search of a meatless diet. Restaurants, catering mostly for tourists, offer set meals (*menus*) concentrating on meat and fish dishes, though meatless items, especially omelettes, can be found on *la carte*. Thanks to the Italian influence, pizza and pasta are widely available too. For drinking, incidentally, the island's red wine is rich, robust and highly palatable.

Self-catering proves far easier than trying to eat out. Any town has a regular local produce market and at least one moderately well-stocked supermarket, with some interesting Corsican cheeses, rice (not brown), beans, vegetables and coarse white bread.

Corsican specialities include:

Brilloli, Brioli   chestnut porridge

Brocciu, Broccio, Bruccio	a cheese rather like Italian *ricotta*, which can be made of whey, skimmed milk whole milk or a mixture; much used in cooking, especially omelettes
Cacca Velli	lemon cheesecake
Fritelle, castagnaci	fritters or pancakes made of chestnut flour
Embrucciate	*brocciu* cheese tart
Falculella	cheesecake
Fiadone	*brocciu* and orange flan
Panizze, Pulenta, Migliassis	cake or bread made of chestnut flour
Tagliarini	same as Italian tagliatelle, i.e. 'shoelaces' of pasta
Torta Castagnina	a nut and dried-fruit tart made of chestnut flour

INFORMATION

Scores of good books have been written about French food. To learn the regional specialities, menu terms, and about French eating and drinking generally, the best little handbook on this huge subject is by Tessa Youell and George Kimball, *The Pocket Guide to French Food and Wine* (Xanadu). Leading the way to fine French eating without meat is the book by the chef Jean Conil, *Cuisine Végétarienne Française* (Thorsons).

The French vegetarian society, L'Union Nationale des Vegetariens, can be contacted at: Auru, Miers, 46500 Gramat, France (phone: 65.33.64.28).

Every town has a Syndicat d'Initiative (SI or OTSI) — a local information centre and tourist office — with encyclopaedic local knowledge and maps available. SI's have addresses of any vegetarian restaurants in their town. This is the best up-to-date source of vegetarian addresses. (French Government Tourist Offices outside France have no useful information.)

Two French health/vegetarian magazines to consult are *La Vie Claire* (BP 77, 94703 Maisons-Alfort Cedex, France [phone: 1/43.78.11.32]) distributed principally through the nationwide chain of health food shops of the same name (full list of their shops in the magazine), and *Vivre en Harmonie* (5, rue Emile-Level, 75017 Paris, France [phone: 1/46.27.54.54]), sold at a selection of health food shops: both have ads. for vegetarian shops, eating places and accommodation around the country. A new magazine, sold through newsagents, is *Le Naturel* (6, rue Jean-Leclaire, 75017 Paris, France).

The Vegetarian, and other British health/vegetarian magazines often carry advertisements for vegetarian holiday accommodation in France.

Greece

Tables set out under sunshades during the day, or in the pleasant balmy air at night . . . the melodic strumming of bazouki music — either live, or more likely, from a tape recorder . . . and a marvellously informal, casual atmosphere: that's Greece, where the price of a restaurant meal is so low that it could not be done cheaper if you bought and cooked the ingredients yourself.

Greeks love to stroll about, chatting, taking the air and enjoying the climate. Perhaps that's why aperitifs and starters, meals and desserts are served in three different establishments. At the aperitif hour, about 8 p.m., people gather to drink an *ouzo* (aniseed liquor) and pick at the *mezedes*, or *meze* — tiny nibbles, often fishy and meaty, but sometimes olives, nuts, working up to vineleaves stuffed with rice, called *dolmades* (for the *meze* get better the more *ouzo* you order!) — which come with the drinks. *Meze* used to be free, but now most places charge for them. After the aperitif, customers gradually move on to continue their meal at a proper restaurant, although it is perfectly possible to make a complete meal of *mezes*.

The way of life involves, for the men at least, spending a great deal of time in the *kafeneion* (which sells mainly strong black coffee, ouzo and brandy, plus the savoury nibbles to go with them) and the *taverna* (which has a wider choice of both drinks and *mezedes*, as well as proper meals). During the afternoon the women sit talking outside their houses on the doorstep or on chairs. At mealtimes the wives send a child to the bar to tell Dad the food is ready, and he'll absent-mindedly say he's coming but won't budge for another half hour. Sometimes you will see the women dashing about in the street with a baking tray of cooked food; this is because ovens are in short supply, so people use a friend's or the local baker's. Eating out is tremendously popular too. The whole family will go out together, perhaps with another family, and they'll pass the evening hours loudly talking and arguing, drinking, gesticulating, and also doing a little eating. Apart from the basic *taverna*, which is a cross between a pub, a social club and a café, other eating places may be called *estiatoria* (theoretically upmarket from a *taverna*, though sometimes the difference is imperceptible) or, more rarely, *psistaria* (which makes each dish to order).

In *tavernas* and *estiatoria*, the usual procedure, in all but the most developed tourist areas, for anyone uncertain what to eat, is to wander into the steamy kitchen and choose a dinner simply by pointing at what you fancy as it simmers in none-too-hot stainless steel pans. The first curious feature of eating-out in Greece is that food is never served hot, only ever warm. The second is that almost every *taverna* throughout the length of the country, apart from those with no menu at all, has more or less exactly the same printed list. Most of the dishes are always 'off' — indeed they were never 'on' — the few which *are* available having two prices scrawled in alongside the name of the dish. The price to be paid is, of course, the higher of the two, which includes service, etc. Because *taverna* fare depends largely on what's in season, on some islands the selection of vegetables is at its most abundant in early summer — in any case the nicest time of year in Greece.

Almost without exception, the food on offer includes: light dips and starters under the heading *Orektika* (ορεκτικα), these sometimes being exactly the same as *mezedes*; tomatoes or green peppers stuffed with a mixture of rice and minced meat (sometimes rice only); vegetables — haricot beans, French beans or courgettes — cooked in highly seasoned, tomatoey olive oil; sautéed potatoes or chips; and a fish or meat dish (usually mutton or goat). Greek 'specialities', such as *moussaka*, make a frequent appearance, but almost all of these contain minced meat. You'll notice that food in Greece is not the same as food in 'Greek' (actually Cypriot) restaurants around the world. *Houmous*, *tahini*, and pitta bread, for example, are not eaten in Greece.

The one dish which is universally available is *Horiatiki*, or

'Greek Salad': sliced green peppers, cuts of huge succulent tomatoes, chunks of sweet Mediterranean cucumber, and big pieces of tangy feta cheese (made from goats' milk). There are occasional variations according to what is available locally. Greek salad is seasoned with olive oil and ground pepper only; with a few hunks of fresh Greek bread it makes a delicious, satisfying lunch, light and cool.

In their homes, most Greeks eat very little meat. This is simply for money reasons, and although the quantities may be small, it does tend to creep into many dishes. For far from being vegetarian, most people wish to eat as much meat as they can afford. Fish, surprisingly for many visitors, is not common in the Aegean. It is even more expensive than meat, so rarely eaten at home. But although vegetarianism for moral or health reasons is unheard-of, people are well acquainted with the idea of abstinence from meat and fish, which they associate with devout religious observance. In the Orthodox calendar, a large proportion of the year consists of these so-called 'fasting' days. Understandably, restaurants — even the most down-home *taverna* — use more meat than would be normal at peoples' homes. After all, they are not catering for people on a fast, and in a country like Greece the eating of meat is a sort of conspicuous consumption, a status symbol, which shows the world that you have money to spend. For all that, there are usually two or three meatless options in any eating place. Most would be acceptable to vegans too, as animal fats are not used — in Greece everything is cooked in olive oil.

Although nothing is cooked in animal fats, and butter is scarce, dairy produce figures largely in the Greek diet. Delicious wholemilk yogurts are eaten daily, milky puddings are traditional, and prodigious quantities of cheese are consumed. Indeed, incredibly, the Greeks eat more cheese per head of population than almost anyone else in the world! Mostly this is *feta*, a pale, crumbly and unique goat cheese. Little *feta* is exported from Greece and in fact it is imported (from Denmark of all places — an inferior brand for cooking only), because not enough is made for the home market.

Cooked *feta* appears, with or without minced meat, in several popular dishes. There are other cheeses too, the most common being Kasseri and Kefalotiri (or Kefalissio), two strong and tangy pale-coloured cheeses with a hard texture and made from ewes' milk; and Graviera, creamier, yellower, served in slices for eating by itself and made of either cow's or ewe's milk. Each locality has its own cheeses — Crete has many — so unless you know what is currently available, just ask for *tyri* (cheese). Ancient traditional methods are still very widely used (*feta* is mentioned by Homer) but unfortunately, as best I can discover, animal rennet (*pitia*) is generally part of the process in most of them.

Breakfast and snacks

Beware the hotel breakfast of a slice of stale bread, a slice of stale cake and a pot of tepid water with which to make your own tea or coffee from teabags or sachets of Nescafé. It's probably vegetarian, not looking too closely at the cake, but it's a terrible way to start the day. Instead, go out to a café for gorgeous fresh white bread, local honey, eggs fried in olive oil (takes getting used to) or omelettes made in olive oil (awful!) and many delicious varieties of yogurt. The coffee though, if you insist on instant, will be just as bad as in the hotel.

Ewes' and cows' milk and mixtures of the two are made into full-fat yogurts which are all wonderful, with or without honey. Local people like them too, but prefer to cover them with white sugar. A couple of companies make 'strained' yogurt — creamed — which is thick and heavy. This is popular with foreigners. Traditionally, yogurt used to be sold in smaller pots, the cream of the milk forming an almost solid layer of skin on top. This can still be bought in out-of-the-way places. It tastes much lighter and more tangy than the strained varieties. Ask for *yaourti helliniki*, Greek yogurt. A modern development is yogurt made with real fruit juice in it — lovely.

An old-fashioned delight worth looking out for is *rizogallo*, a rich rice pudding served cold with a generous sprinkling of cinnamon. These days it is found only in less developed areas, and is regarded as a peasant dish. Ridiculously sweet and utterly gorgeous gateaux, often decorated with something resembling shaving soap, as well as the more traditional flaky syrupy pastries like baclava, are sold everywhere in shops called *Zakaroplasteion* (ζακαροπλαστειου). Most of the pastries are made of thin flakes of filo pastry or shreds of wheat flour, plus almonds and other nuts, and a liberal dousing of sugar, honey and syrup. *Kataifi* is a nutty version which looks like shredded wheat. *Loukoumades* are thin doughnuts sprinkled with cinnamon. *Galaktobureko* is something quite different, a rich custard pie. *Crema* is a light milk pudding. Greek cakes are more enjoyable, incidentally, with a glass of water than with tea or coffee.

Tea and instant coffee are expensive. Greek (never say Turkish) coffee is a thimbleful of strong, gritty black stuff, served very sweet. For less sugar ask for *metrio*. If you want no sugar at all ask for *sketo* (bitter). Fresh milk hardly exists in Greece. For adding to instant coffee, watered down condensed milk is quite usual.

Other useful snacks include *tyropitta*, layers of flaky pastry and white cheese, literally cheese pie; and *spanakopitta*, spinach pie, both sold for a few drachmas from cafés and street stalls. Street vendors also sell delicious roasted nuts and pulses, while others offer ring-shaped bread rolls.

Lunch and dinner

Vegetarians should avoid the most touristy, package-holiday areas with direct charter flights from Britain. From the visitor's point of view, Greece can be divided into three types of regions: very spoiled; reasonably developed but still typically Greek; and very poor and undeveloped. In the most popular resort areas, such as the east coast of Corfu or the north coast of Crete, food is much meatier and Greek dishes may be pushed off the menu altogether by international favourites like chicken and chips or spaghetti bolognese. The best hope for a vegetarian here is pizza and salad. Likewise in the poorest regions — most of the genuinely 'undiscovered' islands — vegetables are in short supply and, ironically, small amounts of meat are harder to avoid.

In such a place, at a remote village on the island of Evia, I sat in a smoky *taverna* where a local delicacy, stuffed goat intestines, was roasting on a spit at a fireplace in the middle of the room. The customers sat with knives, forks and plates, not eating but staring and waiting for the meal to be cooked to perfection. The only other food on offer that evening was sliced tomatoes, chips and bread — which became my dinner that night, together with a bottle of vile local wine!

The best areas for vegetarians are in the second category, quite developed but not spoiled, except in those of the more developed places which have attracted a young and unconventional type of tourism (for example Ios, Mykonos). *Horiatiki* salad with bread is available nearly everywhere. Vegans can simply ask for the salad *horis tyri*, without cheese. But you may have to resort to it again in the evening, depending on what else is on offer at local *tavernas*.

Typically, a Greek meal is not divided into beginning, middle and end. *Orektika*, normally translated as 'starters', are really just small dishes which may come at the same time as, or even after, the so-called 'main dishes'. Your order could be brought to the table in any sequence or all at once. More than one of the *orektika* will be without meat or fish, and you may order as many of them as you want. One of the most common is *Tsatsiki*, a yogurty dip. Vegetables, fried in olive oil, are listed simply as vegetables, and also as *Lathera*, which are vegetable dishes fried in a savoury oily sauce. Most often, these are aubergines, potatoes, courgettes and beans, though okra, mushrooms and peas make an occasional appearance. If perusing the day's fare in the kitchen, which is quite normal except in the most touristy areas, ask if any of the stuffed vegetables are *horis kreas*, without meat. Places with even a small number of tourists may offer pizza, but these, like all foreign dishes, are not done well. In *tavernas* and *estiatoria*, desserts are not served, though they do have fruit.

After you have eaten at the same *taverna* for a night or two, particularly if a tip was left on the table (remember that waiters whose tip is included in the price earn less from vegetarians because the bill is smaller), they might be willing to make something meatless for you for the following night. A simple request, always willingly granted when I have asked, is to have tomatoes or peppers stuffed with rice instead of mixed rice and meat. Always explain, whether by words, gestures or both, that you are vegetarian. As soon as people know the reason for your request they are more ready to help.

The role of wine in such an oily diet is presumably to act as a kind of vinegar. The most famous Greek wine is retsina, rot-gut with pine resin added. It tastes like turpentine, but has many devotees. Other wines range from cheap earthy reds to delicate whites. Demestica is a passable table wine either red or white. Hymettos is just slightly better. Boutari is a company producing several good wines. Their best is from Naoussa, priced accordingly, while a good cheap one is Rotundi.

Self-catering

Quite apart from the cheapness of eating-out, Greece does have a few disadvantages for the self-caterer. On most of the islands (and much of the mainland too) vegetables have to be shipped in without benefit of refrigeration and can be of rather poor quality. They are in any case only available in season, which though a good thing in one way, at times gives a very restricted selection. Fruit, too, is only abundant in its season. Fresh milk is normally unavailable, though there are cans of evaporated milk in the shops.

Most shopping is done in disorganized 'mini-supermarkets' or ordinary village grocers, where a certain amount of Greek vocabulary will be useful. Tinned products ready to eat include beans, lentils and delicacies like rice-stuffed *dolmades*. Health food shops are rare indeed — I don't remember ever seeing one — as are brown rice, wholemeal pasta or bread, and brown flour. However, several types of beans, lentils, peas, nuts and dried fruits, as well as white rice and pasta, are cheap and easy to find.

The white bread, warm and fresh from a bakery, is delicious. Olive oil is top-quality and extremely inexpensive; eggs are free-range; local honeys are excellent; and the yogurt — whether cow's or sheep's — is properly made of whole milk with live culture, and contains no sugar.

What to say

Accented vowels have a dot on. Note that the Greek D — Δ, δ — sounds more like *th*. The Greek G — Γ, γ — is sometimes more like a *y*, sometimes a gutteral *h*.

The essentials

Hello or goodbye	yàssou, yàssas
Do you speak English?	meelàteh Angleekà
Menu	katàlogo, menou
What will you have?	Ti thà pàrete? (what the waiter says to you)
Please	paragalò
Thank you (very much)	efharistò (poli)
Eat, drink	faghitò, potà
I don't want meat/fish	den thelo krèas/psàri
Without meat/fish/ cheese	horis krèas/psàri/tyri
Yes, no	Ne, òhi
(Very) good	(Poli) galà
And	keh
With	meh
Cheers!	stinyàssas!
The bill . . . how much?	O logariasmòs . . . pòsso kàni?

There is no word for a vegetarian. *Hortophagos* means vegetable-eater, and implies 'crazy', rather like calling someone a nutcase! *Phitophagos* means plant-eater and sounds odd when applied to a human being. *Nistia* means a fast, when a person restricts their diet, either cutting out meat and fish only, or in some cases giving up other foods as well.

That/this	aftò

100, 200, 500 grams	ekató, thiakóssia, pendakóssia grammos
Breakfast, lunch, dinner	to próyevma, to yévma, to déepno
Bread	psomi (Ψωμί)
Wholemeal bread	staréniou psomi (Σταρένιου ψωμί) — a rarity
Honey	méli (Μέλι)
Sugar	zákhari (Ζάχαρη)
Coffee — Greek/instant	kaffáy — ellinkó/nes (Καφέ — ελληνικό/νεσ)
(with) Milk	(me) gála (με γάλα)
Tea	tchai (Τσάι)
Water	neró (Νερό)
Ouzo	strong, sweetish anis liquor, very popular (Ούζο)
Metaxa	by far the most popular brand of Greek brandy (Μετasα)
Wine — red/white	krassi — mávro/áspro (Κρασί—άσπρο)
Wine from the barrel, house wine	krassi hima (Χιμα)
Beer	bira (Μπύρα)
Bottle/glass	boukáli/potíri (Μπουκάλι, ποτήρι)
Yogurt — Ewes'/cows'	yaourti — próveio/ayelathos (Γιαούρτι — Πρόβειο/αγελαδοσ) The animal is usually pictured on the carton.
Cheese	Tyri (Τυρί)
Féta	crumbly white goats' cheese (Φέτα)
Kasséri, kafalotiri	types of hard cheese often seen, very salty (Κασέρι, κεφαλοτύρι)
Egg	avga (Αυγά)
Baker	Fournos (Φουρνos) or Artopoleo (Αρτοπολειο) — sells yogurt and other things besides bread.

Café, bar	Kafeneion (Καφενειο)
Cake shop	Zakaroplasteion (Ζακαροπλαστειου)
	– serves coffee, tea, desserts
Grocer	Pakalis (Μπακαλης)
Taverna	*cheap informal restaurant (Ταβερνα)*
Estiatorion, Psistaria	other names for a restaurant
	(Εστιατοριο/Ψησταρια)

On the menu

Orektika (Ορεκτικα)	hors d'oeuvres
Mezedes (Μεζεδες)	small portions of cooked food, appetizers. Also known as *meze(s)* or *mezedakia*. Much the same thing as *orektika*.
Entrades (Εντραδες)	main course
Lathera (Λαδερα)	vegetables cooked in seasoned oil
Salades (Σαλατες)	salads
Lakhanika (Λαχανικα)	vegetables
Soupess (Σουπες)	soups
Tighanita (Τηγανιτά)	fried
Vrasta, vrastes (βραστά)	boiled
Yigantes (Γίγαντες)	white beans
Fava (Φάβα)	split peas, usually cooked almost to a paste
Fasolia (Φασολια)	haricot beans, usually as a soup
Fasolada (Φασολάδα)	a soup of beans and vegetables
Fasolakia (Φασολακια)	French beans, cooked in tomatoes and oil
Melizanasalata (Μελί τζανοσαλάτα)	a cold dip of garlicky aubergines with tomatoes and onion
Tsatsiki (Τζατζίκι)	a dip of yogurt, garlic, cucumber and lemon juice
Skordalia (Σκορδαλία)	tangy potato and garlic dip
Pantzaria salata (Παν τζάρια σαλάτα)	beetroot salad
Ellies (Ελίες)	olives

Horta *(Χόρτα)*	wild fresh green vegetables boiled and served like a salad
Fasolia mavromatika *(Φασολια μαυρομάτικα)*	black-eyed bean salad
Horiatiki *(Χωριατικη)*	called Greek Salad or Peasants' Salad; cucumber, olives, tomato, green pepper, onion, and *feta* (sometimes other vegetables too)
Revithosupa *(Ρεβυθόσουπα)*	chickpea soup
Faki *(Φακές)*	lentil soup
Hortosoupa *(Χορτόσουπα)*	vegetable soup
Burekakia *(Μπουρεκάκια)*	general name for little savoury pastries
Kolokithopitta *(Κολοκυθόπηττα)*	courgette pie
Spanakopitta *(Σπανακοπηττα)*	spinach pie
Tyropitta *(Τυροπηττα)*	cheese pie
Pizza, Pitsa *(Πίτσα)*	Italian-style pizza
Piperies psites *(Πιπεριές ψητες)*	baked peppers with nothing inside them
Strapatsatha *(Στραπατσαδα)*	scrambled eggs with tomatoes; offered in simple little places only
Arakas latheros *(Αρακας λαδερός)*	peas cooked in olive oil
Arakas me anginares *(Αρακας με αγγινάρες)*	artichokes with peas
Anginares a la polita *(Αγγινάρες α λα πολίτα)*	artichokes cooked in oil with carrots and potatoes
Anginares me koukia *(Αγγινάρες με κουκια)*	artichokes with broad beans
Bamies latheres *(Μπάμιεξ λαδερές)*	stewed okra

Yiachni (Γιαχνί)	potato casserole with tomatoes and/or other vegetables
Briam (Μπριαμ)	a vegetable ragout, a bit like ratatouille with potatoes
Saganaki (Σακανακι)	fried *feta*; now rare and old-fashioned, sometimes appears as a *meze*
Rizospanaki (Ριζοσπανάκι)	mixed rice and spinach
Makaronia me saltsa domata (Μακαρόνια με σάλτσα ντομάτα)	spaghetti or macaroni with tomato sauce

Other vegetables

Kolokithia (Κολοκίθια) — courgettes; *Melidzanes (Μελιτζανες)* — aubergines; *Bamies (Μπάμιες)* — okra; *Domates (Ντομάτες)* — tomatoes; *Patates (Πατάτες)* — potatoes; *Piperia (Πιπεριές)* — green pepper; *Radikia (Ραδίκια)* — dandelion leaves; *Spanaki (Σπανάκι)* — spinach.

But beware of

Avgolemono (Αυγολέμονο)	egg-and-lemon soup — the recipe calls for chicken stock
Makaronia pastitsio (Μακαρόνια παστίτσιο)	macaroni cheese baked in the oven with tomato sauce, but often also contains minced meat
Yemistes (Γεμιτς)	stuffed vegetables — these could be stuffed with mixed rice and meat; the same occasionally goes for *Dolmades (Ντολμαδες)*, stuffed vine leaves.

And avoid altogether

Taramasalata (Ταραμασαλατα), a pretty pink dip made of fish roe, and *Calamares (Καλαμαρεs)*, innocuous-looking pieces of fried squid.

Fruit and desserts

Glika (**Γλυκὰ**)	sweets, dessert
Fruta (**Φροὺτα**)	fruit
Pagota (**Παγωτὰ**)	ice cream

Karpuzi (Καρποὺζι) — water melon; *Stafili (Σταφὺλια)* — grapes; *Koromila (Κορομηλα)* — plums; *Fraoules (Φρὰουλεs)* — strawberries; *Mandarinia (Μανταρἱνια)* — tangerines; *Nectarinia (Νεκταρἱνια)* — nectarines; *Portocallia (Πορτοκαλἱα)* — oranges; *Rothakina (Ροδὰκινα)* — peaches; *Verikoka (βερὑκοκα)* — apricots. There are lots of dried fruits and nuts too, not much seen in restaurants but sold from big sacks in shops. The almonds (*amigthala*) and pistachios (*fystikia*) are especially good, and you will also see pine nuts (*koukounari*), marrow seeds (*pasatembo*) and roasted chickpeas (*stragalia*), among many others.

Overleaf is a very typical taverna menu. What could we eat? Among the *Orektika* are *tsatsiki*, olives, and at the bottom of the list, handwritten, *Halva* (a rather unusual thing to feature as an hors d'oeuvres; this could be saved till the end and eaten as a dessert). The fried vegetables tonight are potatoes, courgettes (squashes) and red peppers (*kok* stands for *kokkino*, red). *Lathera* has been rendered as Cooked in Oil, and the dishes (handwritten) have not been translated at all. There's *Yigantes fournos*, which translates nicely as baked beans; *Fava*, the split-pea dish; *Melidzanes Imam*, or baked aubergines; and *Tyropitta*, cheese pie, which isn't cooked in oil at all! In the last column there is a simple tomato salad as well as *Salata Horiatiki*; servings of two kinds of cheese; and to follow, cherries or (handwritten) apricots. The final item scrawled at the end of the drinks is *Krasi kok hima*, red house wine. Red wine is normally called *mavro*, black, but this proprietor has used the word red, as we would. All in all, plenty there to choose from.

TABEPNA - RESTAURANT

Ο ΒΥΡΙΝΗΣ

B' ΚΑΤΗΓΟΡΙΑΣ   CLASS B'
ΑΡΧΙΜΗΔΟΥΣ 11 - ΠΑΓΚΡΑΤΙ
11 ARCHIMIDOUS STR. - PANGRATI
ΤΗΛΕΦ. 70 12 153

ΤΙΜΟΚΑΤΑΛΟΓΟΣ - PRICE LIST

Ποσοστόν Σερβιτόρου 13%
Waiter's percentage 13%

ΤΟ ΚΑΤΑΣΤΗΜΑ ΠΟΙΚΕΙΤΑΙ ΕΙΣ ΑΓΟΡΑΝΟΜΙΚΟΝ ΕΛΕΓΧΟΝ   THE SHOP IS SUBJECT TO THE MARKET POLICE CONTROL
ΑΓΟΡΑΝΟΜΙΚΟΣ ΥΠΕΥΘΥΝΟΣ : ΗΛΙΑΣ Κ. ΒΥΡΙΝΗΣ   PROPRIETOR : ELIAS K. VYRINIS

	ΑΝΕΤ ΦΟΛ. W-OUT TIP	ΜΕΤΑ ΦΟΛ. WITH TIP
'Αρτος λευκός — White bread		
Κουβέρ — Cover per person		
ΟΡΕΚΤΙΚΑ — APPETIZERS		
Τζατζίκι — Tzatziki		
Ταραμοσαλάτα — Tarama Salad		
'Αντζούγιες — Anchovies		
'Ελιές — Olives		
Ρωσική Σαλάτα — Russian Salad		
Μελιτζανοσαλάτα — Eggplant salad		
Φιλέτο Λακέρδα — Tunny fish fillet		
ΤΗΓΑΝΙΤΑ		
Πατάτες — Potatoes		
Κολοκυθάκια — Squashes		
Πιπεριές — Peppers		
Μελιτζάνες — Eggplant		
ΨΑΡΙΑ — FISH		
Βακαλάος τηγανιτός — Fried salted cod		
Γαλέος — galeo		
Μαρίδες τηγανιτές — small fish		
ΕΝΤΡΑΔΕΣ — RAGOUTS		
Μοσχάρι πατάτες — Beef with potatoes		
» μακαρόνια — » spagetti		
» πιλάφι — » rice		
'Αρνάκι πιλάφι — Lamb and rice		
» μακαρόνια — » spagetti		
» πατάτες — » potatoes		
» γιουβέτσι — » youvetsi		
Κατσίκι λαδορίγανη — Lamb in oil & oregano		
Κατσίκι λαδορίγανη — Kid		
Κοτόπουλο — Chicken		

	ΑΝΕΤ ΦΟΛ. W-OUT TIP	ΜΕΤΑ ΦΟΛ. WITH TIP
ΖΥΜΑΡΙΚΑ — PASTAS		
Μακαρόνια σάλτσα — Spaghetti in sauce		
Πιλάφι σάλτσα — Rice in sauce		
ΨΗΤΑ — ROASTED		
Μοσχάρι ψητό — Beef		
Χοιρινό ψητό — Pork		
Κοτόπουλο ψητό — Chicken		
ΣΠΕΣΙΑΛΙΤΕ — SPECIALITIES		
Μοσχάρι έξοχικό — Beef country style		
Μοσχάρι σπιτικό — Beef home made		
Μοσχάρι στιφάδο — Beef stewed & onions		
Κρασάτο — Beef stewed in wine		
ΛΑΔΕΡΑ — COOKED IN OIL		
ΚΥΜΑΔΕΣ ΚΑΤ. — CHOPPED MEAT FR.		
Κεφτέδες — Meat balls		
Γιουβαρλάκια — Meat & rice balls		
Ντολμάδες — Stuffed cabb. leaves		
ΤΗΣ ΩΡΑΣ — ON THE CHARCOAL		
Μπον φιλέ μοσχαρ. — Bon fillet		
Κόντρα φιλέτο μοσχ. — Beef steak		
Κόντρα φιλ. χοιρινό — Pork chops		
Παϊδάκια αρνίσια — Lamb chops		
Παϊδάκια κατσίκι — Kid chops		

	ΑΝΕΤ ΦΟΛ. W-OUT TIP	ΜΕΤΑ ΦΟΛ. WITH TIP
ΣΑΛΑΤΕΣ — SALADS		
Ντομάτα — Tomato	52	58
'Αγγουρουντομάτα — Cucumber - tomato		
Μαρούλι — Lettuce		
Λάχανο — Cabbage		
Χόρτα ραδίκια — Dandelion		
Χόρτα βουνού — Mountain vegetable		
Κουνουπίδι — Cauliflower		
Κολοκυθάκια βραστά — Squashes boiled		
Παντζάρια — Beets	100	113
ΤΥΡΙΑ — CHEESES		
Φέτα 65 γραμ. — Feta 65 gram.	43	49
Κασέρι 56 γραμ. — Kasseri 55 gram.	44	49
Κεφαλίνο 55 γραμ. — Kefalisso 55 gram.		
ΦΡΟΥΤΑ — FRUITS		
Μήλα — Apples		
Πορτοκάλια — Oranges		
'Αχλάδια — Pears		
Καρπούζι — Water melon		
Κεράσια — Cherries	85	94
Φράουλες — Strawberries		
Πεπόνι — Melon		
ΜΠΥΡΕΣ - ΚΡΑΣΙΑ / BEERS - WINES		
'Αμστελ 500 γραμ. — Amstel 500 grem.	89	98
'Αμστελ 330 γραμ. — Amstel 330 grem.	56	63
Henninger 500 γραμ. — Henninger 500 gram.	56	63
Κάιζερ 330 γραμ. — Kaizer 330 gram.	110	
Ρετσίνα κιλ. δι' οίκίας — Retsina kl. for houses		60
Δεμέστιχα 640 γραμ. — Demestica 640 gram.		
Μπουτάρι 700 γραμ. — Boutari 700 gram.		
Κόκα - Κόλα — Coca Cola		
Λεμονάδα — Lemonade		
Αερινόδα — Soda Souroti		
Σουρωτή		

Information

The International Handbook has very few listings in Greece and there is no society or publication for Greek vegetarians. A useful and interesting book is Jack Santa Maria, *Greek Vegetarian Cookery* (Rider).

Italy

An appealing, showy disorder reigns in every area of Italian life. And whether it's architecture, driving a motor car, having a discussion with friends or waiting at table, everything can be turned into a stylish, dramatic performance. In food too, there is a cheerful flamboyance: excellent ingredients are thrown together with flair, to produce — as if quite by accident — a tasty, filling and nutritious repast served up with simple relaxed elegance. Italian cookery has nothing over-refined about it, and remains true to its origins as robust peasant fare. Even though the meat dish has nominal pride of place as the centre of a restaurant meal, in fact grains and vegetables play at least as important a role as the meat. 'Were I to become a vegetarian, which God forbid,' said the food writer Quentin Crewe, 'Italy would be the country where I would choose to indulge my folly.'

Contrary to what most non-Italians seem to think, pasta would rarely be offered as the main course in a restaurant. Rather, it comes as a first or second course before the main dish. But it is simple to change all this: one of the delights of Italy, from the vegetarian point of view, is that little ritual or formality attaches to eating-out, so no one minds much if you want to play around with the menu. Restaurants are often very willing to make something on request. It is not strictly necessary to explain to the waiter that you are vegetarian, but it may be a useful move helping to ensure his co-operation, firstly, in having pasta (or salad or some other dish) as a main course in place of meat, and secondly, in guarding against meat or fish creeping into the rest of your order. In cheaper, snackier eating places you can order as you like anyway, and there are always plenty of meatless possibilities to choose from. Maybe this is one reason why Italy, alone among south European countries, has quite a large number of vegetarians.

In principle, each of Italy's eighteen different regions has its own style of cooking, though in fact this is no longer quite true. Certainly several areas have made great contributions to the national cuisine, regional names are still used and there are local specialities, but nowadays you will find more or less the same dishes everywhere. Up in the north much more butter is used, and more meat, than in the south. On the coasts more fish is eaten. Yet it is southern cooking, particularly the Napolitan style (the area around Naples) which has had the greatest impact on Italian food as a whole. Pizza, pasta and tomato-based sauces all originated from this region, as did the practice of turning milk into ice cream. Among the important additions from other regions, the wide range of exquisite cheeses — most made from ewes' milk — heads the list. Parmesan (from the area around Parma, where it still tastes better than anywhere else), surely the best known of them all, is served as an accompaniment to almost every meal. Travelling around, there are still regional variations to be found, the most important being in the amount of olive oil used, the type of herbs which preponderate in seasoning, the use of local cheeses and a liking for rice in certain areas. Major cities have every kind of restaurant. In Milan, for example, and perhaps elsewhere too, there is a restaurant based on cheese dishes, and others with regional and foreign cooking.

Trying to understand which establishments serve what kind of food is all part of the fun (or the confusion). *Pizzeria*, *Tavola Calda*, *Bar* (maybe), *Trattoria*, *Ristorante*, *Hotel*, *Albergo*, *Rosticceria* are all possible names for a restaurant. Menus are often not displayed outside, partly because much the same food is served in all of them. Occasionally a place has nothing available that would suit a vegetarian — if, for example, all the pasta sauces are meaty: when in doubt, I tend to ask if I can see the menu before sitting down, and if necessary tell the waiter that I am vegetarian. His eyes may roll, but the chances are that if there is something meatless to eat he will point it out. Similar confusion exists in the naming of bars. At a small town where I stayed for a while, two bars faced each other across the street. One was called a *Bar* and the other a *Pasticceria*. The *pasticceria* served hot and cold drinks, cakes and home-made ice cream. So did the bar. Both were clean, comfortable, and had outdoor tables. But *pasticceria* sounds classier than bar, more up-market. And indeed there was one slight difference between the two: the *pasticceria* sold small packets of tea over the counter, and tea is considered a luxury in Italy, something that only rather refined people drink.

Breakfast and snacks

Breakfast, whether at home or in a bar, consists of a milky but strong coffee with a small brioche (plain sweetish pastry) or a *cornetto* (rather like a French croissant, but sweeter, and with unexpected fillings such as marmalade), depending on what's available (in bars, these pastries are displayed on the counter and you help yourself). Hotels offer a distinctly inferior version, often with unashamedly stale bread and stale cake.

Sitting around in bars, or at their outdoor tables, just relaxing, meeting friends and chatting, takes up much of the day for anyone (especially men) with time to spare. Coffee, alcoholic drinks, cakes, ice cream, 'toasts' and biscuity pastries are consumed all day long. Without any doubt, the best of these, at least if made on the premises as it usually would be (*della casa*), is the ice cream — *gelati*. Made of full cream milk, no emulsifiers, not too much sugar and subtle natural flavours, it's delicious and counts as one of Italy's great culinary achievements. Many Italian vegetarians look upon this home-made gelati as a valuable source of protein — anyway, that's the excuse they give for eating plenty of it!

Coffee, called Caffè, is espresso-style: it comes strong and black and in a small cup. Regular doses of this powerful concoction help to keep you in tune with the Italian temperament! A double-sized portion is called a *Doppio*, and a coffee with a shot of liqueur is a *Corretto*. You can have coffee with milk, called *Caffelatte*, or if you prefer, the milk can be frothed up with steam and poured over the coffee to form a white cap like a Capuchin monk, hence the name *Cappuccino* which means 'hood' in Italian. Everywhere else in the world, *cappuccino* is served with a sprinkle of chocolate powder on top. But it is said that this custom originated in Vienna, not Italy, and certainly in Italy (other than in the most touristy places) *cappuccino* does not often have chocolate on it. But for those who want this little extra, sometimes a chocolate sprinkler stands on the counter for customers to use. White coffees are made with UHT ('long life') rather than fresh milk. Most bars and restaurants (not all) have very good decaffeinated coffee too. This is proper ground coffee, not instant; Hag seems to have a monopoly of this market in Italy, and to order a decaffeinated coffee, ask for Hag (pronounced Ag). Decaffeinated coffee can be used to make a *cappuccino* or any other type. Tea and herb teas are also available, at inflated prices, but hot chocolate, most surprisingly, is a rarity (more common in winter).

As a rule Italians do not eat substantial snacks between meals. These do exist though, the pizza being the classic example. Until only a few years ago, the pizza was generally made, sold and eaten at street stalls — a knife and fork were not provided! Nowadays pizza can be bought in every town at popular pizzerias with tablecloths, waiters, clean cutlery, carafes of house wine and dessert to follow. Indeed, most pizzerias, apart from the fact that they make pizza, are no different from any other cheap restaurant, and offer a wide range of pasta, salads, soups and other dishes. Yet pizza remains, as always, an informal, snacky food, available throughout the day and eaten with little ceremony.

Another type of snackbar/cheap restaurant, the *Tavola Calda* ('hot table'), has been the inspiration for those thousands of Italian-run sandwich bars and cafés in British and American cities. A *Tavola Calda* has counter-service or self-service, stays open all day and has an extensive à la carte selection of hot and cold dishes which can be eaten as a snack or light meal, or can be put together as courses to make a complete meal. Much the same can be done in a *Trattoria*, an informal restaurant with waiter service, plenty of dishes to choose from and no obligation to order a complete meal: a bowl of Minestrone, for example, or a plate of salad, with some bread, makes an excellent light meal or snack.

Lunch and dinner

In a country where people have much joie de vivre, and above all love to relate to one another, food and mealtimes naturally have tremendous importance. Lunchtime stretches vaguely right across the middle of the day from about 12 noon until 3 p.m. Dinner takes up the whole evening from 8 p.m. onwards. Of the two, lunch could be considered the more important to most people, but they don't stint themselves over dinner either. Big plates of food and quantities of cheap, but usually palatable, local plonk are enjoyed with gusto at both meals — Italy has the world's highest per capita consumption of wine.

The Italian menu, rather like, let us say, Italian politics, is a hopelessly disorganized attempt to impose order on chaos. On the face of it, the rules could hardly be simpler: a meal normally consists of four courses: starter; pasta; main course plus vegetables and/or salad; dessert or cheese or fruit. But when it comes down to details, numerous problems of definition set in. First, there is the *Antipasto* (before-the-pasta, the hors d'oeuvre), one of which may actually be called *antipasto*, and there might also be a soup on the list; then the pasta course, but this can be replaced with soup unless you had soup as a starter (so this course may be listed under either *Minestre* or *Pasta* or both); then the main dish (called the *Secondo Piatto*, the second course, even though it is actually the third), which is sometimes divided into two sections, and the side dishes (*Contorni*) which as likely as not will be served quite separately from the dish they were intended to accompany, perhaps even after you've finished eating it; finally there is cheese (*Formaggi*) or dessert (which may simply be called Dessert or *Dolci*, or may be divided into *Dolci*, which strictly speaking are puddings and cakes, and *Gelati*, which means ices). Even if you have successfully grasped these principles, be prepared for some surprises when confronted by a real menu, on which any of the courses might have been given quite different names, with further subdivisions like egg dishes (*Uova*), fish dishes (*Pesce*) and dishes of the day (*Piatti del Giorno*), listed separately. Presumably it's all done to clarify a confusing situation, and no doubt it would if one were Italian. Bear in mind too that in Italy, more than most countries, restaurants are happy to make something for you which is not on the menu at all.

Pasta in the UK and elsewhere tends to be made from dried spaghetti or macaroni boiled in salted water for the allotted number of minutes. In Italy the pasta is normally freshly made, and when you taste it you will understand the whole point of pasta. It's delicious, indeed often good enough to eat on its own without sauce or with just a little olive oil or butter. There are scores of varieties — more shapes and sizes than seem possible: long, short, hollow, flat, round, fat, thin, twirly, folded in half, cut into tiny pieces — and there are all the little (or big) pasta cushions or rings stuffed with cheese, vegetables or meat. Pastas are very often made with egg, or can be bright green if made with spinach, red if made with tomatoes, and just occasionally wholemeal flour is used. But the majority of pastas, despite the multitude of styles, are all made of the same basic ingredients: white durum wheatflour and water. Having so many sorts affects not so much the taste as the texture, and gives some small variety to a dish which is eaten daily.

Each shape of pasta has its name, though needless to say these sometimes vary from one region to another. I have listed the commonest of them on page 199. If faced with an unusual type or an unfamiliar name you might have to resort to consulting the waiter (good luck!). The obvious thing to be most careful about are those stuffed pastas and pasta sauces which contain meat. And unfortunately, anchovies make an all-too-frequent intrusion into otherwise perfectly acceptable food (unfortunate for the anchovies as well). On the other hand, always keep an eye open for pasta stuffed with ricotta cheese or with eggs or spinach and other vegetables.

Polenta, risotto and other rice dishes, and dumplings called

Gnocchi (pronounced Nyoki) made of potato and/or maize flour, are all often seen and can be useful for vegetarians. Interesting salads include those with herbs and chunks of mozzarella cheese. Some of the soups (*Zuppe*) are entirely vegetarian, though it is hard to be sure whether or not meat stock was used. In particular, the ever-popular Minestrone is a generous and filling vegetable and noodle soup served with optional Parmesan cheese on top — but meat stock is often used to make it, unfortunately.

Above all else, the standby which makes it so easy to travel as a vegetarian in Italy is the pizza. Here too, watch out for meat and fish toppings, especially salami and anchovies. Pizzas covered with vegetables without any cheese are not common, but because every pizza is freshly made it is no problem to choose one from the menu and order it 'without ham' or 'without cheese'. I have listed (page 201) which pizzas to avoid and which to enjoy. Everywhere, you can always get *Pizza Margherita*, which just has cheese and tomato, one of the cheapest and most basic sorts, and perfectly tasty.

Self-catering and picnics

Extensive street markets enliven many small towns at least once a week, when the whole population turns out, if not to shop then simply to stand around chatting noisily. In fact it is at these cheap markets, rather than chic stores, that Italians buy their stylish shoes and clothes, while other stalls display fresh fruit and vegetables, nuts, dried fruits, olives and herbs, strings of garlic, eggs, and one-hundred-and-one cheeses.

Shops keep flexible hours, but generally open from between 7 and 9.30 a.m. to around 7 p.m., and close between 12 noon and roughly 3 p.m. When going into a shop it is polite to say, or merely mutter if you prefer, *Buon giorno* or *Buona sera*; and when leaving, a quick *Ciao* or *Arrivederci* is correct. Following such customs helps maintain friendly relations between locals and foreigners. Neighbourhood grocery shops, *Alimentari*, have only a limited stock, mostly of the commonest less expensive vegetables — tomatoes, cucumbers, aubergines, green and red peppers, garlic, onions and seasonal fruits.

Among the other small shops, some specialize in *Formaggi e Salumi*, cheese and charcuterie: in London this would be called an Italian Delicatessen. *Pasticceria* means literally 'pastrycook's'. It makes and sells pastries and cakes, which have a biscuity, bready quality totally unlike either British-style cakes or French patisserie. Most *pasticcerie* also make their own ice cream, and indeed most are also bars, where you can have a coffee or alcoholic drink. *Gelaterie* concentrate more on the ice cream. Fresh pasta can be bought at shops with the sign 'Pasta Fresca'. *Panificio* means a bakery, and here you can buy both bread and cakes made on the premises. Most have *pane integrale*, wholemeal bread, as well as cakey white bread in broad flat loaves of varying size.

Supermarkets, even in quite small towns, stock a considerable array of produce. Not all the familiar wholefood and vegetarian foods will be found, but there's plenty to provide a healthy meatless diet. As well as abundant fresh local fruit and vegetables, especially whatever is in season at the moment, in cans there are chick peas, beans and lentils, with or without tomato sauce, all of which make a quick and convenient basis for many meals. There are lots of canned vegetables, including tomato pastes either plain or already seasoned. There's a big choice of local honeys, nuts, dried fruit and several sorts of olives. Mayonnaise comes in large jars and many varieties — some with chopped herbs or vegetables mixed in. Main cooking oils are sunflower, corn and olive oil, including top quality 'extra virgin'.

It's quite usual for big supermarkets to sell fresh pasta and fresh *gnocchi*, as well as ready-prepared salads, all of which it makes sense to use if you are self-catering. On the shelves with the dried pastas you may find some wholemeal pasta in assorted shapes and sizes, costing rather more than ordinary pasta. Pasta *con cruschello* has added bran. Strangely enough, wholemeal flour seems hard to get, even though several other kinds of flour are readily available, such as the flour of chestnuts, chickpeas and potatoes, as well as maize (for *polenta*) and white wheatflour. There are different qualities of rice on sale, all of them white. *Vialone* is an unbleached, less polished sort, but I have not seen proper brown rice. Packet cereals are not popular (because liquid milk is not much liked), but there are sometimes small (and pricey) packs of good quality muesli.

Although Italians do not consume much milk as a drink, it is certainly not true that they don't like dairy produce. Any supermarket has a remarkable selection of yogurts, most low-fat but some whole-milk. In addition to plain unsweetened sorts and fruit yogurts, there are some with what seem to us quite bizarre flavourings — such as Ovaltine. There are sweetened drinking-yogurts too, and desserts made of soft cheese mixed with fruit and sugar. Salted and unsalted butters are both available, and intended to be used for different purposes. (There are vegetable margarines too; but low-cholesterol foods seem almost unheard-of). The cheese counter always has plenty of cows' and sheeps' milk cheeses, huge pieces of the indispensable Parmesan, maybe some smoked cheeses, some Gorgonzola or other blue cheese, and masses of Ricotta, the soft white (rennet-free) cheese much used in cooking.

The shops have dozens of ground coffees or beans to choose from, including *decaffeinato*, decaffeinated, and they can often grind the coffee beans for you on the spot. A useful feature of Italian supermarkets is that many sell very small quantities of certain goods, for example, tiny 25g packs of tea and minute packets of ground coffee, which are handy for short holiday-length stays in an area.

What to say
GL pronounce as double *l*. GN is like *ny*. C before I or E pronounce as *ch*. CH sounds like *k*

The essentials
Hello   Buongiorno (day), Buona sera
                                         (evening).

Goodbye	Arrivederci. Less formal is *Ciao* (pronounced Chow)
Do you speak English?	Parla Inglese?
Menu	Menu, lista. Prezzo Fisso = fixed price meal.
Have you got . . .	Avete . . .
Can we have . . .	Possiamo avere . . ., more polite is *Potremmo avere* . . .
Please	Per piacere, per favore
Thank you (very much)	(Molte) Grazie (pronounced Gratsiay).
Prego	Meaning roughly: can I help you, at your service, you're welcome (what the waiter will say to you)
Eat drink	Mangiare/bere
I am (we are) vegetarian	Sono vegetariano (Siamo vegetariani)
I don't want meat/fish	Non voglio carne/pesce (pronounced: Non volio carn/pesh).
Vegetarian restaurant	Ristorante vegetariano
No ⎫ meat/fish/ Without ⎭ cheese/egg	Niente ⎫ carne/pesce/ Senza ⎭ formaggio/uovo
No meat stock, no animal fat	Niente brodo di carne, niente grasso animale
No ham, no anchovies	Niente prosciutto, niente acciughe (pronounced proshutto, ashuge)
Is there meat in this?	C'è carne in questo?
Vegetable stock	Brodo vegetale
Yes/no	Si/no
(Very) good	(molto) buono
And/with	E/con
Cheers!	Salute! Cin-Cin! (pronounced Chin-chin)
The bill . . . how much?	Il conto . . . quanto?
That/this	Quello/questo

100, 200, 500 grams	Cento, duecento, cinquecento grammi
Breakfast/lunch/dinner	Colazione/pranzo/cena
Bread, flour	Pane, farina
Rye, barley, wheat, oats	Segale, orzo, grano/frumento, avena
Maize, bran	Mais, crusca/cruschello
Wholemeal (bread/pasta)	(Pane/pasta) integrale
(Brown) rice	Riso (integrale)
Honey, sugar	Miele, zucchero. Unrefined brown sugar is *zucchero integrale*.
Yogurt, milk	Yogurt, latte — and if whole milk, *latte intero*.
Butter, cream, eggs	Burro, panna, uova
Cheese (see 'On The Menu' below)	Formaggi. Mild is *dolce*, strong is *piccante*
Salt, pepper, oil	Sale, pepe, olio
Olives, olive oil	Olive, olio d'oliva
Herbs, garlic	Erbe, aglio
Vegetables	Ortaggi/verdura
Fruit (juice)	(Succo di) Frutta
Coffee, tea, Ovaltine	Caffè, tè, ovomaltina
Decaffeinated	Decaffeinato
with milk	con latte. A white coffee is *Caffelatte*.
Hot/cold	Caldo/freddo
Water	Acqua
Wine (red/white/rosé)	Vino (rosso/bianco/rosato).
Bottle, glass, carafe	una bottiglia, un bicchiere, una caraffa
Half-bottle	una mezza-bottiglia
House wine	Vino della Casa. *Vino locale* is local, ordinary, table wine.
Baker	Panificio
Cheeses and Charcuterie	Formaggi e Salumi

Food shop	Alimentari
Fresh pasta	Pasta Fresca
Greengocer	Fruttivendolo
Supermarket	Supermercato

Where to eat:

Gelateria	'Ice cream maker' — often a café, bar or restaurant. *Gelati della Casa* means ice cream made on the premises.
Latteria	'Dairy shop', but often also sells pastries and snacks
Pasticceria	'Pastry maker', cake shop — often also a bar or café
Bar, Caffe-Bar	Bar, selling all hot and cold drinks, usually one or two pastries, and maybe a few other snacks. No age limits. A *bar* generally has more to eat than a *caffe-bar*. The sign 'Panini o Tosts' means light snacks are available.
Pizzeria	restaurant or café specializing in pizza but usually having other food as well
Trattoria	cheap restaurant or café
Taverna	a cheaper and simpler trattoria
Tavola calda	cheap restaurant or café, mostly with counter service only
Rosticceria	cheap restaurant or café
Osteria	rural bar with one or two snacks
Locanda	an inn with food and lodging; usually quite basic, but not always
Ristorante, Restaurant	restaurant, generally with higher prices and much less local character than other eating places
Albergo, Hotel	hotel, but often with a restaurant open to the public

On the menu

Agro-dolce	sweet and sour sauce containing sugar and vinegar
Antipasti	starters, hors d'oeuvre
Antipasto misto	assorted plate of charcuterie, seafood, cooked or raw vegetables in any combination
Arrosti	roasted
Bollita, Lesso	boiled
Calzone	type of rolled-over pizza
a Carrello	from the trolley
della Casa	'of the house', made on the premises
Casalinga	home-made
Contorni	side dishes
Coperto	cover charge
alla Crema	creamed
Crostacei	shellfish
Crostini di . . .	fried bread with . . .
Crudo	raw
Dessert, dolci	dessert
Farinacei	rice dishes and pasta dishes
Formaggi	cheeses: Italy offers a huge range, mostly made with cows' (*Vaca*) or sheep's (*Pecora*) milk, rarely goats' (*Capra*). Heading south, sheep increase in number and cows decrease, and the milk of water buffalo (*Bufala*) which live in parts of the south contributes its own varieties. Among the best and most widely available cheeses are:
Bel Paese	factory-made, mild and creamy, a twentieth-century invention
Caciotta	small soft cheeses locally made, taste depending on the district. *Cacio Fiore* is *caciotta* made with vegetable rennet

Dolcelatte	factory-made, creamy blue cheese, mild but tangy
Fontina	firm, sweetish cheese from Italian Alps
Gorgonzola	rich, tangy, delicious blue cheese from Lombardy
Grana	general name for the many hard, grainy cheeses, all of which foreigners call Parmesan, though that is simply one type of *Grana*
Mozzarella	firm rubbery texture, mild taste, and much used in cooking, especially as the topping for pizza. Also used in salads. It should be made with buffalo milk, but huge demand has made that impossible; nowadays, cows' milk is more usual, though Mozzarella-style cheese made with cows' milk is properly known as *Fior di Latte*. The original version is now specifically called *Mozzarella di Bufala*.
Parmigiano Reggiano	or Parmesan, as it is known abroad. Sharp, hard, grainy; eaten by itself when young, or grated to use as a condiment when more mature. Delicious when freshly grated — packs of ready-grated Parmesan do not compare.
Pecorino	general name for sheep's milk cheeses.
Ricotta	soft white cheese made of whey or full-cream milk or semi-skimmed. No rennet is used. Much used in cooking, especially in pasta, but also in desserts. *Ricotta moliterno* is drier and

	saltier, and *forte* is dry enough to be grated.
al Forno	baked
Frittata	omelettes — generally not much good, especially if fried in olive oil. *Frittata Genovese* is a spinach omelette. *Frittata alla Trentina* is a filled omelette, and can be a dessert
Fritti	fried
Frutta	fruit
Gelati	ice cream
Giardiniera	mixed chopped vegetables
Granite	water ice
Gnocchi	light, small dumplings made into shapes and served with various interesting sauces and accompaniments (see 'Sauces' below). The gnocchi themselves can be made of the flour of potatoes (*di patate*), maize (*di polenta*) or wheat (*di semolino*), or a mixture. They are vegetarian, but be careful with the sauces.
Insalata	salad. What's in the salad is usually self-explanatory, as in *insalata di carciofi* (artichoke hearts, very popular) or *insalata di mozzarella e basilico* (mozzarella and basil), but more obscure is *insalata di finocchi e cetrioli* (fennel, eggs, onion, tomatoes and cucumber).
Melanzene ripiene	baked stuffed aubergines. Could be stuffed with meat, rice, vegetables or cheese, or any combination. *Melanzane ripiene alla parmigiana* is with mozzarella, parmesan and tomato sauce.

Peperoni ripieni	stuffed peppers, as with stuffed aubergines
Pomodori ripieni	stuffed tomatoes, just like peppers and aubergines above
Minestre, minestra	'mixtures', stews, soups
Minestrone	vegetable and noodle soup or stew, with infinitely varied ingredients. I always suspect that there will be a few little pieces of meat bobbing about in this, because it would be so tempting to just throw anything in it that happened to be handy, but so far there never have been! In any case though, *brodo* (meat stock) probably forms the basis of it much of the time. It would be sensible to make sure by asking the waiter. If the menu specifies *Minestrone alla Genovesa*, there should be no pasta and definitely no meat. But the recipe for *Minestrone alla Milanese* says that this version should contain pork.
Misto	Mixed
Ortaggi	vegetables
alla Parmigiani	vegetables *alla Parmigiani* are usually cooked with, or served with, grated parmesan cheese
Pasta, pasta asciutta	pasta (see 'Types of Pasta' below)
Pasta in brodo	meat broth with pasta in it
Piatti di farsi	dishes made to order
Piatti del Giorno	dishes of the day, 'today's specials'
Piatti pronti	ready to serve
Pesce	fish
Piccante	spicy, sharp
Pizza	flat circle of thin bread dough,

	brushed with olive oil and baked with any one of numerous toppings (see 'Pizza Toppings' below)
Polenta	a fairly solid cakey substance made by boiling maize flour. It may then be fried, baked or eaten as it is, with eggs, vegetables or meat, and with or without a sauce. However, beware — in restaurants, most polenta dishes do contain meat.
Polenta fritta	fried polenta
Primi piatti	entrée, first course — but not the starter
Riso	rice. *Riso in bianco* is plain boiled white rice. *Riso giallo* is saffron rice with butter and parmesan. *Al limone* means with lemon juice.
Risotto	sautéed rice cooked together with finely chopped vegetables or meat or both. *Risotto di Magro* means a meat-less risotto. Note that *Risotto Parmigiana* does not mean 'with parmesan' — this risotto has a lot of meat in it.
Salsa	sauce
Salumerie	pork products, sausages, charcuterie
Secondi piatti	main course
Servizio	service charge
Sformati	a vegetable 'mould' or 'shape' like a sort of heavy soufflé — any vegetable puréed, mixed with flour, eggs, milk and seasoning, and steamed or baked.
di Stagione	in season
al Sugo	in sauce
Uova	eggs; *affogate* or *in camicia* is poached; *in padella*, *fritte*, or *affrittal-*

late is fried, also called *occhio di bue*.

Verdura — vegetables

Vini — wines. *Vini inclusivo* on a set menu means table wine is included in the price. Italy produces scores of excellent wines, most of the best being red — Chianti, Barolo, Barbera, etc. — but there are goodish dry whites too, for example Frascati, and sparkling sweeter wines such as Asti Spumante. This is a huge subject which I cannot begin to tackle here, but for enhancing dining pleasure it repays a little reading. Italy produces and drinks more wine than any other nation. Incidentally, if red wines usually disagree with you, it may be worth trying Chianti, said to have the lowest level of histamines of all red wines.

Zuppa — soup. (But *Zuppa Inglese* is trifle).

Zuppa di Verdura — vegetable soup

Vegetables, nuts and herbs

Arachide — peanut; *aglio* — garlic; *asparagi* — asparagus; *barbabietole* — beetroot; *basilico* — basil; *borragine* — borage (used quite a lot in Italian cooking); *broccoli* — broccoli; *carciofi(ni)* — artichoke (hearts); *capperi* — capers, one of the most popular additions to pizza toppings; *carote* — carrots; *castagne* — chestnuts; *cavolfiore* — cauliflower; *cavoli* — cabbage; *ceci* — chickpeas; *cicoria* — chicory; *cipolle* — onions; *cetriole* — cucumbers; *fagioli(ni)* — (green) beans; *fave* — broad beans; *finocchi* — fennel; *fiori di zucca* — marrow flowers; *funghi* — mushrooms (many varieties); *gallinacci* — chanterelle mushrooms; *lattuga* — lettuce; *lenticchie* — lentils; *mais* — sweetcorn; *mandorle* — almonds; *marone* — chestnuts; *melanzane*

— aubergines; *minta* — mint; *nocciole* — hazelnuts; *noci* — nuts, walnuts; *origano* — oregano, marjoram; *patate* — potatoes; *peperoni* — peppers; *pinoli* — pine nuts; *pistacchi* — pistachios; *piselli* — peas; *pomodori* — tomatoes; *porri* — leeks; *prezzemolo* — parsley (much stronger flavour than British sort); *radici* — radishes; *salvia* — sage; *sedano* — celery; *spinaci* — spinach; *tartufi (bianchi/neri)* — (white/black) truffles; *vaniglia* — vanilla; *zucca* — marrow; *zucchine* — courgettes.

Fruit and desserts (apart from ice cream)

Albicocche — apricots; *ananas* — pineapple; *arance* — oranges; *caramellate* — oranges soaked in syrup and kirsch; *banane* — bananas; *castagnaccio* — fruit cake made of chestnut flour; *ciliege* — cherries; *cioccolata* — chocolate; *composta di frutta, frutta coota* — stewed fruit; *crema* — custard; *crostata* — cake, tart, flan; *dattero* — date; *fichi* — figs; *fragole* — strawberries; *frutti di bosca* — forest fruits = blackberries, bilberries, etc.; *limone* — lemon; *mandarini* — mandarins, tangerines; *mele* — apples; *meringa* — meringue; *mirtilli* — bilberries; *monte bianco* — chestnut purée with cream; *pere* — pears; *pere ripiene* — pears filled with Gorgonzola cheese; *pesche* — peaches; *pompelmo* — grapefruit; *profiteroles* — featherlight balls of pastry filled with cream and covered with chocolate sauce; *prugne* — plums; *sfogliatelle* — pastries filled with ricotta and candied fruit; *spumone* — rich, flavoured ices made of cream; *torta* — cake, flan, tart; *uva* — grapes; *zabaglione* — eggs whipped with Marsala and sugar; *zibibbo* — raisins; *zuppa inglese* — sponge cake soaked in liqueur and covered with cream or custard (like trifle).

Types of pasta

As well as plain flour and water, perhaps with oil and salt, pasta can also be made with egg (*pasta all'uovo*), or it can be made green by adding spinach to the mixture (*pasta verde*). *Pasta di grano saraceno* is buckwheat and *pasta con cruschello di grano* has added bran. Here are the usual names of just a few sorts — there are many more! *Acini di pepe* — tiny 'peppercorn' shapes; *alfabeto* — more tiny shapes, letters of the alphabet; *anolini* — small ravioli; *bigoli* — strings of buckwheat or wholewheat pasta (a Venetian speciality); *bucatini* — little tubes; *cannolicchi* — short tubes; *capellini* and *capelli d'Angelo* — extremely thin strings; *cannelloni* — big cylindrical noodles, sometimes of egg pasta, sometimes plain, which can be either empty or else filled with meat and vegetables; *diamante* — tiny diamond shapes; *farfalline* — small butterfly shapes; *fettuccine* — thin flat 'shoelaces' of egg pasta — can be green (*verde*); *fusili* — long and twirly like corkscrews, and folded in half; *gramigna* — small shaped tubes; *linguine* — very narrow tagliatelle or fettuccine; *maccheroni* — only in Naples is this spelt Macaroni — long or short tubes of plain pasta; *maccheroncetti* and *maccheroncini* — smaller versions of macaroni; *paglia e fieno* — mixed white and green tagliatelle/fettuccine (beware meat sauce with which it is usually served); *panzarotti* — little cushions filled with vegetables, cheese and egg, and nearly always served with a cheese-and-nut sauce; *penne* — short big tubes; *ravioli* — little cushions nowadays nearly always filled with meat. Occasionally (and originally) filled with spinach and ricotta. In fact, *ravioli* filled with meat should properly be called *agnolotti*. *Ravioli* with ricotta cheese is *ripieno di ricotta*, spinach-filled is *ripieno di verde*; *rigatoni* — another name for cannelloni; *spaghetti* — long tangly strings of plain pasta; *spaghettini* — extra thin spaghetti-like strings, thinner than vermicelli; *stelle* — tiny stars; *tagliatelle* — the other name for fettuccine; *tagliolini* — smaller tagliatelle, and made without egg; *tortelli* — ravioli-like cushions filled with almost anything at all — artichokes, apples, mushrooms, potatoes, ricotta . . .; *trenette* — smaller than tagliatelle, but otherwise the same; *tubetti* — like macaroni but narrower; *vermicelli* — smaller and thinner than spaghetti, but similar; *zite* — same as tubetti.

Some other types are always served with meat, or contain meat, including *Agnolotti, Cappelletti, Crespolini, Fagottini, Lasagne* and *Tortellini*.

Sauces for pasta and gnocchi

This list could go on forever, but I have kept it down to the sauces you are most likely to encounter. The ones definitely to avoid, because they are made with fish or meat, are *con acciughe*, *alla amatriciana*, *all'arrabbiata*, *alla bolognese*, *alla carbonara*, *con la lepre*, *alla marinara*, *panna e prosciutto*, *alla partenopea*, *al ragu* (or *ragu alla bolognese*), *al salmone*, *con le sarde*, *alla trasteverina* and *alle vongole*.

Always be careful of pasta sauces, because chefs may take it into their heads to make a little impromptu addition of an anchovy or two, but in principle the following is a guide to those without meat or fish:

Aglio e Olio	olive oil and plenty of garlic (beware anchovies)
all'Agrodolce	bitter-sweet sauce, 'sweet-and-sour'
alla Boscaiola	tomatoes, aubergines and mushrooms
ai Broccoli	with broccoli (beware anchovies)
al Burro	with butter
alla Cavalleggera	eggs, nuts and cream
alla Cipola	onion sauce
alla Crema	with cream
al Doppio Burro	butter, cream and cheese
con Fave Fresche	beans and onions
al Forno	baked (could be a meat dish)
ai Funghi	mushrooms
alla Genovese	see *Pesto*
alla Napoletana	tomato, olive oil and garlic
salsa di Noci	any nut sauce (beware other ingredients)
all'Olio e Aglio	same as Aglio e Olio!
all'Ortolana	peas and artichokes
alla Panna	with cream
alla Parmigiani	with parmesan cheese (and probably other things)

al Pesto (or Pesto alla Genovese)	a spicy sauce of garlic, olive oil and basil
Pizzaiola	tomato sauce with herbs and garlic
alla Pomarola (or Pomarola alla Napoletana)	see *Napoletana*
al Pomodoro	tomatoes
al Sugo	with sauce (unspecified: could be meat)
salsa d'Uovo	eggs (beware other ingredients)
salsa Verde	usually spinach (beware anchovies)

Pizza toppings

As with pasta sauces, nothing is ever really certain with pizza toppings. In particular, the cooks may regard a few anchovies as a sort of free bonus. Extras like olives, capers, peppers, are always offered with pizzas, and equally you can have unwanted ingredients left out.

all'Aglio	garlic
Aglio, olio e pomodoro	garlic, tomatoes, olive oil and herbs
Calzone	rolled-over pizza, usually filled with ham and cheese, but not always
Capricciosa	'mixed', surprise
alla Cipola	onions
ai Funghi	mushrooms
Margherita	the commonest and most reliable of them all: cheese and tomato
alla Marinara	tomatoes, garlic, herbs (not the same as *Pasta alla Marinara*)
Napoletana	cheese, tomatoes and usually anchovies
all'Occhio di bue	fried egg
con Olive	with olives
Prosciutto e Funghi	meat
Quatre Staggione	a different topping in each of the

	four quarters — normally at least one of them will be fishy
Romana	cheese and herbs — or should be!
Rustica	variable, but usually onions, tomatoes, and olives. May include anchovies
alla Salsiccia	meat
Siciliana	olives, capers and cheese (and sometimes anchovies)
al Tonno	fish
Vongole	seafood

Other dishes to look out for (or ask for)

But always check whether they contain any fish or meat, especially ham or anchovies

Bruschetta	bread toasted with garlic and olive oil
Caponatina	aubergines in seasoned tomato sauce
Carciofi sott'olio	artichoke hearts marinaded in seasoned olive oil
Crostini	bread with various toppings, or actual sandwiches, fried in oil
Fagioli al fiasco	beans slowly cooked in a special flask with tomatoes and herbs — a Tuscan dish
Fagioli all'uccelletto	beans cooked in seasoned olive oil and tomato sauce
Fagiolini in padella	sautéed french beans, onions and tomatoes
Fitascetta	baked onions and bread
Fonduta	North Italian version of fondue, using fontina cheese and white truffles
Gnocchi Verde	confusingly known as *ravioli* in

	Tuscany, these are gnocchi made with spinach, eggs and cheese, and served with a cheese sauce. *Gnocchi di ricotta* is the same thing without the spinach
Mozzarella in Carrozza	bread and mozzarella, soaked in whisked egg and milk, and fried (served with it comes a little anchovy butter — remember not to make use of this optional extra). Don't have *Pandorato* though, which seems much the same thing but is made with ham or anchovies.
Panzarotti	deep fried cheese pastries
Peperonata	peppers, onions, tomatoes and garlic simmered in olive oil until cooked — served cold
Polenta e Fontina in torta	self-explanatory name: a baked dish of polenta and fontina cheese in layers
Risotto ai Funghi	mushroom risotto
Risotto di Magro	in principle means any risotto without meat or fish
Suppli	rice balls with *mozzarella* in the middle (sometimes meat)
Taralli	baked pastry with fennel seeds
Uova	eggs — done in lots of different ways, including:
— affogate in gratin	baked with cheese
— alla Castellana	chopped boiled eggs mixed with onions and mushrooms and fried in butter
— alla Campagnola	eggs fried with potatoes and onions
— alla Fiorentina	eggs with spinach, in a cheese sauce
— fredde ripiene	cold hard-boiled eggs stuffed with mayonnaise and capers

— mollette con funghi e formaggi	soft boiled eggs with fried mushrooms and cheese
— piatto con patate	eggs, mozzarella and potatoes baked together with parmesan topping
— alla Piemontese	pie of eggs, cheese, and truffles
— al piatto con pomodoro	fried tomatoes and onions, baked or refried with eggs
— stracciate al formaggio	scrambled eggs with cheese

. . . and many more.

Soups: There should be no meat in these soups, but remember that they are very often made with meat stock — to be certain you should ask

Acqua Cotta	soup of peppers and tomatoes
Iota Friulana	bean and vegetable
Pancotto	bread and tomato
Pasta e Fagioli	a thick bean and pasta stew (n.b. sometimes with pork)
Risi e Bisi	hearty rice and pea stew (chicken stock often used)
Ribollita	a stew of beans, vegetables, bread and cheese
Zuppa di Castagne	chestnut soup
Zuppa di Fontina	cheese soup
Zuppa di Veneta	vegetable soup with wine and noodles

But avoid altogether

Acciughe	anchovies — they get into almost everything
Bagna Cauda	a hot garlic dip — made with anchovies
Brodo, Brodo di Carne	a meat broth or stock. Most soups are made with it, including some

	nice-sounding 'vegetable' soups.
Caponata	vegetable stew — with fish
. . . di Cozze	. . . with mussels; don't confuse this with *della Casa*, 'of the house', home-made
Frutti di Mare	shellfish, seafood. Nothing to do with fruit
Olive ripiene fritte	fried stuffed olives — they are stuffed with minced meat
Pomodori farciti, pomodoro ripieni	stuffed tomatoes — often with tuna fish
Prosciutto (di Parma)	(Parma) ham, added to many dishes
col Tonno, di Tonno, Tonnate	with tuna fish

A real menu

Below is an admirably simple menu with a good chance of a meatless meal, though none of the *Antipasti* are suitable (mussels, ham, seafood). On the *Primi Piatti* list, the Lasagne and the Spaghetti are definitely out, and the Agnolotti (I presume that's what 'Agnelloti' is supposed to mean) must be a meat-filled pasta with some sort of asparagus sauce. However, we could probably choose the Minestrone soup, Penne pasta with mushrooms or the Macheroncetti pasta 'with four cheeses'.

Secondi Piatti are as usual unsuitable: here there are rabbits, turkeys, something 'on a skewer', steak, cuttlefish, another fish, prawns and mixed fried fishes. The *Contorni* are fried potatoes, boiled beans, asparagus and mixed salad, which all sound OK. Then follows a typical selection of cheeses (the Stracchino is a bit puzzling since this is the name for a whole range of rich, creamy but firm cheeses of which Gorgonzola is itself an example), and desserts — melon in port, strawberries, cream caramel, and apricot tart.

I would probably order either the Minestrone or the asparagus or the mixed salad as a starter, have pasta as a main dish, and

COPERTO £.1500
SERVIZIO 10%

Antipasti

ZUPPA DI COZZE	5.000
PROSCIUTTO E MELONE	4.500
ANTIPASTO DI MARE	4500

Primi Piatti

MINESTRONE	5000
PENNE AI FUNGHI	6000
AGNELLOTTI AGLI ASPARAGI	6000
SPAGHETTI ALL'AMATRICIANA	3500
LASAGNE AL FORNO	6500
TAGCHE RONCETTI AI 4 FORMAGGI	3500

Secondi Piatti

FESA DI TACCHINO	6000
CONIGLIO ARROSTO	6000
SPIEDINI	8000
BISTECCHE ALLA FIORENTINE	L/900A
PAILLARD	700
SEPPIE CON PISELLI	700
PARAGHI	6000
GAMBERONI AI A GRIGLIA	9000
FRITTO MISTO DI PESCE	8000

Contorni

PATATE FRITTE	2000
FAGIOLI BOLLITI	2000
ASPARAGI	5000
INSALATA MISTA	2500

Formaggi

GORGONZOLA	2000
BEL PAESE	2000
PARMIGIANO	7000
STRACCHINO	7000

Dessert

TIRLONE AL PORTO	2500
FRAGOLE	2000
CREM CARAMEL	
CROSTATA DI ALBICOCCHE	2000

Vini

£.11000

GALESTRO	5.000	1 LT. VINO DELLA CASA
LIBECCHIO	5.000	1 LT. MINERALE 1.500
TREBBIANO	5.000	
CHIANTI CLASS.	5.500	

finish with apricot tart . . . could be a nice three-course meal.

To drink, there's a good white Chianti (Galestro), another white (Trebbiano), a good red (Chianti Classico), as well as one I don't know (Libecchio), a cheaper house wine by the litre (*vino della casa*) and bottles of mineral water. Note that cover and service charges will add around 3,000 to our bill — that's lira, not pounds!

Information

There are vegetarian restaurants dotted about all over Italy but it is hard to get accurate up-to-date information. The head office of the Associazione Vegetariana Italiana, c/o Dr Ferdinand Delor, Viale Gran Sasso 38, 20131 Milano, may be able to help. Or you could contact Ms Lilia Fabretto at their Rome office — Associazione Vegetariana Italiana, via Pietro Cartoni 12/12, 00152 Roma.

Three interesting cookery books, not so much to take on holiday as to consult before you go and then keep you in an Italian mood when back at home, are: Janet Hunt, *The Best of Vegetarian Cooking: Italian Dishes*; Jo Marcangelo, *Italian Vegetarian Cooking*; and Paola Scaravelli and Jon Cohen's excellent *Cooking From an Italian Garden*. All are published by Thorsons.

Malta

In the deep south of the Mediterranean, 60 miles south of Sicily and 220 miles from the Libyan coast, the tiny island of Malta, together with its yet more minute neighbours Gozo and Comino, might be thought terribly remote and insignificant. In fact though, Malta and the Maltese have played a leading part in the history of the Mediterranean. The capital, Valleta, was once headquarters of the mysterious Knights Templar; and the city's harbour numbers among the best defended (and most beautiful) anywhere in the world. A tremendously cosmopolitan little place, Malta remains much affected by a long and close relationship with Great Britain. Traffic drives on the left (or is supposed to! Actually the Maltese admit to driving 'in the shade', whichever side of the road that may be), the currency is in pounds, and English is almost universally spoken. Lately the island has tried to renew a sense of its Arabic past — the extraordinary language is derived from Phoenician, of all things (that's where Lebanon is now), and the Maltese must surely be the only Christians anywhere whose name for God is 'Allah'.

When it comes to food, three different cultural strands dominate the cuisine: British, Italian and native Maltese. Usually all three languages appear on menus, sometimes French as well. Conveniently for vegetarians, the strongest influence is the Italian. Posh tourist restaurants mainly concentrate on fish for main courses. Locals patronize big, splendidly old-fashioned cheap restaurants with long menus on which there is always something meatless. Popular Italian dishes include _Minestra_ (minestrone), pasta with cream or tomato sauces, _Ravjul_ (cheese-filled ravioli), and cheese-stuffed peppers, aubergines and tomatoes. _Pastizzi_ are little fried pastries filled either with cheese and vegetables or with anchovies — be careful to ask which. Italian ice-creams, cakes and pastries are popular too, as are Italian cheeses. The main local cheese is *Gbejna*, made of ewes' milk.

The Maltese language is awesome. English will cover most eventualities. Where it doesn't, try Italian.

Portugal

Stand at the End of the World, the *fim do mondo*, in Portugal's south-western corner where the last lofty rocks of Europe tower above the crashing Atlantic, and it's easy to understand why the Portuguese became such a great seafaring people. The prosperity which that brought has long-ago disappeared, leaving this as an astonishingly poor and undeveloped nation. Yet the Atlantic still dominates Portugal. Its breezes daily sweep across the country, its tides clean the amazing Algarve beaches, and unfortunately its fish provide most of the country's food. Curiously enough, the national favourite is not fresh fish but dried and salted cod, eaten as often as people can afford it. There are traditional meat dishes too, but restaurants, especially in tourist areas, make a feature of fish and seafood, and everywhere eating-out can be difficult for vegetarians, except where omelettes are offered as an alternative, or in those towns — there are a few — which have a vegetarian restaurant.

Luckily, Portugal has always favoured self-catering holidays. The Portuguese, a rather dignified and refined people compared to their other Iberian neighbours, have been anxious to avoid turning their beautiful coastline into anything resembling the overcrowded squalor of the Spanish *costas*. To prevent this, they have firmly encouraged up-market villa holidays instead of hotel packages. And self-catering in Portugal works reasonably well for vegetarians. Markets, with abundant fruit, vegetables and pulses, are big, lively, and well stocked, while grocery shops and supermarkets provide a very adequate selection of other foods. Self-catering gives a base from which to explore an area to discover if there are any restaurants nearby offering meatless and fishless dishes. There may not be; but at least the *casas de cha*, tea houses — for Portugal is one of the few European countries where tea is popular — provide an opportunity to go out and sample some of the extraordinarily rich cakes and puddings of this sweet-toothed nation.

Breakfast, snacks, and sweets

The morning starts, whether at home, in hotel or bar, with fresh bread and strong milky coffee. As usual, the hotel version compares badly to that in any ordinary bar The coffee is good, and there are several words to describe exactly how you like it — big, small, milky, and so on (see page 218 for vocabulary). Tea tends to be drunk only in the afternoon, together with one of the rich eggy puddings or sugary cakes. Afternoon tea, called *lanche* and rather confusingly pronounced 'lunch', is at its best in a tea house or *pasteleria*, cake shop, which will have a selection of these *bolas* and *pasteis*, cakes and pastries. Some of the puddings have saucy names like Nun's Breasts. Among the more popular are *Sonhos* (dreams) made of sugar, egg, cinnamon, almonds, wine and caramel sauce; *Torta de Viana* is like a swiss roll but with a creamier filling made with eggs. *Farofias* are lemony meringues with rich egg custard, sprinkled with cinnamon; *Queijadas de Sintra* is a sort of cheesecake; one of the most straightforward but delicious, items, is *Arroz Doce*, cold rice pudding dusted with powdered cinnamon; and you'll also find the more familiar *Gelado*, ice cream.

In general, it's probably true to say that apart from such sugary concoctions, snacks are not much liked by the Portuguese, and are looked upon as rather a desperate measure by someone who perhaps had to skip lunch for one reason or another. Yet they do exist. Tea rooms, *pastelerias*, and bars have a few savoury fillers, particularly savoury butters to spread on toasted bread or rolls. A sign in the window declaring *Sandes* means sandwiches are available, which can be toasted (*Tosta*). Almost all of these possibilities include meat or fish, but the alternative everywhere is cheese. One excellent rustic snack is a plate with a slice of heavy corn bread, some cheese and a piece of *membrillo*, a firm jelly made of quince.

In simple restaurants, small meals can be ordered — of just one course, say — and almost anywhere it's possible to have half-portions: this is quite respectable and you don't have to be a child — it just means you've a small appetite or are not terribly hungry.

Lunch and dinner

Portuguese mealtimes, quite unlike those in Spain, fit in with the pattern familiar in Northern Europe. Lunch is from about 12.30 to 2 p.m. and dinner between about 8 and 10 p.m. Note, though, that late-comers are offered a restricted choice. Menus usually are displayed outside restaurants and are in English and/or French as well as Portuguese. Just about any café or bar can provide meals, and some turn into proper restaurants at mealtimes then revert to being bars for the rest of the day.

Cooking is done in olive oil, which is of the highest quality, and unrefined. However, a white pork fat called *banha* finds its way into many dishes, and corn oil and cheaper vegetable oils are replacing olive oil to a small extent. Meat or, even more, fish are the centre of any meal and are almost always served with chips (or fried potatoes) or boiled white rice, or both. Salads are quite usual too, so at the very least it should be possible to get a meal of bread, salad and chips at almost any restaurant. Egg dishes crop up fairly often too, so an omelette can often be taken as a main course instead of meat or fish. Since vegetarians will almost without exception be eating 'à la carte', no one will care if you make an eccentric choice of dishes and eat them in an odd order. The end of the meal is nearly always a *pudim flan*, caramel custard, or fresh fruit, though you may in places be offered a wider selection of desserts including chocolate mousse or one of the elaborate egg puddings (which, incidentally, are known as 'Convent Puddings' because they were all developed, interestingly, at the many convents dotted all over the country.)

A distinctive characteristic of Portuguese wines is that many are drunk very young, when they have a light crisp taste and are slightly sparkling: this is what is meant by *Vinho Verde*, green wine. There are other good wines too, which by contrast can be matured over several years. One of the best is Dão. The country's most famous product must surely be Port, which in Britain has a languid, luxurious quality and is drunk at the end of a meal. It plays a very different role in Portugal itself, where instead of the deep red colour of the port exported to Britain, white port is the norm, a crisp dry drink popular as an aperitif. There are scores of varieties of dry white port, though few, if any, are ever exported. The red ports are also available (at very cheap prices).

Self-catering and picnics

Thanks in part to Portugal's offshore possessions, Madeira and the Azores, produce markets are loaded with an amazing profusion of excellent fruit and vegetables, some of them quite exotic. Among the most useful items sold in markets are bags of ready-mixed salad vegetables and herbs. You'll also find bags of ready-grated cabbage in both markets and shops, intended for soup-making. Several types of dried beans and peas are sold and there are different types of rice to choose from, though brown rice is a rarity. It's worth taking a close look at the rice before you buy it, as I discovered when I made rice and vegetables for a group of friends. There being no brown rice in the shop I had picked up a bag of some white rice . . . which turned out to be pudding rice (for making the popular *Arroz Doce*). Pudding rice boiled in salted water turns into a very interesting substance, but not a very pleasant accompaniment to sautéed vegetables!

Shops stock inexpensive, top-quality olive oil, as well as corn oil and other vegetable oils, salted butter and imported sunflower margarine. Herbs are cleverly used in Portuguese cooking, and these can be found in bunches at markets. Coriander leaves (*coentro*) are surprisingly popular and the parsley is of a much more powerful type than is seen in other countries. Tomato chutneys, purées and sauces are widely available. Among the spices there's *colorau*, a hot peppery condiment sometimes known as African paprika. Cinnamon, of course, essential to so many desserts, is easily found. There are huge jars of mayonnaise; *marmelada*, which is not orange marmalade but quince jam; and honeys. Pasta is commonly sold too, but not wholemeal.

Milk products are not a great feature of Portuguese cooking, though among the excellent range of teas and coffees (hardly ever any decaffeinated) there will be a number of instant milk drinks, plus Ovomaltine (as it is called here), etc. French-made yogurts are now being imported in large quantities and are sold mainly in supermarkets. A local type of plain yogurt is sold with a little spoon attached — handy for on-the-spot picnics. Cheese remains to this day mainly a rustic, local product, not widely available. It is mostly made of sheep's milk, with some goats' cheeses and very few cows' cheeses. Stored in vats of olive oil, and often seasoned with herbs or spices, some of the cheeses have intriguing flavours. As well as traditional Portuguese cheeses, you may see far more often imitations of foreign varieties, such as Edam or Cheddar. Good examples of Portugal's own are the soft white *requeijao* or *queijinho fresco*, smooth and soft curd cheeses, such as Tomar (they are a little like cottage cheese) and Cabreiro, a tangy, firm goat's cheese. Most of the country's best are so old-fashioned that they are made using **plant rennet,** including the three excellent sheep's milk cheeses, Azeitão (from near Setúbal), Serpa (from Alentejo), and Serra (from several villages, this is one of Portugal's most widely sold varieties).

From bakers you can buy nice bread and rolls, usually white though occasionally wholemeal (*integral*), and also *broa*, a heavy yellowy corn bread. *Pastelerias* are the place for those awesome Portuguese cakes, and also for ready-mixed savoury butters. Processed baby foods, if you want them, do exist but tend to be sold only in pharmacies.

In Lisbon, Portugal's ornate, colourful, historic capital, there are far more imported goods and shops catering to foreign tastes, including some health foods.

THE ISLANDS

Five hundred miles west into the Atlantic, **Madeira** emerges spectacularly from the water as a dazzling profusion of plant life. Once densely forested — the name means 'wood' in Portuguese — now it is productively cultivated by small-scale peasant farmers. Much of Portugal's produce comes from here, particularly the bananas and other 'tropical' fruits, though the climate is by no means tropical, merely pleasantly warm all year round. The island is well known too for the rich, sweet wine that bears its name. Madeira cake, by the way, is known here as English cake and probably had nothing to do with Madeira originally. Discovered as recently as the fifteenth century, Madeira was settled by destitute immigrants from many parts of Europe who tamed the land through tremendous endurance and labour, giving it a character rather different from the rest of Portugal. The best seasons for a visit are spring and autumn, with winter a close second, high summer being a humid and misty time of year. Mass tourism has had a dire effect on the island's beauty in places and also on its cuisine: in the higher priced restaurants, 'international' cooking prevails, while often the cheaper places too stick to set meals, mostly of fish, calculated to appeal to both locals and tourists.

More remote, and much less known to outsiders, the **Azores** lie several hundred miles further into the ocean. This scattered collection of still-volcanic islands enjoy a climate which is mild and agreeable all year round. Windmills dot the landscape and almost the whole population is employed in small-scale traditional farming of grapes and other fruits and vegetables, rearing dairy cattle or fishing. Island food broadly resembles that of the distant mainland, with 'international' dishes also pushed on to the restaurant menus by visiting yachtsmen and cruise liners. Fish dishes predominate, salads are available, and there are good cows' milk cheeses.

What to say

In written form Portuguese has some reassuring resemblance to Spanish, but in speech it is a dreadful language, losing all consonants and vowels to create a flow of indistinguishable nasal sounds (nevertheless it is mother tongue for over 150 million people worldwide). A few rules help:

Any vowel followed by M or N is nasal — and the M or N is not pronounced; Ã, with the wavy *tilde* over it, is also nasal; ÃO is pronounced like a nasal *ow*; E varies greatly, but Ê sounds more like *ay*; O can be as in English *on* but more usually is like the *o* in English *vote*, and is sometimes more of an *oo* (Lisboa is pronounced Lijbooa); ÕE and OI sound like a nasal *oy*; UI makes a resonant nasal *ooy*; B sounds a bit like *v*; C before E or I is pronounced *s* — otherwise, C is like a *k*; but Ç is like *s* wherever it appears; CH sounds like *sh*; D is more like *th*; G before E or I sounds like a *j* — otherwise can be either like *g* or like a *guttural ch*; H is silent; J actually sounds like *j* — *not h* or *y*; LH is pronounced like *lli* in 'million'; NH, similarly, sounds like *ny*, as in 'bunyon'; QU makes a *k* sound; R is trilled, as if it were written, say, *rrr*; S can be like *s* or *z* or *sh* or *j*; X is usually pronounced like *sh*; Z can be like *z* or *sh* or like *j*. And once you've mastered all that, remember that there are lots of exceptions!

The essentials

Do you speak English/ French/German?	Fala Inglês/Francês/Alemão?
Good morning	Bom dia
Good afternoon, evening	Boa tarde
Hello/Goodbye	Ola/adeus

Say good morning, etc. when entering shops, bars or other small commercial premises, and goodbye when leaving. This is a little touch of politeness that is conventional in Portugal.

Have you got . . ., Is there . . ., Are there . . .?	Há . . .? A very useful and simple word. But more polite for 'Have you got . . .? is 'Tem . . .?', which is

	also quite easy to manage.
Menu	Ementa, Lista, Carta. A set meal is *una ementa fixa*
Wine List	Carta, Lista (de vinhos)
Please	Por favor
Thank you	Obrigado if you are male, Obrigada if female
Waiter/waitress	Criado/criada
Sorry	Desculpe
Eat/drink	Comer/beber
I am (we are) vegetarian	Eu sou (Nos somos) vegetariano
I cannot eat meat or fish	Eu não posso comer carne ou peixe
I don't want meat or fish	Eu não quero carne ou peixe
A vegetarian restaurant	Um restaurante vegetariano
No } meat/fish/ Without } cheese/egg	Não } carne/peixe/queijo/ovo Sem }
Is there meat in this?	Isto tem carne?
Animal fat, meat stock	Gordura, resto de carne
Sausage, lard	Salsicha, banha
Yes/no	Sim/não
(very) good	(muito) bem
And/with	E/com
Cheers!	Saude! (produced Sehooder)
The bill . . . how much?	A conta . . . quanto?
That/this	Este/esse (masculine words), Esta/essa (feminine)
100, 200, 500 grams	Cem, Duzentos, Quinhentos gramas
Breakfast/lunch/dinner	Pequeño almoço/almoço/jantar
(Wholemeal) bread, flour	Pao, farinha (integral). *Broa* is corn bread.
Oats	Aveia
(Brown) rice	Arroz (integral)
Honey, sugar	Mel, Açúcar
Yogurt, cheese, eggs	Yogurt, queijo, ovas
Garlic, mayonnaise,	Alho, maionese

Oil, salt, pepper	Oleo, sal, pimenta
Olive oil	Azeite
Milk, butter, cream	Leite, manteiga, natas
(Hot) chocolate	Chocolate (quente), cacau
Coffee	Café. Black is *puro*; white, *con leite*. *Uma bica* is a small strong black coffee. *Garato* has more hot milk than coffee. *Carioca* is watered-down coffee. *Galao* is a large strong café con leite. *Pingado* is a galao with extra milk.
Iced coffee	Café gelado
Decaffeinated	sem cafeina (rare)
Tea	Cha. Normally served black, with no sugar. If you want lemon/milk/sugar ask for it *com limão/leite/açúcar*
(Mineral) water	água (mineral)
-juice	sumo de -
Lemon, orange	Limao, laranja
Beer (bottle/half-pint glass/pint)	Cerveja (garrafa/caña/caneca)
Wine (red/white/sweet/dry)	Vinho (tinto/branco/doce/seco). Vinho da Casa means House Wine — very cheap and usually good.
Bottle, glass, carafe	Garrafa, copo, jarro
half-bottle	meia garrafa
Baker	Padaria
Cheese and charcuterie	Charateria
Dairy	Leitaria
Food	Comidas (sign hanging in café windows)
Greengrocer	Hortaliceiro
Grocer	Mercearia
Market	Mercado
Small grocery shop	Lugasi

Supermarket	Supermercado

Where to eat

Pasteleria, Confeitaria, Casa de Cha, Salão de Cha	all are cake shops doubling as bars selling small snacks, sweets, cakes and drinks, alcoholic or otherwise, including tea
Casa de Fado, Adega Tipica	bar-restaurants with ordinary Portuguese food, where *fado*, the national folk music — a wailing heartfelt song and haunting guitars — can be heard. Some *fado* places have become terrible tourist traps though.
Cafe, Cafe-Bar, Tasca, Taverna	are all basic café-bars, usually with food
Cervejaria	another sort of bar, specializing in beer
Churrasqueira, Marisqueria	eating places specializing in chicken and seafood respectively
Pensão	modest inn with food and lodging
Pousadas	pricey Government-run hotels in interesting buildings, and always with a restaurant
Estalagem	a classy inn with quality food and lodging
Restaurante	any eating place
Restaurante Tipico	any eating place serving only traditional Portuguese food

Fruit, vegetables, nuts, herbs, etc.

A tremendous variety of fruit and vegetables grows in Portugal and its islands. Amazingly, *all* of these common marketplace foods are home grown:

Agriões — watercress; *aipo* — celeriac, celery root; *alcachofyas* artichokes; *alface* — lettuce; *alho* — garlic; *alperces* — apricots; *ameixas* — plums; *amendoas* — almonds; *amendoim* — peanuts; *ananas* — pineapple (from the Azores); *anona* — 'custard apples', a fruit with sweet , soft inside (from Madeira); *arroz* — rice; *aspargos* — asparagus; *avelãs* — hazelnuts; *azeitonas* — olives; *bananas* — from Madeira or the Algarve; *basilico* — basil; *batatas* — potatoes; *baunilha* — vanilla; *beringelas* — aubergines; *broculos* — broccoli; *canela* — cinnamon; *castanhas* — chestnuts (used in both savoury and sweet dishes); *cebolas* — onions; *cenouras* — carrots; *cereja* — cherries; *coentro* — coriander; *cogumelos* — mushrooms; *couve* — cabbage (very common in the North); *couve flor* — cauliflower; *ervilhas* — peas; *ervilhas tortas* — 'mange tout' (peas with edible pods); *estragão* — tarragon; *espinafres* — spinach; *favas* — broad beans; *feijão* — beans; *feijão branco* — haricot beans; *feijão manteiga* — butter beans; *feijão verde* — green beans; *figos* — figs (much used in sweets); *funcho* — fennel; *grão* — chickpeas; *hortelã* — mint; *laranja* — oranges; *limão* — lemon; *macã* — apple; *maracujá* — passion fruit; *melão* — melon; *membrillo* — quince; *mexirica* — tangerines; *nabos* — turnip tops, not root; *nêspera* — medlars; *noz* — walnut; *passa* — raisin; *pepino* — cucumber; *pera* — pears; *pera abacare* — avocados (from Madeira); *pessego* — peaches; *pimentos* — peppers; *romas* — pomegranates; *salsa* — parsley; *tomate* — tomato; *tomilho* — thyme; *toranja* — grapefruit; *uvas* — grapes.

On the menu

Acepipes	hors d'oeuvres
Açorda (de Alho)	bread soup: a tasty and filling soup of crumbled bread, garlic, water, olive oil and herbs. But beware of variations, particularly *Açorda de Marisco* or *Açorda Alentajana* which both include fish.
Almondegas	not almonds but meatballs

Arroz Doce	cold rice pudding dusted with cinnamon, an Arab dessert introduced during the Moorish rule
Assado	roasted
Beringelas fritas	aubergine fritters
Broa	heavy corn bread
Caldeirada	the ubiquitous fish stew
Caldo	broth, stew
Caldo Verde	thick cabbage and potato soup, with slices of sausage. Lard may be used in cooking.
Caril	curry; quite common, thanks to the Portuguese colonies in the East
Carne	meat: includes *Anho* and *Borrego*, two names for lamb; *Caça*, game, i.e.: animals killed in the wild; *Cabrito*, kid; *Frango* or *Galinha*, chicken; *Vaca*, beef; *Faisão*, pheasant; *Aves*, fowl; *Porco*, pork; *Vitela*, veal; etc.
Cozido	boiled, stewed; if eggs, hard-boiled
Cru	raw
Doces	dessert, sweets
Uma Dose	a portion
Media Dose	half portion: quite common, not just for children
Empada	pastry, pie
Estrelados	fried eggs
Farinheira	note that this is a sort of sausage, not to be confused with *Farinha* (flour).
Feijão	beans, bean stew — but beware: most bean dishes contain ham, pork or lard
Frio	cold
Frito	fried

Fruta	fruit
Gaspacho	this delicious Spanish iced soup of salad vegetables is spoiled in Portugal by the addition of a few pieces of sausage or ham
Grão	chickpeas, or chickpea soup; *Grão com espinafres* is a side dish of chickpea and spinach stew, *Grão com tomates* is chickpea and tomato stew
Guisado	stewed
Legumes	vegetables
Mariscos	seafood, e.g. *Gambas* (prawns); *camaroes* (shrimps).
Mista	mixed
Molho	sauce
No forno	baked; literally, in the oven
Omeleta	omelette; e.g. *omeleta de cogumelos*, mushroom omelette
Ovos	eggs; *Ovos a Minhota* are eggs baked with tomatoes and onions
Panada	bread soup, anything done with bread
Pato	note that this is duck, not potato
Peixes	fish: including *Anchovas*, anchovies; *Atum*, tuna: *Bacalhau*, cod; *Calamares*, squid; *Sardinhas*, sardines; etc.
Piri-piri	spicy red sauce, mainly intended for grilled chicken or pork
a Portugesa	with onions, tomatoes and garlic cooked together in oil or butter
Prato	dish, course, plate. *Prato do Dia* is the Dish of the Day
Prato Combinado	a set combination of eggs, vegetables, meat or fish. May on

	occasion be without meat or fish
Pudim Flan, Pudim Flã	'crême caramel', caramel custard
Queijo	cheese
Quente	hot
Salada	salad
Salsicha	sausage; including Enchidos, Chouriço, Murcela, Linguica, Alheira, Farinheira — much used
Sandes	sandwiches
Sobremesa	dessert
Sopas	soups
Sopa de tomate a Alentejana	soup with garlic and poached egg
Sopa de Agrioes	a rich watercress soup with added cream and egg
Sopa de Legumes	vegetable soup (may include other things)
365	nickname for Pudim Flan — because it's served every day of the year
Tosta	toasted sandwich; *tosta mista* is with cheese and ham

Information

There have long been a few vegetarians in Portugal, and the concept is understood, at least among the educated. Even the first Portuguese phrase book I bought in 1971 thought it worthwhile to include a translation of 'I am a vegetarian'! There are some vegetarian and macrobiotic restaurants in the main towns, especially Lisbon.

However, the Portuguese Vegetarian Society seems to lead only an occasional, ephemeral existence, and could not be traced at the time of writing this book. Up-to-date details of eating places can best be found at local tourist offices.

Carol Wright's *Self-catering in Portugal* (Croom Helm) is by no means for vegetarians and contains a few slightly misleading remarks but could nevertheless prove useful for shopping. Some of the recipes she gives would be easy to adapt.

Spain

**Pues no podemas haber aquello que queremos
Queremos aquello que podremos**
Spanish proverb

*(Since we cannot get what we like,
Let's like what we can get).*

Spain is Europe's most popular holiday destination. Each year millions of Britons, French, Germans and Scandinavians find their way to its shores. Fortunately though, they *only* go to its shores, and to a mere handful of towns at that. So commercialized have these favourite resort areas become — Benidorm, Torremolinos, Lloret del Mar, etc. — that they are now quite risible. German 'Bierkellers' and British 'Pubs' line the streets, and it's all too obvious that the vast majority of the charter-flight army have not the slightest interest in the country they are invading. If Blackpool could guarantee as much summer sunshine as Benidorm, they would never venture abroad again. The Spanish have no objection to these tourist ghettos — they too go on holiday to Benidorm — regarding them as a way of keeping the foreign visitors under control. Phalanxes of tall concrete hotels keep guard behind the beaches and promenades as if preventing the tourists from wandering into the real Spain. One tip if you do want to venture inland: you'll get the best from people if you dress in proper clothes, not swimsuits or shorts.

An astonishing variety of countryside and peoples separates the Pyreneean north of Spain from the parched, barren landscapes of Andalucia in the south, taking in the misty plains of Zaragoza, the snow-capped crests of the Sierra Nevada and extending from primitively rustic woods and farm country in the hills of Galicia in the north-west down to Europe's only genuine desert, Almeria in the arid south-east. Altogether it makes one single fascinating country, unsophisticated, nostalgic, full of strength and emotion, in which the historic blend of East and West, Islam and Christianity, resulting from four centuries of Arab rule, still moulds the nation's character to a considerable degree, while more lately, release from thirty-six years of Franco's fascism still laces the air with a subdued excitement and sense of discovery.

Yet each province asserts its own identity through language, history and culture, and as always it is claimed that food reflects these regional differences. Eating habits do vary from place to place, and it's true, *paella* and other rice dishes originated in Valenciana, *gazpacho* in Andalucia, *tortilla* in Castile; but these and many other regional dishes are now found over the whole country, albeit changed sometimes to suit local ingredients. However, most regional specialities, it must be said, are of little use unless one eats meat and fish.

Some say that the reason the Spanish are so deeply, violently emotional is that they are suffering from the lack of a proper breakfast. Or it could be a melancholy induced by having to wait so long for their dinner. Spanish mealtimes can certainly catch visitors unawares. Breakfast is a very light affair, while lunch does not follow until anything up to four in the afternoon, and the evening meal could be at 9 or 10 p.m. or even as late as midnight. The South keeps later hours than the North, and it is strange indeed to see people going out at eight-thirty or nine in the evening for a glass of beer, an ice-cream or coffee and cake to keep them going until dinnertime, which lies some hours ahead.

Such a system could not work without an endless supply of between-meal snacks. Every bar serves a big selection of *tapas*. These are savoury snacks, some of them fairly substantial, generally of a fishy nature but not always. A few of the standard tapas are OK for vegetarians. For anyone of hearty appetite who just cannot make it to the next meal surviving on nothing but these titbits and glasses of dry sherry, *raciones* are meal-sized portions of *tapas*. In addition, most bars make a variety of extremely filling sandwiches.

In many ways, the real speciality of Spanish cuisine is these *canapés*, little bits and pieces, snacks and nibbles which go with drinks. When it comes to main dishes the Spanish make remarkably care-free cooks, mixing up incongruous ingredients in idiosynchratic proportions. This does not work to the advantage of vegetarians, to whom obviously ingredients are of paramount importance. Many a would-be bowl of rice and vegetables is spoiled by the inclusion of a few pieces of chicken or fish or both. Paella, best known of the national dishes, consists of saffron rice, seafood, meat and vegetables in such unpredictable combinations that it is said that no two plates of it are ever alike. The name, indeed, refers only to the special pan in which it is cooked. For all that, a few items on the average menu are excellent and contain no meat. Olive oil is the principal cooking medium, omelettes are popular and a number of soups contain no stock.

However, if there are meatless dishes to choose from, that certainly does not imply any tradition of vegetarianism. Rather, it stems from poverty and the abundance of vegetables in season. The Spanish, to generalize, have not the slightest sentimentality or concern about animals. This much is obvious from the enthusiasm for bullfighting. At one time, skilled arena games of combat with animals were very widespread in Europe. While they have all but disappeared everywhere else, in Spain not only bullfighting survives; cockfighting too is popular and is a favourite 'sport' in the Canary Islands.

Breakfast

From about seven in the morning, bars open their doors and people drift in for their morning coffee. Perhaps because of the Latin American connection, or for whatever reason, the coffee in Spain is arguably the best in Europe, strong, dark, full-flavoured, delicious. It's served in a glass. At this time of day, it is a *café con leche*, an espresso topped up with plenty of hot milk, taken with the most minimal breakfast of a single dainty little cake from the display on the counter. Everything in Spain is so amusingly macho — even the women are tough, hard-bitten and self-assured — that not surprisingly many people scorn this small breakfast as a mere trifle not worth bothering with. They would rather have nothing at all, and instead of *café con leche* they prefer to begin the day with a *café solo*, black coffee, with or without a dash of liqueur, or perhaps just a shot of fiery *coñac* on its own, knocked back quickly on the way to work. *Café cortado* is a black coffee with a splash of milk. Needless to say, breakfast is taken in a manly way, at the bar, standing up.

For those feeble creatures who fancy something more leisurely, not to mention more filling, other bars do a complete *desayuno*, breakfast, of toasted bread rolls (*tostada*) spread either with olive oil (*con aciete*) or with mixed butter and jam (*con mantequilla y mermelada*), and served with a *café con leche*. *Descafeinado*, de-caffeinated, is available everywhere but is instant coffee and rather flavourless. A *descafeinado con leche* has hardly enough strength to cover the taste of the milk, always UHT, so better to try a *solo* or *cortado* if you want caffeine-free coffee.

Spanish bars have a tremendous atmosphere. A good many retain the elaborate decor, big mirrors and marble reminiscent of another age, while others, newer and less stylish, have a rough down-to-earth clientele and Spanish music playing. If you want to get served at a crowded bar you must speak up. It is quite the custom for everyone to order at once, shouting out, holding a loud conversation with someone else at the same time, and when paying, to bang down their coins assertively on the counter. Equally, of course, barmen and waiters assert *themselves* by being in no hurry to serve you. Don't worry, they will in due course — but first you must wait the allotted time. Not that they are lounging about, these defiant waiters; far from it. They are rushing for all they're worth to deal with orders they ignored ten minutes ago.

Mainly confined to Andalucia, the 'traditional' breakfast is *chocolate y churros*: a glass of hot chocolate, thick, strong, heavy and not sweet, together with a plate of two or three *churros*, hot oily doughnuts (made of flour, water and salt and fried in olive oil), also not sweet, and made on the premises. There's sugar on the counter which can be sprinkled to taste on *chocolate* or *churros*. The intriguing, wiggly random shape of *churros* is said to have fascinated the infant Picasso and to have been the subject of his first drawings.

A bar that makes *churros* calls itself a *churreria*, and has a unique appeal, the air heavy with the hot oil and dough, added to the patience, pleasure and anticipation of the crowd who have gone in to eat them.

Most visitors to Spain stay in hotels where the room price includes the cost of breakfast. The cheaper class of hotels known misleadingly as *hostals* do not include breakfast in the price. Hotels typically give their guests a breakfast of real coffee, a bread roll of indeterminate freshness with butter and jam, and a sticky pastry full of E-numbers. If at all possible, escape from the hotel to have breakfast in a local bar.

Tapas, raciones and snacks

As soon as *desayuno* is over, bars put out their selection of savoury *tapas*, either displayed on the counter or listed on a board. These little fillers supposedly provide the ideal accompaniment to alcoholic drink and help bridge the immense gulf between meals. For many people, wandering from bar to bar eating snacks makes the perfect alternative to a proper sit-down meal, especially in the evening. In fact, some *tapas* could pass for a light meal in themselves, and it is not obligatory to order a drink with them.

The most popular drink, if you do want one, is sherry. Don't just ask for sherry though (*Jerez*, in Spanish), for this would be as meaningless as asking for 'a beer' in an English pub. Instead make it clear whether you want a *Fino* (very dry, clean taste), *Amontillado* (dry, rich flavour), *Oloroso* (sweet and dry elements together), *Pedro Ximenez* (sweet, Muscatel flavour) or better still ask for a particular brand by name — Tio Pepe, for example, which is one of the best finos. The word 'sherry' comes from the name of the town now called Jerez-de-la-Frontera, capital of sherry, which the Moors pronounced Sherish. 'Sack', the old-fashioned English name for sherry, comes from *sacar*, export, written on the barrels shipped to the British Isles. The British are still the main importers of sherry, but special sickly-sweet varieties have to be made for the UK market — 'cream' sherries cannot easily be found in any Spanish bar or shop. Manzanilla is an interesting sherry-like wine, and of course there are numerous other drinks sold in the bars, including beer, local brandies, coffee, lemonade or bottled water. When taking an order for mineral water, *agua mineral*, the waiter will immediately ask '*Con gaz o sin gaz?*', fizzy or still. Either is better than tap water. Sangria, much beloved by holidaymakers, is a punch of red wine and some stronger liquor with a few slices of fruit and is really only a fiesta or party drink not normally drunk at other times, though bars and restaurants in resort areas get through gallons of it.

Despite extensive lists of *tapas*, most are fishy and of no use to vegetarians. Straightforward olives and nuts number among the simplest, but are no longer much seen. A couple of others are *queso*, a selection of cheeses, and wedges of *tortilla* (or *tortilla español*), the layered, oily and tasty potato omelette which contains more fried potato than egg. In effect, bars double-up as restaurants, and most will, on request, put together a salad to go with a hefty tortilla slice. A plain omelette is called *tortilla francesa*. Down south in Andalucia, *tortilla* does not feature among the bar snacks, but its place is taken by *gazpacho*, a refreshing and delicious iced soup made of garlic, tomatoes and cucumber.

As well as *tapas*, there are *raciones* — much the same thing, though in bigger portions. As genuine *tapas*, which properly ought to be *very* small, become rarer, the difference between *tapas* and *raciones* is less obvious. *Bocadillos* are rolls filled with fish, meat, *tortilla* or cheese. If made with sliced bread instead of a roll, it's called a *sandwich*.

Sometimes sweet snacks, desserts and pastries can also be found in a bar, but there are other places specializing in cakes (a *pasteleria* or *confiteria*) or ice cream (a *heladeria*). The cooling, lovely drink called *horchata* is a great summertime tradition. A milky suspension of *chufa* ('a sedge with edible tubers' says Chambers dictionary; 'earth almonds' according to the OED), rich in protein and quite filling, *horchata* is sold in big glasses in ice-cream bars or at streetstalls wherever you see a sign saying 'Hay Horchata', including, of course, places calling themselves *Horchaterias*. Other cold drinks equally popular, and found in the same sort of places, come under the general heading of *granizada* — drinks (for example lemon juice) mixed with lots of crushed ice.

Tapas, raciones and other quick snacks most often available are: *Almejas, Anchoas, Angulas, Arenques, Boquerones, Calamares, Chanquetas, Chipirones, Gambas, Pulpo* and *Sepia* are all fish or seafoods. *Caracoles* are snails. *Croquetas*, croquettes, can be made of anything mixed with mashed potato or breadcrumbs or crushed biscuits and fried in olive oil — generally meat or fish.

Butifarra, Chorizo, Cocida, Empanadilla (fish or meat pie), *Fabada, Jamón, Lomo, Olla, Pinchos, Salchichón* and *York* (ham) are in the main all meat preparations. Perhaps worth considering is *Pan con tomate y jamón* — bread with tomato paste and olive oil, served with a slice of ham which could be left.

Although *huevos* means eggs, most 'egg dishes' include ham or sausage. Beware of *Huevos rellenos a la Española*, halves of hard-boiled eggs stuffed with any one of many possible fillings, most of which are fish-based, and *Huevos a la Flamenca*, baked eggs with vegetables and ham. *Huevos aliñadas* means cods' roe.

The *tapas* to look out for are *aceitunas* — olives; *alcachofas (a la vinagreta)* — artichokes (vinaigrette); *almendras tostadas* — toasted almonds; *champiñones* — mushrooms; *ensalada valenciana* — salad of rice, tomatoes and peppers; *ensaladilla* — Russian salad; *gazpacho (andaluz)* — cold salad soup; *patatas bravas* — spicy potatoes; *quesos* — cheeseboard with bread; and *tortilla (Español)* — a slice of thick potato omelette, served hot or cold. In places, especially up north, you'll come across another café snack of *membrillo*, quince jelly, served with bread and a slice of hard cheese.

Lunch and dinner

This section broadly overlaps with the last, since not only can *tapas* pass as a meal in themselves, but indeed many bars have a choice of *Platos Combinados*, basically a selection of *tapas*, *raciones* or main dishes, specifically intended to constitute a complete light meal. Conveniently enough, often one of the *platos combinados* has no meat or fish. Apart from a written list, bars commonly display pictures of their *platos combinados* outside the premises — very useful if you don't speak Spanish! One of these *platos*, served with bread and a bottle of local wine, followed by a dessert, makes a cheap and satisfying lunch or dinner.

When ordering, in bar or restaurant, unless you are absolutely confident that there are meatless dishes on the menu, it's always worth making the point to the waiter that you cannot eat meat or fish. He may think this most peculiar, he may think it must be for medical reasons, or he might even wonder '¿vegetariano?', but he will, almost without exception, be happy to oblige.

Inexpensive restaurants, or bars with a menu (which amounts to much the same thing) have their *Menu del Dia*, a bargain-priced three-course set meal with table wine. However, this is of little interest to vegetarians. Instead, you will have to choose from *la lista de platos* (the menu). Under a multitude of improbable headings, this enumerates and categorizes the dishes available.

Olive oil and garlic provide the basis of cooked food and sauces. Spanish chefs make scant use of animal fats. Toasted flour is used for thickening and tomatoes, onions and some herbs are liberally employed, although food is not highly seasoned. If all that sounds like a hopeful start, the fact is that the end product in most instances cannot be eaten by vegetarians simply because ham, prawns or sausage have been added somewhere along the way.

Typical menu headings read, from the top, *Ensalada y Sopas* — salads and soups, or *Entremeses y Sopas* — starters and soups;

Legumbres or *Verduras* — vegetables; *Huevos y Tortillas* — eggs and omelettes; *Pescados y Mariscos* — fish and seafood; *Arroz* — rice, perhaps listed earlier as *Entremeses y Arroz*, starters and rice; *Carnes y Aves* — meat and poultry; and it's not unusual to find some pasta dishes, the one Spanish concession to foreign food, under some such heading as *Espaguetis* or *Spagetis* or *Pastas*. Pastas tend to be served without grated cheese. Finally you may find any or all of these possibilities tacked on the end: *Postres*, desserts; *Pasteles*, pastries; *Frutas*, fruit; or *Helados*, ice cream.

Among the acceptable items, all of which it would be well to resign yourself to eating every day, are: *Gazpacho*, delicious iced soup made with oil, vinegar, garlic and blended cucumber, tomato and peppers — that is, at least, in the original Andalucian version, *Gazpacho Andaluz*, but there are scores of variations. All, basically, are cold vegetable soups. *Gazpacho Extremeño* contains eggs. Note though that *Gazpachuelo* is not the same thing at all — this is a fish and egg soup; other vegetable soups include *Ajo Blanco con Uvas*, an iced soup of almonds and grapes, or an unadorned *Sopa de Ajo* (garlic soup). However, if a *Sopa de Ajo* is 'al . . .' something or other, even if only *al huevos*, with egg, that's a sign to watch out for meat stock. There are vegetable starters — similar to *tapas* — like asparagus vinaigrette, vegetable salads; and dishes in the vegetable section, especially *Menestre de Legumbres*, also known as *Panache de Legumbres*, or *Menestre de Verduras*, etc., which is a plate of hot vegetables fried in lots of garlicky olive oil (occasionally a small amount of meat fat is used and sometimes the vegetables are served with chopped egg). In this part of the menu you'll discover, too, tempting dishes of *lentejas*, *judias*, *alubias* and other beans or lentils, but unfortunately these usually contain meat. Here as well may be listed rice dishes, unless under their own heading. All these employ white rice only. The famous paella is saffron rice mixed primarily with seafood and cooked in a special paella pan. A paella of vegetables only, *Paella de la Huerta*, if not exactly mythical, makes only a rare showing in peoples' homes and a rarer one in restaurants. Furthermore, so Spaniards have warned me, chicken stock is normally used in making it.

Best to ignore paella; omelettes, of which the potato-filled *tortilla español* is most reliable and best, are vegetarian possibilities, as are vegetable side dishes like chips and meatless Italian-style pasta dishes.

It's worth adding that in Benidorm, et al., astonishingly non-Spanish food — egg, beans and chips, bread and butter, and a cup of tea, for example — can be found with ease! Likewise, in hotels mainly dealing with full- or half-board package holidaymakers, food tends to an 'international' character, very meaty, though often with good salad buffets. In these places, tea and Nescafé are the normal drinks instead of sherry and Spanish coffee.

Wine always accompanies meals, whether in hotels, restaurants or bars. Apart from sherry, which it would be rather unwise to drink by the wine-glass, Spain produces two well-known reasonable table wines sold all over the country — Valdeñas and, better, Rioja — as well as countless local varieties. In general, a local house wine served by the carafe or litre bottle will be tolerably palatable, a good accompaniment to all that olive oil, and extremely cheap. Personally I'd splash out another 50p and have a first rate bottle of Rioja.

Self-catering and picnics

So long as you are not too far off the beaten track, this is by no means a difficult country for vegetarian self-catering. Although restaurant menus give no hint of the fact, in truth quite a proportion of the Spanish concern themselves with healthy eating. Many major towns have a health food shop, or even a health food restaurant. While ordinary grocery stores have few health-orientated foods, larger shops and supermarkets, especially in urban or holiday areas, stock brown rice, lentils and many kinds of beans, muesli and decaffeinated coffee beans. There are many varieties of pasta, but not wholemeal, and there is rarely any brown sugar, but there are jars of honey.

French-made milk desserts and yogurts are plentiful, although the word to watch out for is *Azucardo*, sweetened, more common here than in other countries. There's a large selection of foreign

Bar FERNANDO
restaurant

FRA. № 04272

Molinos, 8   :-:   Teléfono 22 67 81

MESA Nº ....

IMPORTE	FECHA			DESCRIPCION CLAVES	
		1	ME	-	Menú de la Casa y Sopas
EA 000.700	□ — *asparagus + mayonaise*	2	E y A	-	Entremeses y Arroz
EA 000.250	□ — *mixed veg. fried*	3	H y T	-	Huevos y Tortillas
EA 000.150	□ — *chips*	4	PC	-	Pescados
BO 000.320	□ — *wine + water*	5	CA	-	Carnes
PO 000.200	□ — *ice cream tart*	6	PT	-	Platos Tipicos
VA 000.040	□ — *cover/bread*	7	PO	-	Postres
001.260	□ T 9628 —4 JUL⁴⁰	8	BO	-	Bodega
		9	VA	-	Varios
		10	SA	-	Saldo Anterior
		11	ST	-	Sub. Total
		12	TO	-	TOTAL

Servicios e impuestos incluidos — Service charge and taxes included
Service et taxes compris — Bedienungzuschlac und asgaben inbegriffen

Federico Paternina

BANDA AZUL
Su Rioja

Result of a typical meal in a bar-restaurant. Note that, apart from the dessert, all my food — Esparragos y Mahonesa, Menestre de Legumbres, and Patatas Fritas — is classified on the bill as **Entremeses** *(starters). The asparagus was tinned, not unusual with the more exotic vegetables.*

and domestic cheeses, though cheese in Spain tends to be produced in traditional ways and made available only in its immediate area of production. Many traditional Spanish cheeses are of sheep's milk, and stored in vats of olive oil, giving an intriguing texture and flavour. A few cows' milk cheeses exist in the north, and goats' in mountain districts. One of the most popular cheeses, Manchego, made with sheep's milk, is delicious when cut into chunks and fried in olive oil. Several of the more old-fashioned cheeses are still made with **plant rennet**. Among them are Queso do los Montes San Benito (from Huelva), Serena (from Badajoz), Torte del Casar (from Cáceres) and sometimes Aragon (from Castellón de la Plana and Teruel).

Bakeries make a tasty, rather heavy white bread, and sometimes wholemeal, as well as biscuity pastries and large glazed croissants, while supermarkets also sell inferior packet bread both white and brown (but not wholemeal).

NOT QUITE SPAIN

That the people of **Euskadi**, as the Basques call their homeland, are racially and linguistically unconnected with the Spanish, and indeed come from far more ancient origins, is now thoroughly accepted. There are striking cultural differences too, for example the particular love of cooking among Basque men, who join 'eating clubs' where they can cook dinner for their mates. All Spain admits that, in matters of food, the Basques must be counted their superior. Therefore it hardly comes as a surprise that Basque cuisine is not quite like Spanish. Mild enough elsewhere in Spain, Basque seasoning is even more delicate, ingredients and timing are determined with absolute precision, butter and cream tend to replace olive oil and fish stews are of the greatest popularity. In fact fish is the cornerstone of the region's cookery. In short, Basque food is very interesting but not much use to vegetarians. Fortunately both Spanish and French dishes can be found throughout Euskadi!

Catalonia, in Spain's north-east corner, also has its own distinct dialect, history, culture, art and politics, and the Catalans make no secret of their low opinion of the rest of Spain. Their unilateral declaration of independence as an autonomous anarchist region was one of the starting points of the Civil War, and their sense of separate identity has survived centuries of sometimes merciless repression. However, these days the Catalan lifestyle is not so very different from the rest of Spain. The only nation state with Catalan as its official language is **Andorra**, way up among the peaks of the Pyrenees. here too, nowadays, despite what locals would have you believe, the similarity to Spain is fairly marked. Catalans have a reputation as hearty eaters, particularly of things which have to be caught rather than reared, favouring both fish and game (animals killed in the wild). 'Mushroom hunting' provides a more harmless weekend sport for Catalan families, at least in autumn, and dozens of varieties feature in Catalan food. To make the most of their individual flavours, the more unusual mushrooms are often grilled and served on their own with garlic, oil and herbs. Another favourite wild vegetable is asparagus, gathered in spring, and other local delights include grilled spring onions and young artichokes prepared in a multitude of different ways.

Over the centuries the **Balearic Islands** — Majorca, Minorca, Ibiza and Formentera — have by no means been mere peripheral onlookers to the rise and fall of Spain's might. Their own history has not been inconsequential, and the little island of Majorca was once seat of a kingdom which ruled much of Catalonia and the South of France. Now it has become the focus of a massive annual tourist invasion. In the developed resort areas, eating out can be a nightmare, not just for vegetarians but for anyone who has hoped to see something of the life and customs of the islands. The food runs mainly along the same old 'international' lines, paella, pizza, chicken and chips etc., which would make you scream with boredom even if you could eat it. Yet escape from the crowds is not impossible. Indeed, away from the coastal resorts, Majorca remains in places astonishingly unspoiled and beautiful. Unfortunately, local cuisine in these areas is generally as unsuitable for vegetarians as in the tourist haunts. However, there are some worthy exceptions, such as *Tumbet*: a very oily, tasty mixture of fried aubergines, peppers, tomatoes and onions (slightly reminiscent of ratatouille), and *Sopa Mallorquina*, Majorcan soup, a stew made only of vegetables poured into a bowl lined with slices of bread, which soak up the liquid. Traditional Majorcan bread, widely available, is baked in circular loaves and is low in salt, low in gluten, and made of wholemeal flour. *Mallorquin* pastry cooks assure me that the island's local pastries *ensaimada* (plain and light) and *robiols* (like a Cornish pastie with sweet filling) are made without animal fat. *Coca Mallorquina*, the native version of pizza, may incorporate some fish. Among other Balearic specialities there's *Greixera d'ous*, eggs chopped into mixed vegetables, and *Mahonesa*, mayonnaise, which must be the most famous thing ever to come out of the little island of Minorca.

The Spanish would say that **Gibraltar** is really Spain, but no matter how justified or otherwise their claim to this rocky outcrop of the Iberian mainland, there's no escaping the bizarre Britishness which it has acquired. Actually it is not as totally British as some visitors expect. The people are a fascinating mixture of Arab, Maltese, Spanish, Geonese (Italian), Jewish and English, with a heavy sprinkling of temporary residents from other places. To some small extent restaurants reflect this cosmopolitan diversity, but more often they are geared to British tourists on package holidays or disgorged for the day by cruise liners. There are scores of bars with British beer and restaurants claiming to be Spanish, Italian, Chinese, Indian and British — but once again, it's mainly 'international' food.

The **Canary Islands**, lying off the African coast and long ago conquered by Spain, have a superb climate winter and summer which has attracted a huge tourist industry. The islanders' own food resembles mainland Spanish, with plenty of olive oil and garlic, plus a few local specialities. Tremendously fertile in places, the islands export vast quantities of bananas, apples, grapes and other fruits, tomatoes, potatoes and other vegetables, and also produces a surprising amount of grain. Yet even here, apart from providing the obligatory paella, many restaurants are geared up to the familiar 'international cuisine' presumed to be sought after by tourists. There is hardly any Spanish character in these eating places. Most are fish-orientated, for meat is in short supply, and for vegetarians often the only possibility is a salad, though there may be a vegetable soup. *Potaje Canariense* — a thick spicy vegetable and bean soup; *Sopa Verde* — made of parsley, eggs and bread; *Sopa Berros* — watercress broth; and other unusual vegetable soups, all of which may or may not have a meat stock, number among the island specialities. Others are *Papas Arrugada* — small potatoes in their skins boiled in salt water; *Gofio* — cornbread, or simply the roasted corn flour used as a seasoning or even eaten by itself with milk; *Acelgas Guisados* — a frying pan mixture of chard, raisins, tomatoes, onion, and pine-nuts; and *Mojo* — a sauce, either hot or mild, made of oil, vinegar and spices. *Quesodilla* is a sort of cheesecake made of goats' cheese. *Sopa de Miel*, honey soup, appears as a dessert, as does *Miel de Palma*, date syrup, and perhaps predictably, *Platanos Fritos*, fried bananas. Island wines are expensive and curiously sweet. Fruit liqueurs and rum are both extremely popular in the backstreet bars — more so than sherry. It is said that, as we go to print, there are three vegetarian restaurants in Santa Cruz but none anywhere else. The abundance of fresh produce, and the lack of places to eat out, make self-catering an attractive option, though if you're seeking local colour be warned that self-catering is mostly confined to specially-built complexes with their own supermarkets. The accommodation may not be adequately equipped either, having only a Baby Belling to do all the cooking. Consider camping as an alternative. There are only a couple of official campsites, but local tourist offices will direct you to other spots where camping is permitted.

What to say

There's a certain amount of pronunciation to learn before tackling Spanish words. C before E or I sounds like *th*, but before other letters pronounce it like *k*. G before E or I makes a *guttural h* sound, but before other letters it's a hard *g*. J is another *guttural h*. The letter H itself makes no sound — it is always silent. Pronounce LL as *y* or *ly*. Ñ, with the *tilda* on top, sounds like *ny*, as in the word *mañana*, tomorrow. QU makes another *k* sound. Z is pronounced *th*. The letters V and B are rather strange: they are almost indistinguishable, and produce a muffled *b* sound. And with the vowels, remember that two or more vowels together always keep their separate sounds.

The essentials

Do you speak English?	¿Habla usted inglés?
Hello	Ola (informal)
Good morning/afternoon, evening	Buenos días/tardes. Say this when entering bars, small shops, commercial premises.
Goodbye	Adios. Take your leave from shops etc. with this
Menu	el Menu, la Lista, la Carta. The fixed-price Menu of the Day is *el Menu del Dia*
Have you got . . ., Is there . . ., Are there . . .?	Hay . . .? This is one of the most useful words in the language (the H is silent). More correct for 'Have you got' is *Tiene* . . .?
Please	Por favor
Thank you (very much)	(Muchas) Gracias
Sorry	Perdonne
Eat/drink	Comer/bebida
I am (we are) vegetarian	Soy (somos) vegetariano(s)
I (we) cannot eat meat or fish	No puedo (podemos) comer carne ni pescado
I (we) don't want meat or fish	No quiero (queremos) carne ni pescado
Vegetarian/'Natural' Restaurant	Restaurante Vegetariano/Naturista

No ⎫ meat/fish/ Without ⎭ cheese/egg	No ⎫ carne/pescado/ Sin ⎭ queso/huevos
Is there meat in this?	Hay carne en este
Animal fat, meat stock	Grasso animale, caldo (de carne)
Yes/no	Si/no
OK	Vale
(Very) good	(Muy) bien
And/with	Y/con
Cheers!	Salud!
The bill . . . how much?	La Cuenta . . . ¿Cuanto?
That/this	Esta/eso
100, 200, 500 grams	Cien, Doscientos, quinientos gramos
Breakfast/lunch/dinner	Desayuno/almuerzo/cena
(Wholemeal) bread, flour	Pan, harina (integral)
Rye, wheat	Centeno, trigo
Oats, bran	Avena, salvado
(Brown) rice	Arroz (integral)
(Wholemeal) pasta	Macarrones (integro *or* de harina integral)
Honey, sugar	Miel, azúcar
Yogurt, cheese, eggs	Yogurt, queso, huevos
Milk, butter	Leche, mantequilla
Garlic, mayonnaise	Ajo, mahonesa
Oil, salt, pepper	Aceite, sal, pimiento
Olive oil	Aceite de olivas
Cocoa, coffee, tea	Chocolate, café, té
Decaffeinated	Descafeinado
with milk	con leche. *Café con leche* has a lot of milk in it, *café cortado* has just a dash. The milk is hot. If you prefer cold milk ask for *leche frio*
Herb teas	Tisanas . . . *Manzanilla*, camomile, is most available: not to be confused with sherry-like wine of same name, nor with apples, for the

name means (curiously) little
apples. *Tila* is lime blossom.

(Mineral) water	Agua (mineral). *Con gaz* is sparkling, *sin gaz* is still.
-juice	zumo
Lemon, orange	Limón, naranja
Beer (bottle/glass/large glass)	Cerveza (botella/caña/caña grande)
Wine (red/white/sweet/dry)	Vino (tinto/blanco/dulce/seco). A good mature wine is called Reserva.
Bottle, glass, carafe	Botella, copa, garrafa
Half-bottle	Media botella
House wine, ordinary table wine	Vino de mesa *or* vino corriente
Brandy	Coñac
Sherry	Jerez (see 'SNACKS' on page 229) for more details)

And also you will find:

Granizado	Cold drinks mixed with a glass of crushed ice
Horchata (de chufa)	Cold drink made of 'earth almonds'
'Cocina'	sign displayed meaning, roughly, 'Hot and Cold Dishes'.
Panadería	Baker
(Tienda de) ultramarinos	Grocer
Supermercado	Supermarket
Posada, Fonda, Celler Albergue, Restaurante, Hosteria	all names for a restaurant
Parador	An expensive type of hotel in an unusual building, with a restaurant. State-owned.
Bodega	Place where wine is sold. Wine bar. Any drinking establishment.
Bar, Taberna	Café-bar — all drinks, hot, cold

	and alcoholic, plus *tapas* and perhaps other food
Merenderos	Fish restaurant
Heladeria	Ice-cream bar
Granjas	Milkbar (Catalan)
Salon de té, Pasteleria, Confiteria	Cake shop/bar (larger towns only)
Cafeteria	Coffee bar, snackbar, with set menus

On the menu

See also — 'Dishes to look out for' (page 246)

. . . de ajo	garlic — *Sopa de Ajo* is cold soup of vegetables, egg, and garlic
All-i-Oli, Allioli	garlic and olive oil dressing
Anchoas	anchovies (quite liberally used)
Arroz	rice
Asado	roast, baked
Aves	poultry
Caldo	broth, meat stock. But not always: *Caldo Verde* is entirely vegetable
Caliente	hot
Canalones	pasta tubes stuffed with meat
Carne	meat
Cocido	this means boiled, but is also the word for the many different stews, most of which contain meat
Empanadas	filled pastries (meat, fish, vegetable, or any combination)
Ensalada	salad
Ensaladilla	Russian salad — mixed vegetable and mayonnaise
Entremeses	starters, hors d'oeuvres
Espagueti	spaghetti
Especialidad de la Casa	Speciality of the House
Estilo	style . . . *al estilo de*, in the style of . . .

Estofado	stewed — but can mean specifically a beef stew
Fideos	vermicelli, spaghetti and similar long types of pasta
Frio	cold
Frito	fried
Frutas	fruit
Gazpacho	cold soup of salad vegetables
Helados	ice cream
Hervido	boiled
al horno	baked
Huevos	eggs
Jamon	ham (very common ingredient)
Legumbres	vegetables
Macarrones	macaroni
con Mahonesa	with mayonnaise
Mariscos	shellfish, seafood
Menestre	a mixture containing vegetables or a vegetable stew
Noquis	gnocchi (see ITALY on page 194)
Pan	bread
Pasteles	pastries
Patatas fritas	chips
Pescado	fish
a la Plancha	grilled
Postres	desserts (literally, 'afters')
a la Primavera	'Springtime', i.e. with vegetables. This doesn't necessarily mean there's never any meat, although *Arroz a la Primavera*, rice and vegetables, should have none
Queso	cheese. *Queso del Pais* means local cheese
a la Romana	in batter
Salchida	sausage (very common ingredient)
en Salsa	with sauce

Servicio incluido	service included
Sopa	soup
Spageti	spaghetti
Tartaletas	small open pastries with meat, fish, vegetables or cheese.
Tortilla Español	thick potato omelette
Tortilla Francesa	plain omelette
Vainilla	vanilla
Verduras	vegetables
a la Vinagreta	with vinaigrette dressing

Fruit and vegetables

Aceitunas — olives; *acelga* — chard (much used); *ajo* — garlic; *albaricoque* — apricot; *alcachofas* — artichokes, *almendras* — almonds; *alubias* — beans; *ananas* — pineapple; *apio* — celery; *cebolla* — onion; *champiñones* — mushrooms; *ciruelas* — plums; *col* — cabbage; *espárrago* — asparagus (much used); *espinaca* — spinach; *faves* — Catalan/Balearic word for broad beans; *fresas* — strawberries; *garbanzos* — chick peas; *guisantes* — peas; *habas* — broad beans; *higos* — figs; *judias* — French beans; *lechuga* — lettuce; *lentejas* — lentils; *limon* — lemon; *manzana* — apples; *melocotón* — peach; *melón* — melon; *naranja* — orange; *olivas* — olives; *patata* — potato; *pepino* — cucumber; *pera* — pear; *perejil* — parsley; *pimientos* — peppers, i.e. green or red pimentos or sweet peppers. The word for ground peppercorns, i.e. black pepper, is also pimiento; *pinones* — pine-nuts (much used); *plátano* — banana; *rábanos* — radishes; *sandia* — watermelon; *setas* — mushrooms; *tomate* — tomato (a cornerstone of Spanish cuisine); *uvas* — grapes; *zanahorias* — carrots; *zanahorias negras* — 'black carrots', actually dark red with green interior, rather tough, used in stews.

Desserts

Almendras — almonds (form the basis of many cakes, pastries and desserts); *arroz con leche* — rice pudding, with cinnamon; *brazo de gitano* — like a swiss roll, but nicer; *bunuelos* — fritters, e.g. Bunuelos de Albaricoque, apricot fritters; *flan (caramelo)* — the ubiquitous caramel custard; *flan de naranja* — more interesting orange custard; *helado* — ice cream; *leche frita* — 'fried milk', deep-fried squares of set custard, with cinnamon; *mingolillos* — fritters of almond, hazelnut, honey, egg and cinnamon; *natillas* — egg custard with cinnamon; *sierra nevada* — ice cream with meringue; *tarte helada* — ice cream and sponge cake in layers; *torrijas* — pieces of bread fried with egg then baked with honey; *turrón* nougaty confectionery for fiesta and special occasions, particularly Christmas.

Dishes to look out for

Apart from *Tortilla*, *Gazpacho*, *Sopa de Ajo*, *Arroz a la Primavera* (or *Arroz con Verduras*), the various Italian-style pastas, and starters like asparagus or artichokes, there are plenty of other possibilities which you may come across. The most common is *menestre de legumbres* (also known as *Panache de Legumbres*, *Menestre de Verdures*, *Panache de Verdures*, etc.), mixed vegetables sautéed in garlicky olive oil. From time to time you'll also discover:

Alcachofas a la madrileña	sautéed artichokes and chestnut purée, grilled with breadcrumb and cheese topping
Arroz con adán	cold dish of mixed rice, vegetables, eggs and mayonnaise pressed into a shape
Arroz a la cubana	boiled rice, fried eggs, bananas and tomato sauce
Arroz empedrat	boiled rice, white beans and parsley
Arroz gallego	saffron rice with mushrooms, onion and tomato
Cazuela de habas verdes a la granadina	bean and vegetable stew with eggs

Crema sevillana	tomato, onion and red pepper soup
Escalibada catalana	grilled slices of peppers, aubergines and tomatoes with seasoned oil
Espárragos al estilo de málaga	asparagus covered with mashed red peppers, garlic and parsley, baked with a topping of eggs
Espinacas a la catalana	spinach, pine-nuts, garlic and raisins
Guisado de garbanzos	a stew of chick-peas, vegetables, nuts, eggs and spices but no meat
Guisantes a la bilbaína	peas, onions and potatoes
Huevos	eggs — done in lots of ways
Escalfudos	simple poached eggs
a la Gitanilla	baked eggs with bread, oil and almond paste
al Nido	pieces of bread and eggs fried together
Revueltos	scrambled eggs
Revueltos el coll	scrambled eggs with tomato purée
a la Santanderina	eggs baked with peas and asparagus
a la Valenciana	rice with mushrooms, tomato sauce, cheese and fried eggs
Olla cordobesa	chickpea and cabbage stew
Pastel de tortillas	'omelette pie', different vegetable omelettes in layers with béchamel sauce between them
Patatas catalanas	spicy potatoes — fried with onions, garlic and paprika
Patatas a la judia	potatoes boiled, then baked in wine and served with a spicy egg sauce
Patatas y judias a la extrameña	potato and bean stew with tomatoes, peppers and garlic
Pisto	peppers, tomatoes and courgette stew
Pisto a la bilbaína	a sort of courgette and green pepper omelette

Sopa de coles a la asturiana	cabbage and potato broth with bread and grated cheese
Sopa granadina	liquidy vegetable soup with saffron and bread
Sopa de nueces	nut soup — usually hazelnuts and almonds
Sopa de patata rallada	potato and egg soup
Sopa de primavera	'Springtime soup' — all vegetable
Sopa de vainas	soup of potatoes and green beans
Sopa a la vizcaína	cabbage, beans and pumpkin soup (check no meat)
Tortilla murciana	omelette with red peppers and tomatoes. *Tortilla campesina* is the same thing with mushrooms added

But beware of

Paëlla de la huerta	allegedly a meatless, fishless paella (huerta means a vegetable garden). Even if no meat included, chicken fat may be used in cooking
Berenjos rellenos	stuffed aubergines, normally without meat, though it's sometimes hard to be sure. *Calabacines rellenos* are stuffed courgettes with cheese, and the same thing applies. *Pimientos rellenos*, stuffed peppers, and other stuffed vegetables, more often than not have ham in them
Potaje	potage, should be a thick vegetable soup. But if it is 'a la . . .' anything, this possibly suggests meat or fish have been added. *Potaje de col* is cabbage soup, but *potaje de habas*, *potaje de judias blancas*, *potaje de garbanzos*, and all other bean soups usually do contain meat.

Bean dishes, that is with *habas, judias, lentejas, alubias, garbanzos,* usually have some sausage or ham in them. *Con jamon* or *y jamon* means 'with ham'.

And avoid altogether

Caldo de pimentón   pepper soup, contains fish
Farro   vegetable soup in meat stock
and any *huevos,* egg dishes, which you aren't sure about. Many have some meat in them, for example *huevos a la flamenca,* the deceptively-titled *huevos primavera* and *tortilla primavera* are all made with mixed vegetables and ham. Other *tortillas* with fancy prefixes or suffixes could also mean meat.

Information

There is a small vegetarian movement in Spain, mostly centred around Barcelona where, though they come and go, there are several vegetarian restaurants. If you can read Spanish, the health magazine *Integral* (Paseo Maragall 371, Barcelona 32 [phone: 358.16.11]) is a good source of information. Local tourist offices may be able to provide addresses, but these cannot always be relied upon.

Carole and Chris Stewart's *Self-catering in Spain* (Croom Helm), though aimed at meat-eaters, contains much useful information.

Part Three

1,001 Beans

If not 1,001 different sorts of beans, you will certainly eat well over a thousand individual beans, peas, nuts and seeds on a visit to this part of the world! Most of the countries in the Middle East and North Africa are Islamic. The tiny exceptions are Israel, which is principally Jewish; Lebanon, which has a large Christian minority; and Cyprus, split between Moslem Turks and Christian Greeks. All of them, including these three, have been heavily influenced over the centuries by the nomadic Arab culture and cuisine which came up from what is now Saudi-Arabia. A large amount of meat is eaten, indeed at times, in remote areas, there is little else. For wandering herdsmen, who can still be seen all over this region even today, vegetables and grains could be described as a much-needed luxury. Hardly surprising then that where the Arab world meets the abundance of the Mediterranean coast, all sorts of ingenious preparations — both savoury and sweet — were devised to use the array of pulses, vegetables, spices, fruits, nuts and herbs which grow here. However, heading further west across North Africa, meat again dominates the cuisine in the form of meat and vegetable stews.

The traditional meal, now treated more as a starter, is a large selection of small dishes served all at once, which are placed among the diners who reach over and help themselves in any order. A vine leaf or a piece of bread is used to pick up the food and pop it into one's mouth. It is still the custom among family and friends for everyone to eat from the same large plate in this way.

Eating together has an almost mystical significance among Arabs. Hospitality, even to one's enemies, is a religious duty. On the other hand, to refuse hospitality, no matter whether the reason may be that you are simply not hungry, invites the host's wrath. The polite thing to do is to accept, eat everything with gusto, accept again when second helpings come round as they must, at this stage heaping gratitude and praise upon the host for the abundance and deliciousness of the food, but be quite unable to finish. (If you do completely finish the second helping, the host will feel obliged to serve thirds — and you will be obliged to accept — which could cause him to feel that advantage is being taken of his generosity). The best way to explain one's vegetarianism is to describe it as part of a religious conviction, something clearly understood in today's Islamic countries. Before visiting, find out the dates (different each year) of Ramadan, a whole month during which no food or drink may be served or consumed during daylight hours.

Cyprus

The ancients tell us that Aphrodite, Goddess of beauty, was born from the waves on the seashore of Cyprus. Beautiful it certainly is, but Cyprus has long been troubled and divided. For 'this warlike isle,' to borrow Shakespeare's phrase, is in Asia, not Europe, and is part of the Levant, where different cultures meet head on and do not mix. 80 per cent of the population are Greek, at least in language and religion, and 18 per cent Turkish (the remaining 2 per cent presumably takes in the large number of British forces stationed here). In 1974 the Turkish army invaded the island and took control of the whole of the northern half, expelling all Greeks from the area and seizing their property. Of the Greeks who fled south, 200,000 still live in refugee camps. The Turks have laid a barbed-wire barrier across the middle of the island — no one is permitted to cross it — and have gone so far as to declare the occupied northern region as an 'Independent Turkish State'. In spite of this, normality and civilization continue peacefully in the southern half of the island.

Although the relationship between Greece and Cyprus is very close, at mealtimes one can plainly detect the differences between them. Athens lies about 600 miles away, while Beirut is barely more than 100 miles away and Cypriot food leans distinctly towards the Middle Eastern. Much is already familiar to us from so-called Greek restaurants, actually Cypriot, in Britain and Europe.

Hotels and restaurants reach a higher standard than in Greece; food is more carefully prepared and local wines and spirits are superior. Menus feature more 'international' — principally British — food, and it's not a bad imitation, although that of course does not recommend it to vegetarians. Western dishes on the cheaper menus include the universally popular, and sometimes meatless, pizzas and pasta. This style of 'cuisine' is combined with Turkish, Greek and Arab influences which, unfortunately, are not allowed free rein. Nevertheless, the starter is often *mezze*, a large selection of small dishes; a genuine Cypriot meal might well consist only of this.

Even in a *mezze*, few of the foods can be eaten by a vegetarian. Some can: they are among the many items common in Cyprus but not much seen, if at all, in Greece — such as fried *halloumi* cheese (oily, chewy, tasty); *hoummus* (a dip of chick pea paste mixed with garlic, oil and lemon juice); *tahina* (sesame seed paste); *talatouri* (yogurt, mint, cucumber); wild mushrooms in season; grilled olives; perhaps quails' eggs — and in Cyprus, the flat hollow pitta bread typical of the Levant is eaten. Beware *taramasalata* though, the pink and innocent-looking paste of fish eggs which resembles *hoummus*. Eating in admittedly rather expensive restaurants throughout my stay, and insisting everywhere that I could eat only vegetarian food, I was given excellent meatless meals in the form of *mezze*, salads, and Greek or Italian dishes. Fishy items did usually creep in, as did the popular deep-fried *calamares* (squid — actually not a fish), but it was possible to push these aside. Your chances are even better if you can steer clear of expensive touristy places and choose instead a small family-run *kentron*.

Plant life both wild and cultivated thrives on this fertile island. Although many farmers still sow by hand and till the soil with a horse and wooden plough, their fields help to keep Britain fed throughout the winter and spring. Travelling around in February, I passed for mile after mile between little farms and orchards where grew bananas, grapes, peaches, apples, plums, almonds, oranges and tangerines. Lorries rolling by on the road were heavily loaded with boxes of new potatoes, freshly-picked grapefruit, olives, avocadoes, carob and much more.

Self-catering looks an excellent option (and there are attractive facilities for it), though only if you stick to the island's own abundant produce, which is not only good quality but wonderfully inexpensive. Supermarkets stock plenty of pricey imported goods too, selected especially to appeal to British Army tastes, and a startlingly un-Cypriot range of foods it is too: tins of Ovaltine, packets of Chop-Suey, New Zealand butter, Weetabix and other processed cereals, and everything else that one might expect to find in some mediocre street-corner grocery in Aldershot. Yet the same shops were selling good Cyprus wines, *halloumi* and other local cheeses, excellent citrus fruits, bananas in bunches of twenty or more, artichokes, huge cauliflowers and other vegetables at astonishingly low prices. Local produce is sold by the oke, a strictly Cypriot unit of weight. For more about the language, see GREECE (page 172).

Israel

Israel is extraordinary. It's hard to grasp that such a small area of land — about one tenth the size of the UK — can possess such diversity both of peoples and of landscapes and be so crucial to world politics and world religion. In the south, the barren mountains of the Negev desert touch the clear water of the Red Sea, yet the north is rural, rolling green hills and valleys; new Mediterranean beach resorts and ancient, cosmopolitan cities extend along the west coast, while in the east, poor villages survive in rocky, barely cultivable terrain. As you explore the capital, Jerusalem, the city seems to have three simultaneous existences: the mythical (for example the Dome of the Rock, The Holy Sepulchre); the historical (with the most amazing archaeological sites exposed to view); and the real multi-cultural Middle-Eastern city of today.

The story of Israel has many beginnings. The creation of the modern state by the United Nations in 1948 was but one step in its history. It was a tough battle to bring the nation into being and it remains a tough battle to prevent it from being destroyed. That's why you'll notice that security is tight at airports and that soldiers — both men and women — are a distinct part of everyday life in Israel. Of course, soldiers are inseparable from the very existence of this constantly threatened country, and it is noticeable that they are treated with enormous respect and affection by the public.

Israel is a superb country for vegetarians. Jewish dietary laws, which prohibit the mixing of meat and milk in the same meal, or indeed eating them within six hours of each other, have made meat an inconvenience for many eating establishments. Most staff canteens throughout the country, for example, provide no meat at all, and all but the few non-kosher restaurants have to

decide upon one of two categories, meat or dairy. Larger establishments manage to provide both, keeping them strictly separate. Restaurants in East Jerusalem, Judaea and Samaria (that is,
the occupied areas) may not be kosher and could therefore mix
meat and milk. Sometimes, milk sections of restaurants offer fish,
which is thought of as non-meat (not shellfish though, since that's
also prohibited), though there's no problem avoiding it.

Quite logically, the same prohibition means that cheeses cannot be made with animal rennet. Only plant rennet may be used
to make all Israeli cheeses.

Quite apart from religious law, there's a strong vegetarian
sentiment among Israelis. Vegetarian restaurants are not uncommon, and there are at least two vegetarian hotels (at Ashqelon in
the south and Rosh Pina in the north). More often still, hotels
and restaurants willingly provide an alternative menu for vegetarian customers. Vegans don't do badly either. There is even, in the
hills of Galilee, a village with a vegetarian population: Amirim.
More about that on page 265.

In markets and in shops the array of fresh fruit and vegetables
astonishes the uninitiated. Things considered a luxury elsewhere
cost practically nothing here. Many of the varieties, thanks to the
climate, are in season twice a year. The abundance comes from
Israel's myriad of highly productive small farms, mostly owned
and worked by communes and collectives (*kibbutzim* and *moshavim*).

Israelis have a great love of salads and milk products. The
chickpea, cooked and prepared in several ways, is a staple.
Avocadoes and aubergines form the basis of numerous dishes
both hot and cold. The basic cooking medium is oil, although
schmalz, chicken fat, sometimes has to be avoided. But there are
few rules or limitations on what one may find to eat in this nation
of refugees. Naturally the preponderant style of cooking is Middle
Eastern; yet the ghettoes of Poland and Russia, the Jewish villages
of North Africa and Arabia, and Jewish quarters in cities all
around the world, have given to this small area of land not only
all their sufferings and their hopes, but also, inevitably, their

tastes in food and their methods of cooking. For the vegetarian, this diversity is all to the good.

Snacks

In every town, vendors hawk snacks along the main streets, especially in the more 'Arabic' areas. Still top favourite is the old Middle-Eastern standby, *falafel* in *pitta*. *Falafel* is a deep-fried ball of seasoned chick pea paste. *Pitta* (pronounced pitta, not 'peter') is a hollow round of flat bread. Stallholders put a *falafel* or two inside the *pitta* and customers then help themselves to, quite literally, as much as they want — and at no extra charge! — from containers of lovely fresh chopped salads, orange slices, chillies, sometimes chips, fried aubergine slices and a hot sauce called *khraine*, all of which they cram into the *pitta* on top of the *falafel*. Many falafel stands offer a choice of *Pitta ahad*, meaning one whole pitta, or *Khatzi*, half. Both are incredibly cheap, but the half-size is the better bargain.

As well as falafel stands in the street, there are scores of little falafel snackbars which sell basically the same items, plus a few more, particularly *tahina*, a dryish sesame paste, and *hoummus*, chickpea paste mixed with garlic and lemon juice. *Tahina* and *hoummus* both go deliciously well with salad.

Other stalls and stands sell all sorts of dried fruits, roasted nuts and seeds, freshly-squeezed orange juice and Arab or Middle-Eastern sweets. You'll even see vendors selling single washed carrots — surely one of the healthiest take-aways imaginable! Prices of everything are amazingly low.

Nowadays, depending on the area, pizzerias are springing up, with the usual selection of non-meat pizzas, some without cheese either, and oddities like pizza with mixed fruits and vegetables. Other snackbars, 'creameries' and cheap cafés — keep your eyes open and you'll see lots of them — sell *blintzes* (like crêpes, with savoury fillings), dumplings, little filled pastries, corn on the cob and *latkes*, pronounced 'lutkes' (see 'Dishes to look out for' on page 264). And in certain types of neighbourhoods you'll come across French or Viennese style patisseries serving delicious cakes and coffee (not usually any decaffeinated though). In little cafés and falafel bars, coffee can be either the Turkish type, strong stuff served in a tiny cup half-full of sludgy coffee grounds, or espresso. Tea is weak, laced with mint, and served in a glass.

Meals

Except for rushed city dwellers who just grab some buttered bread and a coffee, the Israeli breakfast is an important meal. On farms, in villages, on the countryside collectives, as well as in hotels, breakfast consists of masses of salads with cheeses, yogurt and other milk products, boiled eggs, fruit and fruit juices and fresh bread. It's generally presented and eaten in a relaxed help-yourself buffet style. The sensible thing to do, unless you can't get used to eating salad first thing in the morning, is fill up on this protein- and vitamin-packed breakfast banquet which, however, is very light and won't slow you down, and settle for one of the cheap and filling snacks at lunchtime.

Different groups of immigrants live in quite different ways. One would not expect, for example, an Ethiopian, an East European and a New Yorker — three typical Israelis — to have much in common. For almost everyone though, the day starts early, say at 6 or 7 a.m. Lunch can be anytime between 12 noon and 4 p.m., and for the majority is the main meal. Shops and businesses close from 1 to 4 p.m., and many people take an hour or two of sleep. In densely-populated areas, it is forbidden to make a noise during this part of the day. The evening meal, for most, is a light 'dairy' meal (that is, without meat), similar to breakfast, sometimes eaten quite late in the evening. These long gaps between meals help to explain why Israelis eat so many snacks.

Classier restaurants, predictably, serve meat. 'Dairy' restaurants tend to be snackier and cheaper. Although eating places can be regarded as either 'meat' or 'dairy', it's not always necessary to seek out a non-meat restaurant to find a vegetarian meal. Vegetable soups, salads and dips, pasta and *latkes* might well feature on the menu of a meat restaurant. Customers are often free to help themselves to unlimited salad from the buffet, while the waiter brings the cooked part of the order. Meat restaurants obviously cannot serve coffee with milk at the end of a meal, there's no cheese course and desserts would have to be made without milk or cream. Vegans may well feel themselves better off in a restaurant which serves meat rather than milk. Remember, too, that in the main cities foreign restaurants abound and there are also a few vegetarian places.

Self-catering and picnics

Huge street markets, the stalls loaded with the very finest produce, start before dawn and continue all day. In villages there might be only a couple of markets each week, while in towns and cities they are there every day except Saturday (Friday sunset to Saturday sunset is the Jewish sabbath).* Normal procedure at markets is for the customers to help themselves. Stallholders expect it — how else could you be sure of getting the best? They price everything in 100 shekels ('Maya') . . . though it might suddenly shoot up to 200 if they think you're a *schlemiel*. In any case, the money involved only amounts to pennies.

By contrast, supermarkets can be frustrating places to do shopping. With rare exceptions they are hopelessly inefficient, disorganized, and often filthy too, with constant awful scenes in checkout 'queues' where everyone tries to push or sneak in front of everyone else. However, supermarkets also have distinct advantages: numerous frozen vegetarian foods, meatless sausages and similar; a massive range of pastas (not wholemeal), rice (brown occasionally available), grains and beans; a good selection of different cooking oils (bottles have a picture showing what they're made of); and a great array of cheeses, quark, sour cream, yogurt and other cultured milk products all loosely referred to as *lében*. The cheeses, of ewes' and cows' milk (and all made without

*Shops and bazaars also observe, to varying degrees, the Islamic and Christian sabbaths (Friday and Sunday respectively).

animal rennet, remember), mostly imitate European varieties. There's Israeli-made feta too, and feta-like cheeses with less salt. A plain white cheese, moist and with a spongy cuttable consistency, sold wrapped in paper, is consumed in vast quantities and could be regarded as one of Israel's staple foods. It's known simply as *Gvina Lavana*, which literally means 'white cheese', and can either be used in cooking or eaten with bread as a between-meals snack.

If there's a product you don't recognize on a supermarket shelf, ask another customer what it is. Israeli shops are full of people questioning each other on what things are and how to cook them. There's always someone who knows from his or her country of origin.

Israel's basic bread is a plain and roughish white loaf, free of additives and with a good taste. Government subsidies keep the price very low. Rounds of inexpensive pitta (not wholemeal), particularly important to the Arabs and Oriental Jews, are equally available. There's a tremendous range of other breads too, best bought from proper bakeries rather than supermarkets. There are lovely brown breads, wholemeal, rye, pumpernickel and excellent rolls and pastries. Pretzel is more 'bready' than the biscuity pretzels sold in the West. One oddity for Jewish visitors is the lack of bagels in the European/American sense; instead the traditional Middle Eastern *bagele*, much larger and breadier, is sold in the street or baker's shops as a popular snack. On Fridays the delicious bread called *chollah* (the 'ch' as in Scottish loch), made of egg dough and baked in a plaited shape, goes on sale in supermarkets and (a better version) in bakeries.

What to say

Israel's national languages are Arabic and Hebrew, the latter properly called Ivrit. Both pose problems for visitors and for a short visit are hardly worth attempting to learn. Fortunately English, French, German and Russian are extremely widely spoken, especially by older people. With any of these it should be quite easy to cope. Nevertheless it's a good idea, and occasionally essential, to know a few words of Ivrit. The following spellings should give some idea of pronunciation. K*h* or C*h* represent a guttural 'h' sound as in Scottish 'loch'.

Hello, goodbye	Shalóm
Good morning/evening	Bóka tov, erev tov
See you soon	La'hitra'ot
Please/thank you	Bavakesha/toda raba
I want . . .	Rótsay
Food/hungry/thirsty	Ohel/ráev/tsamay
What's this?	Má ze?
I am (we are) vegetarian	Ani (Anakhnu) Tzimkhon(im)
I (we) cannot eat meat or fish	Ani (Anaknu) lo okhlim bassar o dagim
No ⎫ meat/fish/ Without ⎬ cheese/egg	Lo ⎫ bassar/dagim/gviná/ Blee ⎬ baitzeem
Yes/no	Ken/lo
OK	Beséder
And/with	Ve/a'eem
Cheers!	Lekhain!
The bill . . . how much?	Heshbon . . . kama olé?
That/this	Zhe/elle
100, 200, 300, grams	Meáh, Matáyim, Shlosh meót, gram
Half-kilo	khatzí kílo
Breakfast/lunch/dinner	Arukhat boker/tzohoraim/erev
(Wholemeal) bread	Lékhem (mekhitta meleah)
Black bread	Lekhem shamoor
Vermicelli ('noodles')	Eetreeyót
Rye, wheat	Lekhem kimelli, chitta
Fruit/vegetables	Pairót/yerakót
(Brown) rice	Orez (choom)
Honey, sugar	Dvash, soocár
Yogurt	Yogoort. Yogurt and similar milk cultures generally are known as *lében*
Cheese, eggs	Gviná, baytzéem

Milk, butter	Khaláv, khemáh
Sour cream, sour milk	Shaménet, eshel
Tea	Tay. With milk = *A'eem khalav*
Coffee	Kaffe, Kaffay. If you ask for this, it'll usually be Turkish, very sweet, strong and gritty. For less sugar ask for it *socar aleel*. *Botz* is a cheap and nasty version of Turkish coffee: just boiling water poured over coffee grounds. 'Fresh-brewed' western-style coffee is weak and tasteless; even instant, called 'Nes', tastes better. Espresso is widely available, if you ask for it by name. Israeli 'cappuccino' is espresso topped with whipped cream. Decaf. is rare.
Salt, pepper	Mélakh, pilpél
Oil, fat, milkfat	Shémen. On all pots of yogurt and soft cheeses, the percentage of shémen is shown. It's also the word for cooking oil
Water, wine, beer	Mayeém, yayéen, béera
-juice	Meetz-; Orange juice is *Meetz Tapuzeen*
Baker	Maafia
Grocer	Makólet
Market(place)	Shook
Supermarket	Sóopermarket
Meat restaurant	Misada Besarit: *Misada* means a restaurant
Dairy restaurant	Misada Halavit
Vegetarian restaurant	Misada Tzimkhonit

Dishes to look out for

Blintz	like a crêpe, with meatless savoury filling. Most popular is a mixed vegetable blintz with sour cream topping; blintzes with cheese are a favourite too
Borekas, kréplakh	little triangular fried pastries filled with cheese or vegetables or meat or something sweet: check which sort are being offered
Borsch, Borsht	beetroot-based vegetable soup with sour cream; sometimes served as a cold drink
Chatzilim béagvaniot	literally, aubergines and tomatoes: deep fried aubergines in a fresh, garlicky tomato sauce
Farfel	a sort of egg pasta in pieces cooked as a pie or put in soup
Khamuzím	pickled vegetables
Krupnik	(East European Jewish) mushroom and barley soup (beware chicken fat)
Latke	(Pronounced 'lutke') a sort of fried cake made with grated potato, matzo meal*, egg and onion
Levivot khalamit	fried spinach cake
Lokshen	egg noodles, boiled and turned into moist chunks — used in soup, cheese dishes, and also as a sweet, something like bread and butter pudding in character, called *lokshen* pudding. Not to be confused with *lox*, American Jewish word for smoked salmon

*Matzo is very dry crisp water biscuit made of wheat flour. Matzomeal is powdered matzo.

Marak avocado	Marak means soup, and *marak avocado* is an intriguing soup made of avocadoes
Marak payrot	fruit soup, served cold
Mayeren Kugel	(East European) carrot cake
Pilpél memulá	stuffed peppers
Salat Khatzilim	a dip of puréed aubergines and onions with lemon juice and tomato
Salat hadarim ve'avocado	also called Caribbean salad, and various other names: a plate of fruits in season arranged as a salad with cottage cheese and lemon juice
Salat hakibbutznikim	kibbutznikim means people who live on a kibbutz, and this salad is called, literally, Kibbutznik's Salad. It's a mixture of everything, raw vegetables, boiled eggs, sour cream, yogurt, and more
Schav	hard-boiled egg soup with sour cream
Tfihat kishuim	marrow soufflé
Toureto	a dip made of puréed cucumbers, oil, bread and lemon juice
Triflach	light doughy pieces to put in soup

Amirim — vegetarian *moshav*

A kibbutz is a village in which all possessions are held in common. Children are brought up communally, and the kibbutzniks work not for themselves but for the wealth of the whole community. Long part of the Zionist ideal, the first kibbutz was set up by Jewish immigrants to Israel in 1909. Many more followed, and more are being started every year. Today, communes are a cornerstone of Israel's economic, political and social life. In a moshav, another type of commune, the villagers own their homes and private gardens and have a measure of individual control

NEVE ILAN — HILLTOP RESORT
Gateway to Jerusalem

Vegetarian Menus

1. Mushroom & cheese casserole with Noodles

2. Quiche

3. Corn Fritters / Cauliflower fritters

4. Blintzes: Mushroom / Spinach / Cheese

5. Vegetarian Lazagna

6. Stuffed Cabbage
    " Eggplant
    " Squash
    " Peppers

7. "Shichshuki" — eggs simmered in a mixture of onions, peppers, tomatoes, 'oriental style'

8. "Borekas" oriental sty puff-pastry 'stuffed' with mushrooms, spinach, cheese, potato

9. fish if desired

A typical selection of non-meat dishes . . . from a hotel-restaurant owned and run by an English-speaking kibbutz near Jerusalem over their income and day-to-day lives, but much of the wealth of the village is held in common and communal decisions are made concerning its economic and social activity. At first, most kibbutzim and moshavim lived partly from meat production, particularly the rearing of chickens. Nowadays many have found other sources of income, notably light industry.

In the hills of Galilee in northern Israel, the moshav of Amirim manages to survive without rearing meat. All Amirim's sixty-three families are vegetarian, which has been a requirement for membership of the moshav since 1958. Now Amirim plans to leave the moshav movement and become an ordinary village. As well as keeping orchards of plums, apples and avocadoes, and growing vegetables organically, half the families in the village supplement their income by taking in paying guests, who must also be vegetarian. The total capacity for English-speaking guests is about thirty to forty. Visitors stay in their own comfortable self-contained private rooms and chalets with or near their host family. There's no self-catering: the host family does all the cooking, 'partly', as it was explained to me, 'to avoid people cooking up a fish or something, perhaps in the genuine belief that it would be OK'. Guests eat with their hosts, and there's a family for just about every type of vegetarian.

For example, people staying with Phillip and Aleet Campbell, and Aleet's family the Lamdans, stay in simply but comfortably furnished chalets with a sun-catching porch looking far across the tranquil hills and valleys of Galilee. The meals provided are supremely healthy, with plenty of fruits, salads and vegetables. No sugar is used, and they don't provide coffee or tea other than herb teas. By contrast, guests of Boaz and Yael Goldman, a few minutes walk away, eat rich hearty meals with a wholefood bias — brown rice, cereals, plenty of savoury roasts, sauces, home-made bread and substantial desserts. Other families cater for vegans, and yet others for a free-and-easy diet which takes in white flour, sugar and processed foods. When writing to Amirim for more information or to make a booking, specify what kind of food you like.

Set in the midst of gorgeous flower-strewn countryside, peaceful Amirim (the name means 'treetops') has a view extending clear across this tiny nation, from the Golan Mountains in the east as far as the shimmering Mediterranean in the west. Spread out below the village lies tranquil farmland around the Sea of Galilee. Twenty minutes away, Sfat is a lively town full of Middle-Eastern character. Amirim itself, of course, offers absolutely no 'night life' at all — apart from folk-dancing once a week in the village hall — except looking at the stars shining in a crystal-clear sky.

Write to the Campbells or the Goldmans, or simply address your letter to: Amirim, Marom Hagalil Mobile Post, Israel; or POB 20115, Karmiel, Israel.

Information

For more information, contact:

The Vegetarian and Vegan Movement in Israel, 41 King George Street, Tel-Aviv 63299, Israel.

Mr Phillip Pick (President), The Jewish Vegetarian Society, 855 Finchley Road, London NW3 (phone: (01) 455 0692).

Vegetarian holiday specialists Israel Holidays Ltd., POB 2045, Herzliya 46120, Israel (phone: (972-52) 556729).

A useful book, either for self-catering while in Israel, or to recapture the taste of it when you return home, is: Rose Friedman, *Jewish Vegetarian Cooking* (Thorsons).

If you want to try a working holiday on a kibbutz — most cater for vegetarians — the essential handbook is: John Bedford, *Kibbutz Volunteer* (Vacation Work, 9 Park End Street, Oxford).

The Levant

(See also: Turkey, Israel and North Africa). Syria and Lebanon, neighbours on the eastern shore of the Mediterranean, share much the same food and methods of preparation. Levantine cooking broadly follows the Arabic style, but with the advantage of more choice of ingredients and consequently less emphasis on meat. Many of the dishes found in Egypt could equally appear in Lebanon or Syria.

It is a tragedy, not only for Lebanon itself but for everyone, that this supremely cosmopolitan and civilized society has shattered into a mass of social fragments, each of which has taken up weapons against all the others. For the next few years at least, it seems likely that the only people paying a visit to this country will be members of the Syrian, Israeli or other foreign armies. If ever it returns to normality, vegetarians will discover a wealth of delicious and suitable foods. The staple grain is *bulgar*, or cracked wheat, served with or included in many of the dishes. The bread is in round flat wholewheat loaves. Although the national dish is *Tibbeh*, mixed meat and bulgar, it is aubergines, vine leaves and other vegetables, spices, mint and other herbs, beans, pulses, lemon juice, *samneh* (clarified butter, like Indian *ghee*) and olive oil which are the essentials of the region's cuisine.

Mezza, lots of small dishes served all together, constitutes the traditional meal, or can be served as a first course (the second would then normally be meat). It comprises, for example, among other things, bite-size pastries filled with cheese or vegetables; vegetable pickles; *hoummus* (seasoned chickpea paste); *moutabal* (grilled aubergines with oil, lemon and spices); *baba khannouj* (aubergine dip); *falafel* (chickpea 'croquettes'); *warak inab* (vine leaves stuffed with rice, tomatoes and spices); and — what must be the only dish in the world whose principal ingredient is parsley —

tabouleh (bulgar wheat, parsley, tomatoes, onion, lemon and oil). Everything is eaten with pitta bread or by using a vine leaf as a sort of edible plate. Other Lebanese and Syrian foods are full-fat yogurt, buttermilk and ewes' milk cheeses, like the rubbery salt-tasting *haloumi*, which can be served fried. All food is usually bought fresh in markets rather than in shops.

For language, see Egypt (page 276).

Two excellent books by David Scott: *Traditional Arab Cookery* and *Middle Eastern Vegetarian Cookery* (Rider).

North Africa

Islam's hierarchy which places men at the top, animals at the bottom and women between the two makes itself unpleasantly apparent across the whole Arab world. Horses, sheep and goats, the most common creatures in North Africa, can be seen everywhere in conditions of unspeakable suffering, and it's made none the less shocking by reflecting that centuries ago the situation was hardly any better in Europe. Vegetarianism is unknown in North Africa, and not catered for. However, there's an abundance of traditional meatless snacks which, if only they can be found when they are needed, give great delight as well as nourishment.

Culturally, linguistically and gastronomically, North Africa divides into two distinct regions, for the three western-most countries, Morocco, Algeria and Tunisia, known together as the Maghreb, differ considerably from Libya and Egypt, their neighbours to the east. How vegetarians fare in either region depends upon whether they eat as package tourists in hotel restaurants (most package holidays to North Africa include full or half board), or instead take their chances at the smoky tavernas and street stalls in the *medinas* of Arab cities. European-style hotels vary considerably. Most set out to provide set meals on international lines, with the occasional appearance of a toned-down local dish. A few can manage some excellent buffets, especially for lunch. In some, an omelette, boiled vegetables, chips or salad may be made available on request. By contrast, in the back alleys of the *medina* (old quarter), though they are far more interesting, it's no easy matter to find a complete meal without meat; there is, however, every possibility of finding a succession of suitable small dishes — though not necessarily at just the right moment to satisfy the need for a lunch or dinner!

MAGHREB

In Morocco, Algeria and Tunisia the basic meal is steamed large-grain semolina (wheat) called cous-cous, covered with a mixed stew of meat and vegetables. In theory, a vegetables-only cous-cous could exist. In practice it is hardly ever seen except in Algeria. In second place comes *tajjine*, a mixed meat and vegetable stew done in any way at all, which similarly need not contain the meat but always does. Pavement stalls and wandering street sellers hawk *sfanje* (doughnuts), Arab sweets, fresh fruit juices and dense little cakes (the ones with hashish in them are kept underneath the others). In the swarming *souks* or markets, vendors with little stalls or simply squatting with their produce on blankets sell herbs, spices, yogurt, fresh fruit and dried fruit, nuts, vegetables and pulses, and roasted beans and seeds. Small open-fronted snackbars or tearooms, where men sit together drinking sugary mint tea and sharing a hookah (water pipe), sell fried or roasted vegetable and bean dishes with meatless sauces. In Morocco, the bread, a rough wholewheat with the odd hair or insect's wing mixed into it, comes in flat loaves. In Algeria and Tunisia, a white French loaf is more usual.

Of the three, Morocco has the most ethnic character and eats the most meat. Algeria has few tourists, much less charm or character and rather uninteresting food, although it uses the least meat. Tunisia has, in the main towns at least, the greatest awareness of tourists' preferences and its hotels provide bland international food quite competently, while snackbars and street sellers have the widest variety of appealing Arab titbits, many without meat. Self-catering plays a bigger part in Tunisian holiday options than in the other countries. For a month in Morocco I lived mainly on oranges, nuts, cakes and mint tea. For three months, self-catering in Tunisia, I added to this, boiled cous-cous as a kind of porridge for breakfast, then had it again for dinner, steamed, with a selection of vegetables from the local market. There were opportunities to find out what locals eat when I was occasionally invited to people's homes. Once, dusk falling fast as I walked through a village near the Libyan border, a family invited me to spend the night at their house. In the morning I was given a breakfast of some impossibly dry powder, over which we poured weak tea and ate the mixture with a spoon. I have never found out what it was!

Dishes to look out for

Barkoukess, boufawar	cous-cous stews without meat
Chakchouka	a stew of peppers, tomatoes, onions and eggs
Lablali	chick-pea soup; this and some other soups may contain no meat: always check first
'Salad Marocaine'	a completely French idea (not Moroccan!), mixed vegetable salad.

Small filled pastries play a big part in the diet: *Bourak* are little baked pastries filled with meat, eggs, cheese or vegetables — check which; *Brik* (in Tunisia) are fried pastry triangles stuffed with cheese, vegetables or meat, and an egg — check which sort is being offered; *Mahdjouba* have a filling of peppers and tomatoes; there are sweet pastries too, such as *Briouat*, which is like a sort of almond-filled croissant; *Samsa* is layers of pastry with almond and sesame paste. *Halwa* is a hard sweet block of honey and nut paste.

LIBYA

In Libya, distances are vast and facilities few. The only main road continues for hour after hour with sea on one side and sand on the other. Makeshift villages grow up around gas stations, and dusty small towns punctuate the route. These places seem far beyond the reach of any refinement or culture. The only refreshment I came across was bread, meat, water and warm soft drinks. Alcohol is illegal, like much else (even Coca-Cola is forbidden here, because, or so I was told, it is 'a Jewish company'), yet I was furtively invited into one man's house to share a bottle of whisky which he opened specially for me. We had no language in common but sat together in silence solemnly drinking, more as act of defiance than of pleasure. Travelling on, a lorry driver drove me for half a day, stopping every so often to prostrate himself in prayer and then brew up in a tiny metal pot some acidic drops of powerful black tea. The main towns, their walls plastered with anti-Jewish posters, seem relatively unpopulated compared with the rest of the Middle East. Small restaurants, neat and clean, sell Arabic-style snacks, some of them meatless (see EGYPT below). Hotels — even the cheapest — have every modern comfort and, though not much patronized by Europeans, give their guests 'international' food. The only option for vegetarians was to leave the meat untouched.

EGYPT

Mezza, a selection of many small dishes served all at once, is the traditional meal. Restaurants, particularly those dealing with foreigners, treat *mezza* as a starter, to be followed by stews of meat and beans or grilled meat dishes. *Mezza* consists of salads; sauces; meat, fish and vegetable dishes; tahina and other dips. These are scooped up with pieces of *aiysh*, bread made into thin hollow loaves. Desserts are often awesomely sugary pastries drenched in syrup. Tea, *shai*, is weak, sweet and laced with mint or other herbs. Coffee, *kahwa*, comes in the Turkish style and with a touch of spice. If you don't ask to the contrary, it'll be *ziyada*, very sweet; for less sugar, ask for it *mazbout*, and for no sugar at all (which can be too bitter), say *saada*. Fruit juice is called *asir fakh*: interesting local types include *doom*, a cold natural juice tasting like maple syrup, and *karkade*, another natural juice, served hot or cold. *Aryaan*, like India's 'salt lassi', is a cool drink made of yogurt, water and salt. Despite the religious prohibitions on alcohol, the anis-flavoured aperitif found all round the Mediterranean is popular here as in other countries: in Egypt it's called *Zibib* or *Arak*.

Egyptian breakfast is light, and snacks keep people going until their main meal in mid-afternoon. More snacks follow in early evening and an evening meal, if taken at all, could be as late as 10 or 11 p.m. Large hotels follow a more European pattern, with the dreadful 'continental' breakfast (not actually eaten by the inhabitants of any known continent) and poorly-prepared 'international' meals.

Dishes to look out for

Babakhanoug	puréed aubergines mixed with tahina and yogurt with garlic and lemon juice
Falafel	deep-fried balls of seasoned chickpea paste
Fataya	baked spinach pastry
Fattett moulukhiya	cooked moulukhia (a leafy green vegetable) chopped into rice
Fool medhammes, ful medames, (or even, as I have seen it written, foul madames)	a staple of the Egyptians, yet rarely seen in tourist restaurants — black beans stewed in seasoned oil until almost become a paste
Gibna beida	a cheese like Greek feta
Hoummus	chickpea purée
Moummus bi tahina	mixed hoummus and tahina
Laban, leban, leban zabadi	rich, full-flavoured yogurt
Labna	a thick, soft, white yogurt-like cheese
Meshshi	'stuffed' . . . particularly aubergines, but also courgettes or vine leaves: the filling is rice, with or without minced meat;
Mish	spiced cheese paste
Salata	'salad': typically chopped cucumbers, tomato and lettuce with yogurt
Salata beladi	green salad

Sambousek	small pastries filled with cheese, parsley and/or vegetables
Ta'amia	something like *falafel*, but made of large broad beans called *nabed*
Tahina	sesame seed paste
Taratoor	a dip or dressing made of tahina mixed with garlic and lemon
Turshi	mixed vegetables pickle
Waraq anab	vine leaves stuffed with meat, rice, lentils, or some combination (check which).

What to say

In Morocco and Algeria, French is widely spoken as a second language. In Tunisia, French, English and Italian could all be useful. In Libya and Egypt, English and French can be helpful. You may, however, need a few words of Arabic. Note that local pronunciation in the Maghreb is quite different from that used in Libya and Egypt, although the words are actually the same. Rendering Arabic script into Roman letters, spellings are necessarily only approximate. Pronounce KH, HH, or GH as a guttural *h*.

I (we) cannot eat any meat or fish	Makush lakhma wa samak
Is there meat in this?	Fi hatha'l tamam lakhma?
No / Without } meat or fish	Bidoon lakhma wa samak
Eggs, cheese, milk	Beid, jibne, haleeb
Fruit/vegetables	Thimaar/khudra (wash both carefully)
Nuts/beans	jowzaat/fasouliah, ful
Omelette	Ijjeh
Bread	Khoobz. There are different types, wholewheat pitta being the most common, made into various forms,

Pastries

called variously Aiysh, Pitta, Kesra, Khoobiz-Arabiya, Kmaj, or Shrak
Ka'ek

Turkey

In Istanbul and Turkey's other cities, although grilled goat and mutton form the basis of the diet, it is not difficult to avoid meat by eating light meals and snacks rather than full meals and making the most of the delicious yogurt and milk puddings. Enticing unpretentious eating places display many such items: half are meatless, and you choose by pointing. In any case, in all but the classier restaurants and in the most tourist-frequented areas, it's normal practice to step (after being invited) into the kitchen to inspect and choose the food as it simmers in big pans. Numerous little backstreet café-restaurants have meals all day, with eggs done in various ways, bread, and milky Middle-Eastern puddings. Main courses are meaty but hors d'oeuvres — which generally means *meze*, a selection of small delicious spicy items — can be extended to become the whole meal. Some good salads are made too, with parsley, tomatoes and cucumber. Many dishes are based on aubergines. *Dolma*, baked vegetables or vine leaves stuffed with mixed rice and herbs (or mixed rice and meat — check which) appear often. *Börek* are delicate fried pastries filled with either meat or white cheese. Besides the puddings in their glass bowls, desserts can be syrup-soaked sticky pastries filled with nuts.

The more rural the region, and the further east, the more meat is eaten. It was heading out to the eastern parts of Turkey that a tough, unshaven lorry driver, the tips of his proud moustache pointing skyward, managed with minimal vocabulary, but plenty of smiles and gestures, to invite me to eat at his home village. This turned out to be, when we arrived, no more than a poor and dusty collection of simple dark cottages. A long rough wooden table with benches stood on the earth outside one of the houses. The driver was welcomed with great joy by a crowd of men and women, and soon we sat down at the table and plates were put in front of us. Cheerful toasts of a stiff liquor were knocked back from small glasses. Our meal that night consisted of roasted goat's meat and pieces of bread. There was nothing else. The head of the animal was placed ceremoniously on the table. Seeing that it offended me, another diner jocularly placed it on the ground, from which position nevertheless its dead eyes continued to gaze dreadfully at the revelry.

Fortunately you can easily avoid adventures like this. If all else fails, hotel dining rooms are usually quite adequate. The hotel breakfast is bread and butter, honey, a handful of olives and some white cheese, and tea. Turks themselves would be more likely to eat a savoury cooked vegetable dish for breakfast.

Although nominally Moslem, Turkey scorns the prohibition on alcohol. One of the most popular drinks is a rough anis-flavoured spirit called *raki*, often drunk with *meze*. Despite the fame (or notoriety) of Turkish coffee, the national drink is actually tea, weak and refreshing, served in glasses. *Boza* is a curious Balkan drink made from fermented millet. *Bademli süt* is almond-flavoured milk. *Ayran* is a lovely cool yogurt drink. In the bazaars you'll find excellent fruit and nuts sold from big bags, large flat loaves of bread, circular sesame rolls (*simit*), doughnuts, filled pastries and other snacks, and sellers with fresh juice.

What to say

Turkish is a difficult language with terribly complicated pronunciation. Note that Ç sounds as English *ch*; Ğ is silent but lengthens the preceeding vowel and shortens following vowels; I is just like *ee*, but I (with no dot) sounds something like *uh*; J is pronounced like the '*s*' in *pleasure*; Ö sounds like *ur*; Ş is pronounced *sh*; U sounds like *oo*, but Ü comes somewhere between *ee* and *oo*.

Hello	Merhaba
Goodbye	Allahaısmarladık (said by the person who's leaving), Güle Güle

	(said by someone who's staying)
Please/thank you	Lütfen/teşekkür ederim
Yes/no	Evet/hayır
And/with	Ve/İle
I want . . ., May I have . . .	. . . İstiyorum
Hungry/thirsty	Acıktım/susadım
I (we) are vegetarian	'Et Yemez' im (iz)
I (we) cannot eat any meat or fish	Et veya balık yiyemem (yiyemeyiz)
Without meat, no meat	Etsiz
Without fish, no fish	Balıksız
Animal fat/meat stock	Hayvani yağ/et suyu
Cheers!	Şerefe!
The bill . . . how much?	Hesap . . . Ne kadar?
Breakfast/lunch/dinner	Kahvaltı/öğle yemeği/akşam yemeği
Bread/flour	ekmek/un
Fruit/vegetables	Meyve/sebzeler
Pickled vegetables	Tursu
Rice/beans	Pirinç/fasulye
Honey/sugar	Bal/şeker
Yogurt	Yoğurt (pronounced yo-oort)
Milk/cheese	Süt/peynir
White cheese like Greek *feta*	Beyaz peynir
Cream/butter	Krema/tereyağı
Oil/eggs	Yağ/yumurta
Salt/pepper	Tuz/bıber
(Mineral) Water/fruit juice	(Maden) suyu/meyve suyu
Tea	Çay
Coffee	Kahve. Not surprisingly, coffee in Turkey is Turkish coffee — a sweet strong potion in a tiny cup. For no sugar ask for it *sade* or *sekersiz*; for a

little sugar only ask for *orta sekerli*.
Otherwise it will come *sekerli*,
sugary.

Restaurant	Lokanta. This can be anything from the most humble to the most luxurious. *Kabapçi*, *Köfteci*, *İşkembeci* are all specialist meat restaurants.
'Pudding Shop'	Muhallebici — specializes in pastries and milk desserts
Snackbar, cheap restaurant	Büfe

Dishes to look out for

Beyaz peynir	white goats' milk cheese similar to *feta*, used in cooking, salads, etc.
Böreği, börek	little fried pastries filled with either meat or cheese; *peynirli* means 'with cheese'
Cacık	a dip of yogurt mixed with very finely chopped cucumber, garlic and olive oil
Çoban Salatasi	a salad of cucumber, peppers, tomato and onion, dressed with olive oil and lemon
Domatesli Fasulye	stewed haricot beans in tomato sauce
Fasulye Pilâkısı	cold meze dish of haricot beans stewed with onions
Humus	a dip or sauce of puréed chickpeas, garlic, oil and tahini
İmam Bayıldı	baked stuffed aubergines — no meat
Karışık Salata	mixed vegetable salad
Kuru Fasulye Pujaz	cold butter beans as a salad

Marul	a whole lettuce, served in a glass
Menemen	spicy omelette with green peppers and tomatoes
Pahaça	pastry balls filled with cheese and parsley
Patlican Salatası	aubergine purée with garlic and olive oil
Pirinçli İspanak	baked rice and spinach with tomatoey sauce
Sebze Bastısı	thick vegetable stew served with yogurt
Tarhana Çorbası	*çorbası* means soup: this one is a Turkish classic — made of a thick paste of yogurt thickened with flour and mixed with tomatoes and peppers
Tavası Yoğurtlu	fried aubergines with yogurt
Turlu	garlicky stew of beans, potatoes and onions
and one to **avoid** — Pilâv	rice dishes: they sound good but the rice is normally boiled in meat stock

Pastries and puddings

Aşure	a sweet made of chickpeas, haricot beans and rice, mixed with fruit and nuts
Baklava	layers of paper-thin pastry and crushed nuts: soaked in syrup
Hanım Göbeği	little fried pastry balls soaked in syrup
Helva	halva: a hard sweet block made of sugar, flour, butter, and honey
Kadayif, Bülbül Yuvası	'shredded wheat' pastries filled with crushed nuts and soaked in syrup

Keşkül	pudding made of milk, potato starch, eggs, sugar and nuts
Loukoum, lakoum	Turkish Delight
Sütlaç, muhallebi	two versions of cold rice pudding — both lovely!
Yoğurt Tatlısı	yogurt cake soaked in syrup

Information

There are no vegetarian facilities or information that I am aware of. One interesting book: Nezih Simon, *Eats without Meats — Turkish vegetarian cookery* (Tredolphin Press).

Of further interest . . .

FRENCH VEGETARIAN COOKING

Here are over 120 completely new and original recipes from the authors of the highly-acclaimed CUISINE VÉGÉTARIENNE FRANCAISE. Having established beyond doubt that French vegetarian cuisine is a gourmet experience not to be missed. **Jean Conil** and **Fay Franklin** now turn their attention to family fare. Dishes that are delicious and exciting, but that are also time-saving and simple to prepare, are the essence of this book. From lunchtime snacks for the family on the move to easy yet impressive dishes for informal entertaining, the French love of good food shared with friends shines through every page to create yet another unique collection of French natural cooking.

MEDITERRANEAN VEGETARIAN COOKING

Recipes from the Sun

Colin Spencer, cookery columnist for the 'Guardian' newspaper, here presents a dazzling collection of recipes from the sun-kissed shores of the Mediterranean. Designed to appeal to vegetarians, travellers – armchair or otherwise – and all lovers of gourmet food, the recipes are all delicious, and rich in the produce of the area. Exotic vegetables, pulses, grains and goats milk abound in these dishes which include both traditional recipes and the author's favourite variations. *The very first wholly vegetarian Mediterranean cookbook.*

ITALIAN VEGETARIAN COOKING

A wealth of traditional Italian dishes using all the goodness of natural wholefood ingredients

Jo Marcangelo. A collection of recipes featuring the finest Italian regional cooking. Alongside well-known dishes such as Genoese Minestrone and Pizza Margherita you will find recipes which the Italian people have long treasured, such as Fettucine with Gorgonzola sauce and Panzanella, a delicious Tuscan bread and vegetable salad. In addition to this, the author includes an introduction to the cheese, herbs and other ingredients which serve to make Italian cuisine unique throughout the world.

GREEK VEGETARIAN COOKING

Colourful Dishes from the Eastern Shores of the Mediterranean

Alkmini Chaitow. Delicious recipes from traditional Greek cuisine, making imaginative use of fresh fruit, vegetables and other wholefood ingredients. Includes menu suggestions, recipes for children. Recipes cover *mezze* ('bits and pieces') appetizers, main meals, side dishes and sweets. *Part contents:* Yogurt and cucumber dip (refreshing in summer!); Bechamel sauce (plus alternative soya milk recipe for vegans); Roasted butter beans (traditional Greek dish); Vegetarian moussaka; Strawberries with orange juice and brandy; Exotic fruit salad.